## DATE DUE

| | | | |
|---|---|---|---|
| | | | |
| | | | |
| | | | |
| | | | |
| | | | |
| | | | |
| | | | |
| | | | |
| | | | |
| | | | |
| | | | |
| | | | |
| | | | |
| | | | |
| | | | |
| | | | |
| | | | |
| | | | |
| | | | |
| | | | |
| | | | PRINTED IN U.S.A. |

# LITERARY SYMBOLISM

An Introduction
to the
Interpretation
of Literature

edited by Maurice Beebe
*Purdue University*

WADSWORTH PUBLISHING COMPANY, INC.
SAN FRANCISCO

L. C. Cat. Card No.: 60-8657

Printed in the United States of
America.

Manufactured by American Book-
Stratford Press, Inc.

# PREFACE

This book is not only an anthology of writings on literary symbolism, but a manual designed to serve as an introduction to the art of literary interpretation. In the broadest sense, *symbolism* refers to the *meanings* of things. Almost everyone would agree that a word is a symbol of what it represents and that any particular thing stands for the family group of which it is a part—that in a sense each man is Everyman is Man. Whether the reader stops short at what he takes to be the literal meaning or whether he immediately turns from "the actual soil of the County of Essex" to "the clouds overhead," as Hawthorne put it in his Preface to *The House of the Seven Gables,* he cannot read actively without asking, what does it mean? Most importantly, what does it mean for me? Then, for reassurance, what does it mean for others?

Thus far we can, hopefully, all agree. Beyond this point everything is subject to argument. One of the best teachers I have known liked to shock his students by saying, "*Moby-Dick* is a first-rate whaling story, and that's all it is, and anyone who tries to see more in it than that is a downright fool!" One of the authors represented in this book writes, "It is almost safe to say that a poem is never about what it seems to be about." Between these two extremes lie practically all levels of interpretation. To help the reader distinguish between them in developing his own critical approach to literature is the main function of this collection of essays.

This book raises some of the basic questions about the interpretation of literature. It does not answer them, though I hope that it contains materials by means of which the reader can arrive at his own tentative answers. In selecting discussions, I have tried to give representation to widely divergent points of view. The essays by Saul Bellow and Mary McCarthy, for example, may be considered protests against the kind of criticism represented by some of the readings of particular works in the second part. Some of the selections are easy, some are difficult, but I think that even the easy ones ought to provoke thought and discussion on important issues in criticism.

*Literary Symbolism* may be used as a supplementary handbook, as a collection of materials for a long research paper or a series of shorter critical essays, or as a primary textbook in courses in criticism or the techniques of literary study. In addition, it should prove useful as a unit of study in the introduction-to-literature course or as a bridge between composition and literature in those full-year courses in which a semester is devoted to the reading of literature accompanied by the writing of papers dealing with literature. Often the student is at a loss for information on the procedures and techniques of criticism. Most composition handbooks contain chapters on writing the research paper; few, if any, provide the type of information on the writing of critical papers that I have attempted to present in the appendix. Used early in the curriculum, this book could improve the student's performance in more advanced courses and free his instructor from having to devote too much class time to preliminary considerations.

The materials have been organized to suggest a progression. Part One consists of readings on the interpretation of literature in general by means of which the student is encouraged to develop methods and standards which he may apply to particular works such as those in Part Two. Part One is subdivided into four sections. The first raises immediately the key question of the limits of symbolic interpretation, while the second faces the problem of the author's intention as a standard of evaluation. The third section presents various statements on symbolism which the student may consider in developing his own definition. The fourth section suggests different kinds of approaches to symbolic interpretation. The problems in Part Two—literary works accompanied by alternate critical readings —are arranged from the fairly easy to the more difficult. None of the literary works chosen has a meaning so simple that it is "exhausted" by the critical explanations which follow it. In each case the student is expected not merely to judge and choose among the readings offered, but to go beyond them.

To facilitate the proper documentation of papers using the materials of this book, I have indicated the original pagination in brackets. The texts have been transcribed as accurately as possible, with two exceptions: (1) I have corrected obvious typographical errors and, in several places, errors of fact at the request of the authors; and (2) whenever a page ended with a broken word, I have ignored the break and placed the page reference after the complete word. Unspaced ellipses...are by the original author; spaced ellipses . . . indicate that I have omitted part of the text.

For help and advice of various kinds, it is a pleasure to record my gratitude to Floyd Stovall and Lee Harris Potter of the University of Virginia; John C. Broderick of Wake Forest; Edward Stone of Ohio University; and Mark Rowan, William T. Stafford, Barriss Mills, William Braswell, Robert A. Miller, and Erin Marcus of Purdue University.

# CONTENTS

## Part One: The Nature of Symbolism

1. THE BOUNDARIES OF SYMBOLISM   .   .   .   .    3

Charles Dickens—"The One Thing Needful," from *Hard Times*   .  .  .  .  .  .  ..  .  .    3
Saul Bellow—"Deep Readers of the World, Beware!"  .    4
Ralph Waldo Emerson—from "The Poet"   .   .   .    7
Arthur Symons—from *The Symbolist Movement in Literature*  .  .  .  .  .  .  .  .    8
James K. Feibleman—from *Aesthetics* .   .   .   .    9
Edmund Wilson—from *Axel's Castle* .   .   .   .   10

2. INTENTION—STANDARD OR FALLACY?   .   .   .  11

J. E. Spingarn—from "The New Criticism"   .   .   .  11
W. K. Wimsatt and M. C. Beardsley—from "The Intentional Fallacy" .   .   .   .   .   .  12
Rudolph von Abele—from "Symbolism and the Student" 14
Walter Havighurst—from "Symbolism and the Student" 15
Robert Frost—from "The Constant Symbol"   .   .  16

3. DEFINITIONS AND TOUCHSTONES   .   .   .  18

M. H. Abrams—from "Symbol" in *A Glossary of Literary Terms* .  .  .  .  .  .  .  .  .  18
Samuel Taylor Coleridge—from *The Statesman's Manual* 19
Thomas Carlyle—"Symbols," from *Sartor Resartus*  .  .  20
Charles Baudelaire—"Correspondences"   .   .   .  25
William Butler Yeats—from "The Symbolism of Poetry" 25

D. H. Lawrence—from "The Dragon of the Apocalypse"    31
James Joyce—from *Stephen Hero*    .    .    .    .    .    32

4. THE INTERPRETATION OF SYMBOLS .    .    .    .    34

Herman Melville—"The Doubloon," from *Moby-Dick*    .    34
Charles Child Walcutt—from "Interpreting the Symbol"    39
Mary McCarthy—"Settling the Colonel's Hash"    .    .    43

## Part Two: Problems in Symbolism

1. HUMPTY DUMPTY    .    .    .    .    .    .    .    .    57

Bernard M. Knieger—"Humpty Dumpty and Symbolism"    57

2. HENRY DAVID THOREAU—A Hound, a Bay Horse, and a Turtledove    .    .    .    .    .    .    .    .    .    59

Walter Harding—"Hound, Bay Horse, and Turtledove"    59

3. ROBERT FROST—"Stopping by Woods on a Snowy Evening"    .    .    .    .    .    .    .    .    .    .    63

Earl Daniels—from *The Art of Reading Poetry*    .    .    64
Leonard Unger and William Van O'Connor—from *Poems for Study* .    .    .    .    .    .    .    .    .    .    66
John Ciardi—from "Robert Frost: The Way to the Poem"    67

4. JONAH AND THE WHALE    .    .    .    .    .    .    73

The Book of Jonah .    .    .    .    .    .    .    .    73
Traditional Jewish Folklore—from Joseph Gaer, *The Lore of the Old Testament*    .    .    .    .    .    .    .    76
Herman Melville—"The Sermon," from *Moby-Dick*    .    78
Herman Melville—"Jonah Historically Regarded," from *Moby-Dick*    .    .    .    .    .    .    .    .    .    85
Harold H. Watts—from *The Modern Reader's Guide to the Bible* .    .    .    .    .    .    .    .    .    .    86
Erich Fromm—from *Man for Himself*    .    .    .    .    87
Erich Fromm—from *The Forgotten Language*    .    .    .    88

5. NATHANIEL HAWTHORNE—"Young Goodman Brown"    91

Austin Warren—from *Nathaniel Hawthorne*    .    .    .    101
Richard Harter Fogle—from *Hawthorne's Fiction*    .    .    102

D. M. McKeithan—from "Hawthorne's 'Young Goodman Brown': An Interpretation" . . . . . . 104

Roy R. Male—from *Hawthorne's Tragic Vision* . . 105

Thomas E. Connolly—"Hawthorne's 'Young Goodman Brown': An Attack on Puritanic Calvinism" . . 107

6. JAMES JOYCE—"Clay" . . . . . . . 112

Richard B. Hudson—"Joyce's 'Clay'" . . . . . 117

Marvin Magalaner—from "The Other Side of James Joyce" 119

William T. Noon, S. J.—"Joyce's 'Clay': An Interpretation" 125

7. FRANZ KAFKA—"A Country Doctor" . . . . . 130

Basil Busacca—from "A Country Doctor" . . . . 135

Margaret Church—"Kafka's 'A Country Doctor'" . . 138

Stanley Cooperman—from "Kafka's 'A Country Doctor': Microcosm of Symbolism" . . . . . . 140

8. WILLIAM BLAKE—"The Mental Traveller" . . . 143

W. M. Rossetti—from *The Poetical Works of William Blake* 146

S. Foster Damon—from *William Blake, His Philosophy and Symbols* . . . . . . . . . . 147

Mona Wilson—from *The Life of William Blake* . . 148

Joyce Cary—from *The Horse's Mouth* . . . . 149

**Suggestions for Study** . . . . . . . 155

**Appendix: Writing the Critical Paper** . . . 171

# PART ONE
## THE NATURE OF SYMBOLISM

# 1. THE BOUNDARIES OF SYMBOLISM

## CHARLES DICKENS

"The One Thing Needful." Chapter One of *Hard Times for These Times* [1854], edited by William W. Watt. New York: Rinehart, 1958.

"Now, what I want is, Facts. Teach these boys and girls nothing but Facts. Facts alone are wanted in life. Plant nothing else, and root out everything else. You can only form the minds of reasoning animals upon Facts: nothing else will ever be of any service to them. This is the principle on which I bring up my own children, and this is the principle on which I bring up these children. Stick to Facts, sir!"

The scene was a plain, bare, monotonous vault of a schoolroom, and the speaker's square forefinger emphasised his observations by underscoring every sentence with a line on the schoolmaster's sleeve. The emphasis was helped by the speaker's square wall of a forehead, which had his eyebrows for its base, while his eyes found commodious cellarage in two dark caves, overshadowed by the wall. The emphasis was helped by the speaker's mouth, which was wide, thin, and hard set. The emphasis was helped by the speaker's voice, which was inflexible, dry, and dictatorial. The emphasis was helped by the speaker's hair, which bristled on the skirts of his bald head, a plantation of firs ·to keep the wind from its shining surface, all covered with knobs, like the crust of a plum pie, as if the head had[1] scarcely warehouse-room for the hard facts stored inside. The speaker's obstinate carriage, square coat, square legs, square shoulders,—nay, his very neckcloth, trained to take him by the throat with an unaccommodating grasp, like a stubborn fact, as it was,—all helped with the emphasis.

"In this life, we want nothing but Facts, sir; nothing but Facts!"

The speaker, and the schoolmaster, and the third grown person present, all backed a little, and swept with their eyes the inclined

3

plane of little vessels then and there arranged in order, ready to have imperial gallons of facts poured into them until they were full to the brim.[2]

## SAUL BELLOW

"Deep Readers of the World, Beware!" *New York Times Book Review*, LXIV (February 15, 1959). Reprinted by permission of the author and the publisher.

Interviewed as he was getting on the train for Boston, E. M. Forster was asked how he felt on the eve of his first visit to Harvard. He replied that he had heard that there were some particularly deep readers of his books to be found in Cambridge. He expected to be questioned closely by them, and this worried him. The reason is perfectly understandable.

In this age of ours serious people are more serious than they ever were, and lightness of heart like Mr. Forster's is hard to find. To the serious a novel is a work of art; art has a role to play in the drama of civilized life; civilized life is set upon a grim and dangerous course —and so we may assume if we are truly serious that no good novelist is going to invite us to a picnic merely to eat egg salad and chase butterflies over the English meadows or through the Tuscan woods. Butterflies are gay, all right, but in them lies the secret of metamorphosis. As for eggs, life's mystery hides in the egg. We all know that. So much for butterflies and egg salad.

It would be unjust to say that the responsibility for this sort of thing belongs entirely to the reader. Often the writer himself is at fault. He doesn't mind if he *is* a little deeper than average. Why not?

Nevertheless deep reading has gone very far. It has become dangerous to literature.

"Why, sir," the student asks, "does Achilles drag the body of Hector around the walls of Troy?" "That sounds like a stimulating question. Most interesting. I'll bite,'" says the professor. "Well, you see, sir, the 'Aeneid' is full of circles—shields, chariot wheels and other round figures. And you know what Plato said about circles. The ancients were all mad for geometry." "Bless your crew-cut head," says the professor, "for such a beautiful thought. You have exquisite sensibility. Your approach is both deep and serious. Still I always believed that Achilles did it because he was so angry."

It would take an unusual professor to realize that Achilles *was* angry. To many teachers he would represent much, but he would not *be* anything in particular. To be is too obvious. Our professor how-ever is a "square," and the bright student is annoyed with him. Anger! What good is anger? Great literature is subtle, dignified, profound. Virgil is as good as Plato anytime; and if Plato thought, Virgil must surely have done so, too, thought just as beautifully circle for circle.

Things are not what they seem. And anyway, unless they repre-sent something large and worthy, writers will not bother with them. Any deep reader can tell you that picking up a bus transfer is the *reisemotif* (journey motif) when it happens in a novel. A travel folder signifies Death. Coal holes represent the Underworld. Soda crackers are the Host. Three bottles of beer are—it's obvious. The busy mind can hardly miss at this game, and every player is a winner.

Are you a Marxist? Then Herman Melville's Pequod in "Moby Dick" can be a factory, Ahab the manager, the crew the working class. Is your point of view religious? The Pequod sailed on Christmas morn-ing, a floating cathedral headed south. Do you follow Freud or Jung? Then your interpretations may be rich and multitudinous. I recently had a new explanation of "Moby Dick" from the young man in charge of an electronic brain. "Once and for all," he said. "That whale is everybody's mother wallowing in her watery bed. Ahab has the Oedipus complex and wants to slay the hell out of her."

This is deep reading. But it is only fair to remember that the best novelists and poets of the century have done much to promote it. When Mairy (in James Joyce's "Ulysses") loses the pin of her drawers, she doesn't know what to do to keep them up, the mind of Bloom goes from grammar to painting, from painting to religion. It is all ac-complished in a few words. Joyce's genius holds all the elements in balance.

The deep reader, however, is apt to lose his head. He falls wildly on any particle of philosophy or religion and blows it up bigger than the Graf Zeppelin. Does Bloom dust Stephen's clothes and brush off the wood shavings? They are no ordinary shavings but the shavings from Stephen's cross.

What else? All the little monkish peculiarities at which Robert Browning poked fun in the "Soliloquy in a Spanish Cloister," crossing knife and fork on the platter at the end of a meal and the rest of it, have become the pillars of the new system.

Are we to attach meaning to whatever is grazed by the writer? Is modern literature Scripture? Is criticism Talmud, theology? Deep readers of the world, beware! You had better be sure that your serious-ness is indeed high seriousness and not, God forbid, low seriousness.

A true symbol is substantial, not accidental. You cannot avoid it, you cannot remove it. You can't take the handkerchief from "Othello," or the sea from "The Nigger of the Narcissus," or the disfigured feet from "Oedipus Rex." You can, however, read "Ulysses" without suspecting that wood shavings have to do with the Crucifixion or that the name Simon refers to the sin of Simony or that the hunger of the Dubliners at noon parallels that of the Lestrygonians. These are purely peripheral matters; fringe benefits, if you like. The beauty of the book cannot escape you if you are any sort of reader, and it is better to approach it from the side of *naïveté* than from that of culture-idolatry, sophistication and snobbery. Of course it's hard in our time to be as naïve as one would like. Information does filter through. It leaks, as we have taken to saying. Still the knowledge of even the sophisticated is rather thin, and even the most wised-up devils, stuffed to the ears with arcana, turned out to be fairly simple.

Perhaps the deepest readers are those who are least sure of themselves. An even more disturbing suspicion is that they prefer meaning to feeling. What again about the feelings? Yes, it's too bad. I'm sorry to have to ring in this tiresome subject, but there's no help for it. The reason why the schoolboy takes refuge in circles is that the wrath of Achilles and the death of Hector are too much for him. He is doing no more than most civilized people do when confronted with passion and death. They contrive somehow to avoid them.

The practice of avoidance is so widespread that it is probably not fair to single out any group for blame. But if nothing is to be said or done, we might as well make ready to abandon literature altogether. Novels are being published today which consist entirely of abstractions, meanings, and while our need for meanings is certainly great our need for concreteness, for particulars, is even[1] greater. We need to see how human beings act after they have appropriated or assimilated the meanings. Meanings themselves are a dime a dozen. In literature humankind becomes abstract when we begin to dislike it. And...

Interruption by a deep reader: Yes, yes, we know all that. But just look at the novels of the concrete and the particular, people opening doors and lighting cigarettes. Aren't they boring? Besides, do you want us to adopt a program to curtail the fear of feeling and to pretend to *like* the creature of flesh and bone?

Certainly not. No programs.

A pretty pass we have come to!

We must leave it to inspiration to redeem the concrete and the particular and to recover the value of flesh and bone. Meanwhile, let Plato have his circles and let the soda crackers be soda crackers and the wood shavings wood shavings. They are mysterious enough as it is.[34]

## RALPH WALDO EMERSON

From "The Poet" [1844]. In *Essays, Second
Series*. Concord Edition. Boston: Houghton
Mifflin, 1904. Pp. 1-42.

. . . . Things admit of being used as symbols because nature is
a symbol, in the whole, and in every part. Every line we can draw in
the sand has expression; and there is no body without its spirit or
genius. All form is an effect of character; all condition, of the quality
of the life; all harmony, of health; and for this reason a perception of
beauty should be sympathetic, or proper only to the good. The beautiful rests on the foundations of the necessary.[13] The soul makes the
body, as the wise Spenser teaches:—

> "So every spirit, as it is most pure,
> And hath in it the more of heavenly light,
> So it the fairer body doth procure
> To habit in, and it more fairly dight,
> With cheerful grace and amiable sight.
> For, of the soul, the body form doth take,
> For soul is form, and doth the body make."

Here we find ourselves suddenly not in a critical speculation but in a
holy place, and should go very warily and reverently. We stand before
the secret of the world, there where Being passes into Appearance and
Unity into Variety.

The Universe is the externization of the soul. Wherever the life
is, that bursts into appearance around it. Our science is sensual, and
therefore superficial. The earth and the heavenly bodies, physics and
chemistry, we sensually treat, as if they were self-existent; but these
are the retinue of that Being we have. "The mighty heaven," said Pro-
clus, "exhibits, in its transfigurations, clear images of the splendor
of intellectual perceptions; being moved in conjunction with the unap-
parent periods of intellectual natures." Therefore science always goes
abreast with the just elevation of the man, keeping step with[14] religion and metaphysics; or the state of science is an index of our self-
knowledge. Since every thing in nature answers to a moral power, if
any phenomenon remains brute and dark it is because the correspond-
ing faculty in the observer is not yet active.

No wonder then, if these waters be so deep, that we hover over
them with a religious regard. The beauty of the fable proves the im-

portance of the sense; to the poet, and to all others; or, if you please, every man is so far a poet as to be susceptible of these enchantments of nature; for all men have the thoughts whereof the universe is the celebration. I find that the fascination resides in the symbol. Who loves nature? Who does not? Is it only poets, and men of leisure and cultivation, who live with her? No; but also hunters, farmers, grooms, and butchers, though they express their affection in their choice of life and not in their choice of words. The writer wonders what the coachman or the hunter values in riding, in horses and dogs. It is not superficial qualities. When you talk with him he holds these at as slight a rate as you. His worship is sympathetic; he has no definitions, but he is commanded in nature by the living power which he feels to be there present.[15] No imitation or playing of these things would content him; he loves the earnest of the north wind, of rain, of stone and wood and iron. A beauty not explicable is dearer than a beauty which we can see to the end of. It is nature the symbol, nature certifying the supernatural, body overflowed by life which he worships with coarse but sincere rites.

The inwardness and mystery of this attachment drive men of every class to the use of emblems. The schools of poets and philosophers are not more intoxicated with their symbols than the populace with theirs. In our political parties, compute the power of badges and emblems. . . . See the power of national emblems. Some stars, lilies, leopards, a crescent, a lion, an eagle, or other figure which came into credit God knows how, on an old rag of bunting, blowing in the wind on a fort at the ends of the earth, shall make the blood tingle under the rudest or the most conventional exterior. The people fancy[16] they hate poetry, and they are all poets and mystics![17]

## ARTHUR SYMONS

From *The Symbolist Movement in Literature.* Revised and enlarged edition. New York: E. P. Dutton, 1919. Reprinted by permission of the publisher.

Without symbolism there can be no literature; indeed, not even language. What are words themselves but symbols, almost as arbitrary as the letters which compose them, mere sounds of the voice to which we have agreed to give certain significations, as we have agreed to

translate these sounds by those combinations of letters? Symbolism began with the first words uttered by the first man, as he named every
living thing; or before them, in heaven, when God named the world
into being. And we see, in these beginnings, precisely what Symbolism
in literature really is: a form of[1] expression, at the best but approximate, essentially but arbitrary, until it has obtained the force of a
convention, for an unseen reality apprehended by the consciousness. It
is sometimes permitted to us to hope that our convention is indeed
the reflection rather than merely the sign of that unseen reality. We
have done much if we have found a recognisable sign.

"A symbol," says Comte Goblet d'Alviella, in his book on *The
Migration of Symbols*, "might be defined as a representation which
does not aim at being a reproduction." Originally, as he points out,
used by the Greeks to denote "the two halves of the tablet they divided
between themselves as a pledge of hospitality," it came to be used of
every sign, formula, or rite by which those initiated in any mystery
made themselves secretly known to one another. Gradually the word
extended its meaning, until it came to denote every conventional
representation of idea by form, of the unseen by the visible.[2]

JAMES K. FEIBLEMAN

From *Aesthetics*. New York: Duell, Sloan and
Pearce, 1949. Copyright 1949 by James K.
Feibleman. Reprinted by permission of the
publisher.

It is no accident that the method of art involves symbolism.
For the artist must work with single instances; he can tell only one
story at a time, paint only one picture or sing one song. The story,
the picture or the song, would mean nothing artistically unless it
dragged in its wake a wide penumbra of meaning. Behind every concrete object of art is reflected the shadow of countless absent particulars which it affectively symbolizes. The hold upon us of a character
in fiction, for instance, is its ability to remind us of all those actual
people who are therein described. It is not the particularity of such a
figure but rather its valuational generality which carries the appeal. We
have never met Polonius nor shall we ever meet him: there is no such
person. Yet we meet him every day and he lives for us because we have
met so many dull, busy-body, meddling bores in high places. Needless

to emphasize, the abstract qualities which are embodied in a fictional character do not of themselves constitute the artistic property, and indeed they are incapable by themselves of carrying it. They require embodiment, embodiment in a particular symbolism; and it is just this step which the artist is obliged to furnish.[405]

## EDMUND WILSON

From *Axel's Castle: A Study in the Imaginative Literature of 1870-1930.* New York: Charles Scribner's Sons. Reprinted with the permission of the publisher, copyright 1931 Charles Scribner's Sons; renewal copyright 1959 Edmund Wilson.

The assumptions which underlay Symbolism lead us to formulate some such doctrine as the following: Every feeling or sensation we have, every moment of consciousness, is different from every other; and it is, in consequence, impossible to render our sensations as we actually experience them through the conventional and universal language of ordinary literature. Each poet has his unique personality; each of his moments has its special tone, its special combination of elements. And it is the poet's task to find, to invent, the special language which will alone be capable of expressing his personality and feelings. Such a language must make use of symbols: what is so special, so fleeting and so vague cannot be conveyed by direct statement or description, but only by a succession of words, of images, which will serve to suggest it to the reader. The Symbolists themselves, full of the idea of producing with poetry effects like those of music, tended to think of these images as possessing an abstract value like musical notes and chords. But the words of our speech are not musical notation, and what the symbols of Symbolism really were, were metaphors detached from their subjects —for one cannot, beyond a certain point, in poetry, merely enjoy color and sound for their own sake: one has to guess what the images are being applied to. And Symbolism may be defined as an attempt by carefully studied means—a complicated association of ideas represented[21] by a medley of metaphors—to communicate unique personal feelings.[22]

# 2. INTENTION—STANDARD OR FALLACY?

## J. E. SPINGARN

From "The New Criticism" [1910]. In Irving
Babbitt and others. *Criticism in America: Its
Function and Status*. New York: Harcourt,
Brace, and Company, 1924. Pp. 9-45. Re-
printed by permission of Columbia Univer-
sity Press.

. . . ."There is a destructive and a creative or constructive
criticism," said Goethe; the first measures and tests literature according to mechanical standards, the second answers the fundamental questions: "What has the writer proposed to himself to do? and how far
has he succeeded in carrying out his own plan?" Carlyle, in his essay
on Goethe, almost uses Goethe's own words, when he says that the
critic's first and foremost duty is to make plain to himself "what the
poet's aim really and truly was, how the task he had to do stood before
his eye, and how far, with such materials as were afforded him, he has
fulfilled it."

This has been the central problem, the guiding star, of all
modern criticism. From Coleridge to Pater, from Sainte-Beuve to
Lemaître,[23] this is what critics have been striving for, even when
they have not succeeded; yes, even when they have been deceiving
themselves into thinking that they were striving for something else.
This was not the ideal of the critics of Aristotle's day, who, like so
many of their successors, censured a work of art as "irrational, impossible, morally hurtful, self-contradictory, or contrary to technical
correctness." This was not Boileau's standard when he blamed Tasso
for the introduction of Christian rather than pagan mythology into
epic poetry, nor Addison's, when he tested *Paradise Lost* according to
the rules of Le Bossu; nor Dr. Johnson's when he lamented the absence
of poetic justice in *King Lear,* or pronounced dogmatically that the
poet should not "number the streaks of the tulip." What has the poet
tried to do, and how has he fulfilled his intention? What is he striving

11

to express and how has he expressed it? What vital and essential spirit animates his work, what central impression does it leave on the receptive mind, and how can I best express this impression? Is his work true to the laws of its own being rather than to laws formulated by[24] others? These are the questions that modern critics have been taught to ask when face to face with the work of a poet. Only one *caveat* must be borne in mind when attempting to answer them; the poet's aim must be judged at the moment of the creative act, that is to say, by the art of the poem itself, and not by the vague ambitions which he imagines to be his real intentions before or after the creative act is achieved. For to create a work of art is the goal of every artist; and all questions in regard to his achievement resolve themselves into this: Has he or has he not created a work of art?[25]

## W. K. WIMSATT and M. C. BEARDSLEY

From "The Intentional Fallacy." *Sewanee Review*, LIV (Summer 1946), 468-488. Reprinted by permission of the authors.

. . . . We argued that the design or intention of the author is neither available nor desirable as a standard for judging the success of a work of literary art, and it seems to us that this is a principle which goes deep into some differences in the history of critical attitudes. It is a principle which accepted or rejected points to the polar opposites of classical "imitation" and romantic expression. It entails many specific truths about inspiration, authenticity, biography, literary history and scholarship, and about some trends of contemporary poetry, especially its allusiveness. There is hardly a problem of literary criticism in which the critic's approach will not be qualified by his view of "intention."

"Intention," as we shall use the term, corresponds to *what he intended* in a formula which more or less explicitly has had wide acceptance "In order to judge the poet's performance, we must[468] know *what he intended*." Intention is design or plan in the author's mind. Intention has obvious affinities for the author's attitude toward his work, the way he felt, what made him write.

We begin our discussion with a series of propositions summarized and abstracted to a degree where they seem to us axiomatic, if not truistic.

1. A poem does not come into existence by accident. The words of a poem, as Professor Stoll has remarked, come out of a head, not out of a hat. Yet to insist on the designing intellect as a *cause* of a poem is not to grant the design or intention as a *standard*.

2. One must ask how a critic expects to get an answer to the question about intention. How is he to find out what the poet tried to do? If the poet succeeded in doing it, then the poem itself shows what he was trying to do. And if the poet did not succeed, then the poem is not adequate evidence, and the critic must go outside the poem—for evidence of an intention that did not become effective in the poem. "Only one *caveat* must be borne in mind," says an eminent intentionalist in a moment when his theory repudiates itself; "the poet's aim must be judged at the moment of the creative act, that is to say, by the art of the poem itself."

3. Judging a poem is like judging a pudding or a machine. One demands that it work. It is only because an artifact works that we infer the intention of an artificer. "A poem should not mean but be." A poem can *be* only through its *meaning*—since its medium is words—yet it *is*, simply *is*, in the sense that we have no excuse for inquiring what part is intended or meant. Poetry is a feat of style by which a complex of meaning is handled all at once. Poetry succeeds because all or most of what is said or implied is relevant; what is irrelevant has been excluded, like lumps from pudding and "bugs" from machinery. In this respect poetry differs from practical messages, which are successful[469] if and only if we correctly infer the intention. They are more abstract than poetry.

4. The meaning of a poem may certainly be a personal one, in the sense that a poem expresses a personality or state of soul rather than a physical object like an apple. But even a short lyric poem is dramatic, the response of a speaker (no matter how abstractly conceived) to a situation (no matter how universalized). We ought to impute the thoughts and attitudes of the poem immediately to the dramatic *speaker*, and if to the author at all, only by a biographical act of inference.

5. If there is any sense in which an author, by revision, has better achieved his original intention, it is only the very abstract, tautological, sense that he intended to write a better work and now has done it. (In this sense every author's intention is the same.) His former specific intention was not his intention. "He's the man we were in search of, that's true"; says Hardy's rustic constable, "and yet he's not the man we were in search of. For the man we were in search of was not the man we wanted."[470]

RUDOLPH VON ABELE

From "Symbolism and the Student." *College English*, XVI (April, 1955), 424-429. Reprinted by permission of the author and the publisher.

. . . . what are we to say when the philistines among our students object that the symbolic readings we suggest cannot be shown to have been "intended" by the authors of the works under contemplation? Did William Faulkner "intend," for instance, that *The Sound and the Fury* should be read as a symbolic enactment of the Passion of Our Lord? And if he did not so "intend" it, by what right may we so read it? This question in turn suggests another; but let me comment on it first. The rightful answer is that the only "intention" with which we, as readers, have any business is what might be called "intention realized," or the work as it exists in its presumably final form, not the work as it might have been had its author done other things than those he in fact did do. How do we know what he might have done? Sometimes he tells us what he is going to do, or what he is doing, or what he has done; but it is perfectly clear that all these asseverations yield precedence to the work itself. It is true that we may make inferences from a work's characteristics as to the motives out of which it was composed; but here intention, or "motive," is wholly derivative from the testimony of the text, which is the court of first as well as of last resort. Perhaps the author may have said that he intended to write a tragedy; and if we find that he did not we may say that from his own point of view he failed. Yet from our point of view he may have succeeded in doing something quite different, and just as valuable. Because a hit-and-run driver protests that his intention was not to kill his victim, we do not therefore say that the victim is not dead.

The suggestion that the author's interpretation of his own work may differ from that of the reader implies that readers, too, may differ among themselves. What then? Does the possibility of plural readings of the same work break down the argument that readings[428] may be justifiable and unjustifiable? I think not. I have said that the ideal of an "objective" reading is impossible, and so it is; at least, it becomes more impossible the more complex the work in question happens to be What seem like plural readings, of equal validity, may not be so much plural as partial. We readers come together, as it were, holding our various partial meanings like pieces of a puzzle in our hands. The continual danger is that we should see them, in the pride of discovery, as more than partial, save where works of a low order of complexity are concerned. It is not hard to exhaust the meaning of Hawthorne's *Young Goodman Brown*. But on the other hand, the real problems of apparently rival and justifiable interpretation arise only with the great works; for only the great works are able to generate such problems. . . .[429]

## WALTER HAVIGHURST

From "Symbolism and the Student." *College English*, XVI (April, 1955), 429-434, 461. Reprinted by permission of the author and the publisher.

The writer's intention—Here I have a difference with Mr. Von Abele. Instead of dismissing that intention as something that cannot be tracked and is[429] ambiguous and irrelevant anyway, I believe that awareness of the writer's intention, in matters both large and small, is the basis of valid reading. The act of reading, which calls upon mind, memory, and emotion, is as personal as the act of writing, and no readers will find precisely the same things in a work of literature. But this cannot mean that a poem or a story is an elaborate ink-blot, signifying only what it evokes in a reader's consciousness. A work of literature is a person-to-person communication. It is the business of the writer to have an intention and to make his intention known. If he is successful he does make it known, not only by his context but by his feeling, his over-tones, his point of view. "Seat thyself sultanically among the moons of Saturn," says Ishmael in *Moby-Dick*, "and take a high abstracted man alone; and he seems a wonder, a grandeur, and a woe. But...take mankind in mass, and for the most part they seem a mob of unnecessary duplicates, both contemporary and hereditary." Here are the alternatives, and Melville leaves no doubt as to his intention. Nor does a Zola or a Dreiser, taking the other view of man. Symbolic meanings grow out of the intention. Melville hoped that no one would read *Moby-Dick* as a "damned allegory," but he made it impossible to read as a *Two Years Before the Mast*. . . .[430]

## ROBERT FROST

From the essay "The Constant Symbol." In *The Poems of Robert Frost*. New York: Modern Library, 1946. Reprinted by permission of Henry Holt and Company, Inc.

There are many other things I have found myself saying about poetry, but the chiefest of these is that it is metaphor, saying one thing and meaning another, saying one thing in terms of another, the pleasure of ulteriority. Poetry is simply made of metaphor. So also is philosophy—and science, too, for that matter, if it will take the soft impeachment from a friend. Every poem is a new metaphor inside or it is nothing And there is a sense in which all poems are the same old metaphor always.

Every single poem written regular is a symbol small or great of the way the will has to pitch into commitments deeper and deeper to a rounded conclusion and then be judged for whether any original intention it had has been strongly spent or weakly lost; be it in art, politics, school, church, business, love, or marriage—in a piece of work or in a career. Strongly spent is synonymous with kept.

We may speak after sentence, resenting judgment. How can the world know anything so intimate as what we were intending to do? The answer is the world presumes to know. The ruling passion of man is not as Viennese as is claimed. It is rather a gregarious instinct to keep together by minding[xvi] each other's business. Grex rather than sex. We *must* be preserved from becoming egregious. The beauty of socialism is that it will end the individuality that is always crying out mind your own business. Terence's answer would be all human business is my business. No more invisible means of support, no more invisible motives, no more invisible anything. The ultimate commitment is giving in to it that an outsider may see what we were up to sooner and better than we ourselves. The bard has said in effect, Unto these forms did I commend the spirit. It may take him a year after the act to confess he only betrayed the spirit with a rhymster's cleverness and to forgive his enemies the critics for not having listened to his oaths and protestations to the contrary. Had he anything to be true to? Was he true to it? Did he use good words? You couldn't tell unless you made out what idea they were supposed to be good for. Every poem is an epitome of the great predicament; a figure of the will braving alien entanglements.

Take the President in the White House. A study of the success of his intention might have to go clear back to when as a young politician, youthfully step-careless, he made the choice between the two parties of our system. He may have stood for a moment wishing he knew of a third party nearer the ideal;[xvii] but only for a moment, since he was practical. And in fact he may have been so little impressed with the importance of his choice that he left his first commitment to be made for him by his friends and relatives. It was only a small commitment anyway, like a kiss. He can scarcely remember how much credit he deserved personally for the decision it took. Calculation is usually no part in the first step in any walk. And behold him now a statesman so multifariously closed in on with obligations and answerabilities that sometimes he loses his august temper. He might as well have got himself into a sestina royal.[xviii]

. . . .

Here is where it all comes out. The mind is a baby giant who, more provident in the cradle than he knows, has hurled his paths in life all round' ahead of him like playthings given—data so-called. They are vocabulary, grammar, prosody, and diary, and it will go hard if he can't find stepping stones of them for his feet wherever he wants to go. The way will be zigzag, but it will be a straight crookedness like the walking stick he cuts himself in the bushes for an emblem. He will be judged as he does or doesn't let this zig or that zag project him off out of his general direction.

Teacher or student or investigator whose chance on these defenseless lines may seize, your pardon if for once I point you out what ordinarily you would point me out. To some it will seem strange that I have written my verse regular all this time without knowing till yesterday that it was from fascination with this constant symbol I celebrate. . . .[xxiii]

## 3. DEFINITIONS AND TOUCHSTONES

M. H. ABRAMS

From the article "Symbol" in *A Glossary of Literary Terms*. New York: Rinehart, 1957. Reprinted by permission of the author.

A symbol, in the broadest use of the term, is anything which signifies something else; in this sense, all words are symbols. As commonly used in criticism, however, "symbol" is applied only to a word or phrase signifying an object which itself has significance; that is, the object referred to has a range of meaning beyond itself. Some symbols are "conventional," or "public"; thus "the Cross," "the Red, White, and Blue," "the Good Shepherd" are terms which signify objects of which the symbolic meanings are widely known. Poets, like all of us, use these conventional symbols; but some poets also use "private symbols," which are not widely known, or which they develop for themselves (usually by expanding and elaborating pre-existing associations of an object), and these set a more difficult problem in interpretation.

Take as an example the word "rose," which in its literal meaning is a kind of flower. In Burns's line, "O my love's like a red, red rose," the word is used as a simile, and in the version "O my love is a red, red rose," it is used as a metaphor. William Blake wrote:

O Rose, thou art sick!
The invisible worm
That flies in the night,
In the howling storm,

Has found out thy bed
Of crimson joy,
And his dark secret love
Does thy life destroy.

This rose is not the vehicle for a simile or a metaphor, because it lacks the paired subject—"my love," in the examples just cited—which is[95] characteristic of these figures. . . . Blake's rose *is* a rose—yet it is also something more; words like "bed," "joy," "love," indicate that the described object has a further range of significance which makes it a symbol. But Blake's rose is not, like the symbolic rose of Dante's *Paradiso* and other medieval poems, an element in a complex set of traditional religious symbols which were widely known to contemporary readers. Only from the clues in Blake's poem itself, supplemented by a knowledge of parallel elements in his other poems, do we come to see that Blake's worm-eaten rose symbolizes such matters as the destruction wrought by furtiveness, deceit, and hypocrisy in what should be a frank and joyous relationship of physical love.[96]

## SAMUEL TAYLOR COLERIDGE

From *The Statesman's Manual* [1816]. In *The Complete Works of Samuel Taylor Coleridge,* edited by W. G. T. Shedd. New York: Harper & Brothers, 1884. Vol. I.

It is among the miseries of the present age that it recognizes no *medium* between literal and metaphorical. Faith is either to be buried in the dead letter, or its name and honors usurped by a counterfeit product of the mechanical understanding, which in the blindness of self-complacency confounds symbols with allegories. Now an allegory is but a translation of abstract notions into a picture-language, which is itself nothing but an abstraction from objects of the senses; the principal being more worthless even than its phantom proxy, both alike unsubstantial, and the former shapeless to boot. On the other hand a symbol . . . is characterized by a translucence of the special in the individual, or of the general in the special, or of the universal in the general; above all by the translucence of the eternal through and in the temporal. It always partakes of the reality which it renders intelligible; and while it enunciates the whole, abides itself as a[437] living part in that unity of which it is the representative.[438]

## THOMAS CARLYLE

> "Symbols." In *Sartor Resartus: The Life and Opinions of Herr Teufelsdrockh* [1835], edited ·by Charles Frederick Harrold. New York: The Odyssey Press, 1937.

Probably it will elucidate the drift of these foregoing obscure utterances, if we here insert somewhat of our Professor's speculations on *Symbols*. To state his whole doctrine, indeed, were ·beyond our compass: nowhere is he more mysterious, impalpable, than in this of 'Fantasy being the organ of the God-like', and how 'Man thereby, though based,[217] to all seeming, on the small Visible, does nevertheless extend down into the infinite deeps of the Invisible, of which Invisible, ·indeed, his Life is properly ·the bodying forth.' Let us, omitting these high transcendental aspects of the matter, study to glean (whether from the Paper-bags or the Printed Volume) what little seems logical and practical, and cunningly arrange it into such degree of coherence as it will assume. By way of proem, take the following not injudicious remarks:

'The benignant efficacies of Concealment,' cries our Professor, 'who shall speak or sing? SILENCE and SECRECY! Altars might still be raised to them (were this an altar-building time) for universal worship. Silence is the element in which great things fashion ·themselves ·together; that at length they may emerge, full-formed and majestic, into the daylight of Life, which they are thenceforth to rule. Not William the Silent only, but all the considerable men I have known, and the most undiplomatic and unstrategic of these, forbore to babble·of what they were creating and projecting. Nay, in thy own mean perplexities, do thou thyself but *hold thy tongue for one day:* on the morrow, how much clearer are thy purposes and duties; what wreck and rubbish ˙have those mute workmen within thee swept away, when intrusive noises were shut out! Speech is too often not, as the Frenchman defined it, the art of concealing Thought; but of quite stifling and suspending Thought, so that there is none to conceal. Speech too is great, but not the greatest. As the Swiss Inscription says: *Sprechen ist silbern, Schweigen ist golden*[218] (Speech is silvern, Silence is golden); or as I might rather express it: Speech is of Time, Silence is of Eternity.

'Bees will not work except in darkness; Thought will not work except in Silence: neither will Virtue work except in Secrecy. Let not

thy left hand know what thy right hand doeth! Neither shalt thou
prate even to thy own heart of "those secrets known, to all." Is not
Shame (*Schaam*) the soil of all Virtue, of all good manners and good
morals? Like other plants, Virtue will not grow unless its root be
hidden, buried from the eye of the sun. Let the sun shine on it, nay, do
but look at it privily thyself, the root withers, and no flowers will
glad thee. O my Friends, when we view the fair clustering flowers that
overwreathe, for example, the Marriage-bower, and encircle man's life
with the fragrance and hues of Heaven, what hand will not smite the
foul plunderer that grubs them up by the roots, and with grinning,
grunting satisfaction, shows us the dung they flourish in! Men speak
much of the Printing-Press with its Newspapers: *du Himmel!* what
are these to Clothes and the Tailor's Goose?'

'Of kin to the so incalculable influences of Concealment, and
connected with still greater things, is the wondrous agency of *Symbols.*
In a Symbol there is concealment and yet revelation: here therefore, by
Silence and by Speech acting together, comes a double significance.
And if both the Speech be itself high, and the Silence fit and noble,
how expressive will their union be! Thus in many a painted Device,
or simple Seal-emblem, the commonest Truth stands out to us, proclaimed with quite new emphasis.

'For it is here that Fantasy with her mystic wonderland[219]
plays into the small prose domain of Sense, and becomes incorporated
therewith. In the Symbol proper, what we can call a Symbol, there is
ever, more or less distinctly and directly, some embodiment and revelation of the Infinite; the Infinite is made to blend itself with the Finite,
to stand visible, and as it were, attainable there. By Symbols, accordingly, is man guided and commanded, made happy, made
wretched. He everywhere finds himself encompassed with Symbols,
recognized as such or not recognized: the Universe is but one vast
Symbol of God; nay if thou wilt have it, what is man himself but a
Symbol of God; is not all that he does symbolical; a revelation to
Sense of the mystic god-given force that is in him; a "Gospel of Freedom," which he, the "Messias of Nature," preaches, as he can, by act
and word? Not a Hut he builds but is the visible embodiment of a
Thought; but bears visible record of invisible things; but is, in the
transcendental sense, symbolical as well as real.'

'Man,' says the Professor elsewhere, in quite antipodal contrast
with these high-soaring delineations, which we have here cut-short
on the verge of the inane, 'Man is by birth somewhat of an owl. Perhaps, too, of all the owleries that ever possessed him, the most owlish,
if we consider it, is that of your actually existing Motive-Millwrights.
Fantastic[220] tricks enough man has played, in his time; has fancied
himself to be most things, down even to an animated heap of Glass:
but to fancy himself a dead Iron-Balance for weighing Pains and
Pleasures on, was reserved for this his latter era. There stands he, his

Universe one huge Manger, filled with hay and thistles to be weighed against each other; and looks long-eared enough. Alas, poor devil! Spectres are appointed to haunt him: one age he is hagridden, bewitched; the next, priestridden, befooled; in all ages, bedevilled. And now the Genius of Mechanism smothers him worse than any Nightmare did; till the Soul is nigh choked out of him, and only a kind of Digestive, Mechanic life remains. In Earth and in Heaven he can see nothing but Mechanism; has fear for nothing else, hope in nothing else: the world would indeed grind him to pieces; but cannot he fathom the Doctrine of Motives, and cunningly compute these, and mechanise them to grind the other way?

'Were he not, as has been said, purblinded by enchantment, you had but to bid him open his eyes and look. In which country, in which time, was it hitherto that man's history, or the history of any man, went-on by calculated or calculable "Motives"? What make ye of your Christianities and Chivalries, and Reformations, and Marseillese Hymns, and Reigns of Terror? Nay, has not perhaps the Motive-grinder[221] himself been *in Love*? Did he never stand so much as a contested Election? Leave him to Time, and the medicating virtue of Nature.'

'Yes, Friends,' elsewhere observes the Professor, 'not our Logical, Mensurative faculty, but our Imaginative one is King over us; I might say, Priest and Prophet to lead us heavenward; or Magician and Wizard to lead us hellward. Nay, even for the basest Sensualist, what is Sense but the implement of Fantasy; the vessel it drinks out of? Ever in the dullest existence there is a sheen either of Inspiration or of Madness (thou partly hast it in thy choice, which of the two), that gleams-in from the circumambient Eternity, and colours with its own hues our little islet of Time. The Understanding is indeed thy window, too clear thou canst not make it; but Fantasy is thy eye, with its colour-giving retina, healthy or diseased. Have not I myself known five-hundred living soldiers sabred into crows'-meat for a piece of glazed cotton, which they called their Flag; which, had you sold it at any market-cross, would not have brought above three groschen? Did not the whole Hungarian Nation rise, like some tumultuous moon-stirred Atlantic, when Kaiser Joseph pocketed their Iron Crown; an Implement, as was sagaciously observed, in size and commercial value little differing from a horseshoe? It is in and through *Symbols* that man, consciously or unconsciously, lives, works, and has his being: those ages, moreover, are accounted the noblest which can the best recognize symbolical worth, and prize it the highest. For is not a Symbol ever, to him who has eyes for it, some dimmer or clearer revelation of the God-like?

'Of Symbols, however, I remark farther, that they have both an extrinsic and intrinsic value; oftenest the former only. What, for instance, was in that clouted Shoe, which[222] the Peasants bore aloft with them as ensign in their *Bauernkrieg* (Peasants' War)? Or in the Wallet-and-staff round which the Netherland *Gueux,* glorying in that nickname of Beggars, heroically rallied and prevailed, though against King Philip himself? Intrinsic significance these had none; only extrinsic; as the accidental Standards of multitudes more or less sacredly uniting together; in which union itself, as above noted, there is ever something mystical and borrowing of the Godlike. Under a like category, too, stand, or stood, the stupidest heraldic Coats-of-arms; military Banners everywhere; and generally all national or other sectarian Costumes and Customs: they have no intrinsic, necessary divineness, or even worth; but have acquired an extrinsic one. Nevertheless through all these there glimmers something of a Divine Idea, as through military Banners themselves, the Divine Idea of Duty, of heroic Daring; in some instances of Freedom, of Right. Nay the highest ensign that men ever met and embraced under, the Cross itself, had no meaning save an accidental extrinsic one.

'Another matter it is, however, when your Symbol has intrinsic meaning, and is of itself *fit* that men should unite round it. Let but the Godlike manifest itself to Sense; let but Eternity look, more or less visibly, through the Time-Figure (*Zeitbild*)! Then is it fit that men unite there; and worship together before such Symbol; and so from day to day, and from age to age, superadd to it new divineness.

'Of this latter sort are all true Works of Art: in them (if thou know a Work of Art from a Daub of Artifice) wilt thou discern Eternity looking through Time; the Godlike rendered visible. Here too may an extrinsic value gradually superadd itself: thus certain *Iliads,* and the like, have, in three-thousand[223] years, attained quite new significance. But nobler than all in this kind are the Lives of heroic god-inspired Men; for what other Work of Art is so divine? In Death too, in the Death of the Just, as the last perfection of a Work of Art, may we not discern symbolic meaning? In that divinely transfigured Sleep, as of Victory, resting over the beloved face which now knows thee no more, read (if thou canst for tears) the confluence of Time with Eternity, and some gleam of the latter peering through.

'Highest of all Symbols are those wherein the Artist or Poet has risen into Prophet, and all men can recognize a present God, and worship the same: I mean religious Symbols. Various enough have been such religious Symbols, what we call *Religions;* as men stood in this stage of culture or the other, and could worse or better body-forth the Godlike: some Symbols with a transient intrinsic worth; many with only an extrinsic. If thou ask to what height man has carried it in this manner, look on our divinest Symbol: on Jesus of Nazareth, and his Life, and his Biography, and what followed therefrom. Higher has the human Thought not yet reached: this is Christianity and Christendom; a Symbol of quite perennial, infinite character; whose significance will ever demand to be anew inquired into, and anew made manifest.

'But, on the whole, as Time adds much to the sacredness of Symbols, so likewise in his progress he at length defaces, or even desecrates them; and Symbols, like all terrestrial Garments, wax old. Homer's Epos has not ceased to be true; yet it is no longer *our* Epos, but shines in the distance, if clearer and clearer, yet also smaller and smaller, like a receding Star. It needs a scientific telescope, it needs to be reinterpreted and artificially brought near us, before we can so much as know that it *was* a Sun. So likewise a day comes when the Runic Thor, with his Eddas, must withdraw into[224] dimness; and many an African Mumbo-Jumbo and Indian Pawaw be utterly abolished. For all things, even Celestial Luminaries, much more atmospheric meteors, have their rise, their culmination, their decline.'

'Small is this which thou tellest me, that the Royal Sceptre is but a piece of gilt-wood; that the Pyx has become a most foolish box, and truly, as Ancient Pistol thought, "of little price." A right Conjuror might I name thee, couldst thou conjure back into these wooden tools the divine virtue they once held.'

'Of this thing, however, be certain: wouldst thou plant for Eternity, then plant into the deep infinite faculties of man, his Fantasy and Heart; wouldst thou plant for Year and Day, then plant into his shallow superficial faculties, his Self-love and Arithmetical Understanding, what will grow there. A Hierarch, therefore, and Pontiff of the World will we call him, the Poet and inspired Maker; who, Prometheus-like, can shape new Symbols, and bring new Fire from Heaven to fix it there. Such too will not always be wanting; neither perhaps now are. Meanwhile, as the average of matters goes, we account him Legislator and wise who can so much as tell when a Symbol has grown old, and gently remove it.

'When, as the last English Coronation was preparing,' concludes this wonderful Professor, 'I read in their Newspapers that the "Champion of England," he who has to offer[225] battle to the Universe for his new King, had brought it so far that he could now "mount his horse with little assistance," I said to myself: Here also we have a Symbol well-nigh superannuated. Alas, move whithersoever you may, are not the tatters and rags of superannuated worn-out Symbols (in this Ragfair of a World) dropping off everywhere, to hoodwink, to halter, to tether you; nay, if you shake them not aside, threatening to accumulate, and perhaps produce suffocation?'[226]

## CHARLES BAUDELAIRE

"Correspondences." In *French Symbolist Poetry*, translated by C. F. MacIntyre. Berkeley: University of California Press, 1958. Reprinted by permission of the publisher.

Nature is a temple of living pillars
where often words emerge, confused and dim;
and man goes through this forest, with familiar
eyes of symbols always watching him.

Like prolonged echoes mingling far away
in a unity tenebrous and profound,
vast as the night and as the limpid day,
perfumes, sounds, and colors correspond.

There are perfumes as cool as children's flesh,
sweet as oboes, as meadows green and fresh;
—others, triumphant and corrupt and rich,

with power to fill the infinite expanses,
like amber, incense, musk, and benzoin, which
sing the transports of the soul and senses.[13]

## WILLIAM BUTLER YEATS

From "The Symbolism of Poetry." [1900]. In *Essays*. New York: Macmillan, 1924. Pp. 188-202. [Originally published in *Ideas of Good and Evil*, 1896-1903.] Reprinted by permission of Mrs. W. B. Yeats, the Macmillan Co., New York, and the Macmillan Co. of Canada Ltd.

. . . . In 'Symbolism in Painting,' I tried to describe the element of symbolism that is in pictures and sculpture, and described a little the symbolism in poetry, but did not describe at all the continuous indefinable symbolism which is the substance of all style.

There are no lines with more melancholy beauty than these by Burns—

> The white moon is setting behind the white wave,
> And Time is setting with me, O!

and these lines are perfectly symbolical. Take from them the whiteness of the moon and of the wave, whose relation to the setting of Time is too subtle for the intellect, and you take from them their beauty. But, when all are together, moon and wave and whiteness and setting Time and the last melancholy cry, they evoke an emotion which cannot be evoked by any other arrangement of colours and sounds and forms. We may call this metaphorical writing, but it is better to call it symbolical writing, because metaphors[191] are not profound enough to be moving, when they are not symbols, and when they are symbols they are the most perfect of all, because the most subtle, outside of pure sound, and through them one can the best find out what symbols are. If one begins the reverie with any beautiful lines that one can remember, one finds they are like those by Burns. Begin with this line by Blake—

> The gay fishes on the wave when the moon sucks up the
> dew;

or these lines by Nash—

> Queens have died young and fair,
> Brightness falls from the air,
> Dust hath closed Helen's eye;

or these lines by Shakespeare—

> Timon hath made his everlasting mansion
> Upon the beached verge of the salt flood;
> Who once a day with his embossed froth
> The turbulent surge shall cover;

or take some line that is quite simple, that gets its beauty from its place in a story, and see how it flickers with the light of the many symbols that have given the story its beauty, as a sword-blade may flicker with the light of burning towers.

All sounds, all colours, all forms, either because of their preordained energies or because of long association, evoke indefinable[192] and yet precise emotions, or, as I prefer to think, call down among us certain disembodied powers, whose footsteps over our hearts we call emotions; and when sound, and colour, and form are in a musical relation, a beautiful relation to one another, they become as it were one sound, one colour, one form, and evoke an emotion that is made out of their distinct evocations and yet is one emotion. The same relation exists between all portions of every work of art, whether it be an epic or a song, and the more perfect it is, and the more various and numerous the elements that have flowed into its perfection, the more powerful will be the emotion, the power, the god it calls among us. Because an emotion does not exist, or does not become perceptible and active among us, till it has found its expression, in colour or in sound or in form, or in all of these, and because no two modulations or arrangements of these evoke the same emotion, poets and painters and musicians, and in a less degree because their effects are momentary, day and night and cloud and shadow, are continually making and unmaking mankind. It is indeed only those things which seem useless or very feeble that have any power, and all those things that seem useful or strong, armies, moving wheels, modes of architecture, modes of government, speculations of[193] the reason, would have been a little different if some mind long ago had not given itself to some emotion, as a woman gives herself to her lover, and shaped sounds or colours or forms, or all of these, into a musical relation, that their emotion might live in other minds. A little lyric evokes an emotion, and this emotion gathers others about it and melts into their being in the making of some great epic; and at last, needing an always less delicate body, or symbol, as it grows more powerful, it flows out, with all it has gathered, among the blind instincts of daily life, where it moves a power within powers, as one sees ring within ring in the stem of an old tree. This is maybe what Arthur O'Shaughnessy meant when he made his poets say they had built Nineveh with their sighing; and I am certainly never certain, when I hear of some war, or of some religious excitement or of some new manufacture, or of anything else that fills the ear of the world, that it has not all happened because of something that a boy piped in Thessaly. I remember once telling a seer to ask one among the gods who, as she believed, were standing about her in their symbolic bodies, what would come of a charming but seeming trivial labour of a friend, and the form answering, 'the devastation of peoples and the overwhelming of cities.' I doubt indeed if the crude circumstance[194] of the world, which seems to create all our emotions, does more than reflect, as in multiplying mirrors, the emotions that have come to solitary men in moments of poetical contemplation; or that love itself would be more than an animal hunger but for the poet and his shadow the priest, for unless we believe that outer things are the reality, we must believe that the gross is the shadow of the subtle, that things are wise before they become foolish, and secret before they cry out in the market-place. Solitary men in moments of contemplation receive, as I think, the creative impulse from the lowest of the Nine Hierarchies, and so make and unmake mankind, and even the world itself, for does not 'the eye altering alter all'?

> Our towns are copied fragments from our breast;
> And all man's Babylons strive but to impart
> The grandeurs of his Babylonian heart.

The purpose of rhythm, it has always seemed to me, is to prolong the moment of contemplation, the moment when we are both asleep and awake, which is the one moment of creation, by hushing us with an alluring monotony, while it holds us waking by variety, to keep us in that state of perhaps real trance, in which the mind liberated from[195] the pressure of the will is unfolded in symbols. If certain sensitive persons listen persistently to the ticking of a watch, or gaze persistently on the monotonous flashing of a light, they fall into the hypnotic trance; and rhythm is but the ticking of a watch made softer, that one must needs listen, and various, that one may not be swept beyond memory or grow weary of listening; while the patterns of the artist are but the monotonous flash woven to take the eyes in a subtler enchantment. I have heard in meditation voices that were forgotten the moment they had spoken; and I have been swept, when in more profound meditation, beyond all memory but of those things that came from beyond the threshold of waking life. I was writing once at a very symbolical and abstract poem, when my pen fell on the ground; and as I stooped to pick it up, I remembered some phantastic adventure that yet did not seem phantastic, and then another like adventure, and when I asked myself when these things had happened, I found that I was remembering my dreams for many nights. I tried to remember what I had done the day before, and then what I had done that morning; but all my waking life had perished from me, and it was only after a struggle that I came to remember it again, and as I did so that more powerful and startling life perished in its[196] turn. Had my pen not fallen on the ground and so made me turn from the images that I was weaving into verse, I would never have known that meditation had become trance, for I would have been like one who does not know that he is passing through a wood because his eyes are on the pathway. So I think that in the making and in the understanding of a work of art, and the more easily if it is full of patterns and symbols and music, we are lured to the threshold of sleep, and it may be far beyond it, without knowing that we have ever set our feet upon the steps of horn or of ivory.

Besides emotional symbols, symbols that evoke emotions alone, —and in this sense all alluring or hateful things are symbols, although their relations with one another are too subtle to delight us fully, away from rhythm and pattern,—there are intellectual symbols, symbols that evoke ideas alone, or ideas mingled with emotions; and outside the very definite traditions of mysticism and the less definite criticism of certain modern poets, these alone are called symbols. Most things belong to one or another kind, according to the way we speak of them and the companions we give them, for symbols,[197] associated with ideas that are more than fragments of the shadows thrown upon the intellect by the emotions they evoke, are the playthings of the allegorist or the pedant, and soon pass away. If I say 'white' or 'purple' in an ordinary line of poetry, they evoke emotions so exclusively that I cannot say why they move me; but if I bring them into the same sentence with such obvious intellectual symbols as a cross or a crown of thorns, I think of ,purity and sovereignty. Furthermore, innumerable meanings, which are held to 'white' or to 'purple' by bonds of subtle suggestion, and alike in the emotions and in the intellect, move visibly through my mind, and move invisibly beyond the threshold of sleep, casting lights and shadows of an indefinable wisdom on what had seemed before, it may be, but sterility and noisy violence. It is the intellect that decides where the reader shall ponder over the procession of the symbols, and if the symbols are merely emotional, he gazes from amid the accidents and destinies of the world; but if the symbols are intellectual too, he becomes himself a part of pure intellect, and he is himself mingled with the procession. If I watch a rushy pool in the moonlight, my emotion at its beauty is mixed with memories of the man that I have seen ploughing by its margin, or of the lovers[198] I saw there a night ago; but if I look at the moon herself and remember any of her ancient names and meanings, I move among divine people, and things that have shaken off our mortality, the tower of ivory, the queen of waters, the shining stag among enchanted woods, the white hare sitting upon the hilltop, the fool of faery with his shining cup full of dreams, and it may be 'make a friend of one of these images of wonders,' and 'meet the Lord in the air.' So, too, if one is moved by Shakespeare, who is content with emotional symbols that he may come the nearer to our sympathy, one is mixed with the whole spectacle of the world; while if one is moved by Dante, or by the myth of Demeter, one is mixed into the shadow of God or of a goddess. So too one is furthest from symbols when one is busy doing this or that, but the soul moves among symbols and unfolds in symbols when trance, or madness, or deep meditation has withdrawn it from every impulse but its own. 'I then saw,' wrote Gérard de Nerval of his madness, 'vaguely drifting into form, plastic images of antiquity, which outlined themselves, became definite, and seemed to represent symbols of which I only seized the idea with difficulty.' In an earlier time he would have been of that multitude, whose souls austerity withdrew, even more perfectly than madness[199] could withdraw his soul, from hope and memory, from desire and regret, that they might reveal those processions of symbols that men bow to before altars, and woo with incense and offerings. But being of our time, he has been like Maeterlinck, like Villiers de l'Isle Adam in *Axèl*, like all who are preoccupied with intellectual symbols in our time, a foreshadower of the new sacred book, of which all the arts, as somebody has said, are begging to dream. How can the arts overcome the slow dying of men's hearts that we call the progress of the world, and lay their hands upon men's heart-strings again, without becoming the garment of religion as in old times?

If people were to accept the theory that poetry moves us because of its symbolism, what change should one look for in the manner of our poetry? A return to the way of our fathers, a casting out of descriptions of nature for the sake of nature, of the moral law for the sake of the moral law, a casting out of all anecdotes and of that brooding over scientific opinion that so often extinguished the central flame in Tennyson, and of that vehemence that would make us do or not do certain things; or, in other words, we[200] should come to understand that the beryl stone was enchanted by our fathers that it might unfold the pictures in its heart, and not to mirror our own excited faces, or the boughs waving outside the window. With this change of substance, this return to imagination, this understanding that the laws of art, which are the hidden laws of the world, can alone bind the imagination, would come a change of style, and we would cast out of serious poetry those energetic rhythms, as of a man running, which are the invention of the will with its eyes always on something to be done or undone; and we would seek out those wavering, meditative, organic rhythms, which are the embodiment of the imagination, that neither desires nor hates, because it has done with time, and only wishes to gaze upon some reality, some beauty; nor would it be any longer possible for anybody to deny the importance of form, in all its kinds, for although you can expound an opinion, or describe a thing when your words are not quite well chosen, you cannot give a body to something that moves beyond the senses, unless your words are as subtle, as complex, as full of mysterious life, as the body of a flower or of a woman. The form of sincere poetry, unlike the form of the popular poetry, may indeed be sometimes obscure, or ungrammatical as in some of[201] the best of the Songs of Innocence and Experience, but it must have the perfections that escape analysis, the subtleties that have a new meaning every day, and it must have all this whether it be but a little song made out of a moment of dreamy indolence, or some great epic made out of the dreams of one poet and of a hundred generations whose hands were never weary of the sword.[202]

# D. H. LAWRENCE

From "The Dragon of the Apocalypse" [1930].
In his *Selected Literary Criticism*, edited by
Anthony Beal. London: William Heinemann,
1955. Copyright 1936 by Frieda Lawrence.
Reprinted by permission of The Viking Press,
Inc.

You can't give a great symbol a "meaning," any more than you
can give a cat a "meaning." Symbols are organic units of consciousness
with a life of their own, and you can never explain them away, because
their value is dynamic, emotional, belonging to the sense—consciousness of the body and soul, and not simply mental. An allegorical
image has a *meaning*. Mr. Facing-both-ways has a meaning. But I defy
you to lay your finger on the full meaning of Janus, who is a
symbol.[157]

It is necessary for us to realise very definitely the difference between allegory and symbol. Allegory is a narrative description using,
as a rule, images to express certain definite qualities. Each image means
something, and is a term in the argument and nearly always for a
moral or didactic purpose, for under the narrative of an allegory lies
a didactic argument, usually moral. Myth likewise is descriptive narrative using images. But myth is never an argument, it never has a
didactic nor a moral purpose, you can draw no conclusion from it.
Myth is an attempt to narrate a whole human experience, of which
the purpose is too deep, going too deep in the blood and soul, for
mental explanation or description. We *can* expound the myth of
Chronos very easily. We can explain it, we can even draw the moral
conclusion. But we only look a little silly. The myth of Chronos lives
on beyond explanation, for it describes a profound experience of the
human body and soul, an experience which is never exhausted and
never will be exhausted, for it is being felt and suffered now, and it
will be felt and suffered while man remains man. You may explain the
myths away: but it only means you go on suffering blindly, stupidly,
"in the unconscious," instead of healthily and with the imaginative
comprehension playing upon the suffering.

And the images of myth are symbols. They don't "mean some·
thing". They stand for units of human *feeling*, human experience. A

complex of emotional experience is a symbol. And the power of the symbol is to arouse the deep emotional self, and the dynamic self, beyond comprehension. Many ages of accumulated experience still throb within a symbol. And we throb in response. It takes centuries to create a really significant symbol: even the symbol of the Cross, or of the horseshoe, or the horns. No man can invent symbols. He can invent an emblem, made up of images: or metaphors: or images: but not symbols. Some images, in the course of many generations of men, become symbols, embedded in the soul and ready to start alive when touched, carried on in the human consciousness for centuries. And again, when men become unresponsive and half dead, symbols die.[158]

## JAMES JOYCE

From *Stephen Hero,* edited by Theodore Spencer. A New Edition, Incorporating the Additional Manuscript Pages in the Yale University Library, edited by John J. Slocum and Herbert Cahoon. New York: New Directions, 1955. Copyright 1944 by New Directions. Reprinted by permission of the publisher.

—You know what Aquinas says: The three things requisite for beauty are, integrity, a wholeness, symmetry and radiance. Some day I will expand that sentence into a treatise. Consider the performance of your own mind when confronted with any object, hypothetically beautiful. Your mind to apprehend that object divides the entire universe into two parts, the object, and the void which is not the object. To apprehend it you must lift it away from everything else: and then you perceive that it is one integral thing, that is *a* thing. You recognise its integrity. Isn't that so?
—And then?
—That is the first quality of beauty: it is declared in a simple sudden synthesis of the faculty which apprehends. What then? Analysis then. The mind considers the object in whole and in part, in relation to itself and other objects, examines the balance of its parts, contemplates the form of the object, traverses every cranny of the structure. So the mind receives the impression of the symmetry of the structure. The

mind recognises that the object is in the strict sense of the word, a *thing*, a definitely constituted entity. You see?

        . . . .    [212]

—Now for the third quality. For a long time I couldn't make out what Aquinas meant. He uses a figurative word (a very unusual thing for him) but I have solved it. *Claritas* is *quidditas*. After the analysis which discovers the second quality the mind makes the only logically possible synthesis and discovers the third quality. That is the moment which I call epiphany. First we recognise that the object is *one* integral thing, then we recognise that it is an organised composite structure, a *thing* in fact: finally, when the relation of the parts is exquisite, when the parts are adjusted to the special point, we recognise that it is *that* thing which it is. Its soul, its whatness, leaps to us from the vestment of its appearance. The soul of the commonest object, the structure of which is so adjusted, seems to us radiant. The object achieves its epiphany.[213]

# 4. THE INTERPRETATION OF SYMBOLS

HERMAN MELVILLE

> "The Doubloon." Chapter 99 of *Moby-Dick;
> or, The Whale,* edited by Luther S. Mansfield
> and Howard P. Vincent. New York: Hen-
> dricks House, 1952.

Ere now it has been related how Ahab was wont to pace his
quarter-deck, taking regular turns at either limit, the binnacle[426] and
mainmast; but in the multiplicity of other things requiring narration
it has not been added how that sometimes in these walks, when most
plunged in his mood, he was wont to pause in turn at each spot, and
stand there strangely eyeing the particular object before him. When he
halted before the binnacle, with his glance fastened on the pointed
needle in the compass, that glance shot like a javelin with the pointed
intensity of his purpose; and when resuming his walk he again paused
before the mainmast, then, as the same riveted glance fastened upon
the riveted gold coin there, he still wore the same aspect of nailed
firmness, only dashed with a certain wild longing, if not hopefulness.

But one morning, turning to pass the doubloon, he seemed to
be newly attracted by the strange figures and inscriptions stamped on
it, as though now for the first time beginning to interpret for himself
in some monomaniac way whatever significance might lurk in them.
And some certain significance lurks in all things, else all things are
little worth, and the round world itself but an empty cipher, except
to sell by the cartload, as they do hills about Boston, to fill up some
morass in the Milky Way.

Now this doubloon was of purest, virgin gold, raked somewhere
out of the heart of gorgeous hills, whence, east and west, over golden
sands, the head-waters of many a Pactolus flows. And though now
nailed amidst all the rustiness of iron bolts and the verdigris of copper
spikes, yet, untouchable and immaculate to any foulness, it still preserved its Quito glow. Nor, though placed amongst a ruthless crew
and every hour passed by ruthless hands, and through the livelong
nights shrouded with thick darkness which might cover any pilfering

34

approach, nevertheless every sunrise found the doubloon where the sunset left it last. For it was set apart and sanctified to one awe-striking end; and however wanton in their sailor ways, one and all, the mariners revered it as the white whale's talisman. Sometimes they talked it over in the weary watch by night, wondering whose it was to be at last, and whether he would ever live to spend it.

Now those noble golden coins of South America are as[427] medals of the sun and tropic token-pieces. Here palms, alpacas, and volcanoes; sun's disks and stars; ecliptics, horns-of-plenty, and rich banners waving, are in luxuriant profusion stamped; so that the precious gold seems almost to derive an added preciousness and enhancing glories, by passing through those fancy mints, so Spanishly poetic.

It so chanced that the doubloon of the Pequod was a most wealthy example of these things. On its round border it bore the letters, REPUBLICA DEL ECUADOR: QUITO. So this bright coin came from a country planted in the middle of the world, and beneath the great equator, and named after it; and it had been cast midway up the Andes, in the unwaning clime that knows no autumn. Zoned by those letters you saw the likeness of three Andes' summits; from one a flame; a tower on another; on the third a crowing cock; while arching over all was a segment of the partitioned zodiac, the signs all marked with their usual cabalistics, and the keystone sun entering the equinoctial point at Libra.

Before this equatorial coin, Ahab, not unobserved by others, was now pausing.

"There's something ever egotistical in mountain-tops and towers, and all other grand and lofty things; look here,—three peaks as proud as Lucifer. The firm tower, that is Ahab; the volcano, that is Ahab; the courageous, the undaunted, and victorious fowl, that, too, is Ahab; all are Ahab; and this round gold is but the image of the rounder globe, which, like a magician's glass, to each and every man in turn but mirrors back his own mysterious self. Great pains, small gains for those who ask the world to solve them; it cannot solve itself. Methinks now this coined sun wears a ruddy face; but see! aye, he enters the sign of storms, the equinox! and but six months before he wheeled out of a former equinox at Aries! From storm to storm! So be it, then. Born in throes, 't is fit that man should live in pains and die in pangs! So be it, then! Here's stout stuff for woe to work on. So be it, then."

"No fairy fingers can have pressed the gold, but devil's claws must have left their mouldings there since yesterday," murmured Starbuck to himself, leaning against the bulwarks. "The old[428] man seems to read Belshazzar's awful writing. I have never marked the coin inspectingly. He goes below; let me read. A dark valley between three mighty, heaven-abiding peaks, that almost seem the Trinity, in some faint earthly symbol. So in this vale of Death, God girds us round; and over all our gloom, the sun of Righteousness still shines a beacon and a hope. If we bend down our eyes, the dark vale shows her mouldy soil; but if we lift them, the bright sun meets our glance half way, to cheer. Yet, oh, the great sun is no fixture; and if, at midnight, we would fain snatch some sweet solace from him, we gaze for him in vain! This coin speaks wisely, mildly, truly, but still sadly to me. I will quit it, lest Truth shake me falsely."

"There .now's the old Magul," soliloquized Stubb by the try-works, "he's been twigging it; and there goes Starbuck from the same, and both with faces which I should say might be somewhere within nine fathoms long. And all from looking at a piece of gold, which did I have it now on Negro Hill or in Corlaer's Hook, I'd not look at it very long ere spending it. Humph! in my poor, insignificant opinion, I regard this as queer. I have seen doubloons before now in my voyagings; your doubloons of old Spain, your doubloons of Peru, your doubloons of Chili, your doubloons of Bolivia, your dubloons of Popayan; with plenty of gold moidores and pistoles, and joes, and half joes, and quarter joes. What then should there be in this doubloon of the Equator that is so killing wonderful? By Golconda! let me read it once. Halloa! here's signs and wonders truly! That, now, is what old Bowditch in his Epitome calls the zodiac, and what my almanack below calls ditto. I'll get the almanack and as I have heard devils can be raised with Daboll's arithmetic, I'll try my hand at raising a meaning out of these queer curvicues here with the Massachusetts calendar. Here's the book. Let's see now. Signs and wonders; and the sun, he's always among 'em. Hem, hem, hem; here they are—here they go—all alive:—Aries, or the Ram; Taurus, or the Bull and Jimimi! here's Gemini himself, or the Twins. Well; the sun he wheels among 'em. Aye, here on the coin he's just crossing the threshold between two of twelve sitting-rooms all in a ring. Book! you lie there; the fact is, you books must know your[429] places. You'll do to give us the bare words and facts, but we come in to supply the thoughts. That's my small experience, so far as the Massachusetts calendar, and Bowditch's navigator, and Daboll's arithmetic go. Signs and wonders, eh? Pity if there is nothing wonderful in signs, and significant in wonders! There's a clue somewhere; wait a bit; hist—hark! By Jove, I have it! Look you, Doubloon, your zodiac here is the life of man in one round chapter; and now I'll read it off, straight out of the book. Come, Almanack! To begin: there's Aries, or the Ram—lecherous dog, he begets us; then, Taurus, or the Bull—he bumps us the first thing; then Gemini, or the Twins—that is, Virtue and Vice; we try to reach Virtue, when lo! comes Cancer the Crab, and drags us back; and here, going from Virtue, Leo, a roaring Lion, lies in the path—he gives a few fierce bites and surly dabs with his paw; we escape, and hail Virgo, the Virgin! that's our first love, we marry and think to be happy for aye, when pop comes Libra, or the Scales—happiness weighed and found wanting; and while we are very sad about that, Lord! how we suddenly jump, as Scorpio, or the Scorpion, stings us in rear, we are curing the wound, when whang come the arrows all round, Sagittarius, or the Archer, is amusing himself. As we pluck out the shafts, stand aside; here's the battering-ram, Capricornus, or the Goat; full tilt, he comes rushing, and headlong we are tossed; when Aquarius, or the Water-bearer, pours out his whole deluge and drowns us; and to wind up with Pisces, or the Fishes, we sleep. There's a sermon now, writ in high heaven, and the sun goes through it every year, and yet comes out of it all alive and hearty. Jollily he, aloft there, wheels through toil and trouble; and so, alow here, does jolly Stubb. Oh, jolly's the word for aye! Adieu, Doubloon! But stop, here comes little King-Post, dodge round the try-works, now, and let's hear what he'll have to say. There; he's before it; he'll out with something presently. So, so; he's beginning."

'    "I see nothing here, but a round thing made of gold, and whoever raises a certain whale, this round thing belongs to him. So, what's all this staring been about? It is worth sixteen dollars, that's true; and at two cents the cigar, that's nine hundred and [430] sixty cigars. I wont smoke dirty pipes like Stubb, but I like cigars, and here's nine hundred and sixty of them; so here goes Flask aloft to spy 'em out."

    "Shall I call that wise or foolish, now; if it be really wise it has a foolish look to it; yet, if it be really foolish, then has it a sort of wiseish look to it. But, avast; here comes our old Manxman—the old hearse-driver, he must have been, that is, before he took to the sea. He luffs up before the doubloon; halloa, and goes round on the other side of the mast; why, there's a horse-shoe nailed on that side; and now he's back again; what does that mean? Hark! he's muttering—voice like an old worn-out coffee-mill. Prick ears, and listen!"

    "If the White Whale be raised, it must be in a month and a day, when the sun stands in some one of these signs. I've studied signs, and know their marks; they were taught me two score years ago, by the old witch in Copenhagen. Now, in what sign will the sun then be? The horse-shoe sign; for there it is, right opposite the gold. And what's the horse-shoe sign? The lion is the horse-shoe sign—the roaring and devouring lion. Ship, old ship! my old head shakes to think of thee."

    "There's another rendering now; but still one text. All sorts of men in one kind of world, you see. Dodge again! here comes Queequeg—all tattooing—looks like the signs of the Zodiac himself. What says the Cannibal? As I live he's comparing notes; looking at his thigh bone; thinks the sun is in the thigh, or in the calf, or in the bowels, I suppose, as the old women talk Surgeon's Astronomy in the back country. And by Jove, he's found something there in the vicinity of his thigh—I guess it's Sagittarius, or the Archer. No: he don't know what to make of the doubloon; he takes it for an old button off some king's trowsers. But, aside again! here comes that ghost-devil, Fedallah, tail coiled out of sight as usual, oakum in the toes of his pumps as usual. What does he say, with that look of his? Ah, only makes a sign to the sign and bows himself; there is a sun on the coin—fire worshipper, depend upon it. Ho! more and more. This way comes Pip—poor boy! would he had died, or I; he's half horrible to me. He too has been watching all of these interpreters—myself included—and look now, he comes to read,[431] with that unearthly idiot face. Stand away again and hear him. Hark!

"I look, you look, he looks; we look, ye look, they look."

"Upon my soul, he's been studying Murray's Grammar! Improving his mind, poor fellow! But what's that he says now—hist!"

"I look, you look, he looks; we look, ye look, they look."

"Why, he's getting it by heart—hist! again."

"I look, you look, he looks; we look, ye look, they look."

"Well, that's funny."

"And I, you, and he; and we, ye, and they, are all bats; and I'm a crow, especially when I stand a'top of this pine tree here. Caw! caw! caw! caw! caw! caw! Ain't I a crow? And where's the scare-crow? There he stands; two bones stuck into a pair of old trowsers, and two more poked into the sleeves of an old jacket."

"Wonder if he means me?—complimentary!—poor lad!—I could go hang myself. Any way, for the present, I'll quit Pip's vicinity. I can stand the rest, for they have plain wits; but he's too crazy-witty for my sanity. So, so, I leave him muttering."

"Here's the ship's navel, this doubloon here, and they are all on fire to unscrew it. But, unscrew your navel, and what's the consequence? Then again, if it stays here, that is ugly, too, for when aught's nailed to the mast it's a sign that things grow desperate. Ha, ha! old Ahab! the White Whale; he'll nail ye! This is a pine tree. My father, in old Tolland county, cut down a pine tree once, and found a silver ring grown over in it; some old darkey's wedding ring. How did it get there? And so they'll say in the resurrection, when they come to fish up this old mast, and find a doubloon lodged in it, with bedded oysters for the shaggy bark. Oh, the gold! the precious, precious gold!—the green miser'll hoard ye soon! Hish! hish! God goes 'mong the worlds blackberrying. Cook! ho, cook! and cook us! Jenny! hey, hey, hey, hey, hey, Jenny, Jenny! and get your hoe-cake done!"[432]

CHARLES CHILD WALCUTT

From "Interpreting the Symbol." *College English*, XIV (May, 1953), 446-454. Reprinted by permission of the publisher and the author.

General statements can be made about any particular fact or situation, such as "The cow is a herbivorous mammal." But the cow does not symbolize the idea of herbivorous mammal. Most early student statements of what a poem symbolizes are versions of this error. A student writes, for example, of Housman's "To an Athlete Dying Young," "The athlete who is reduced to nothing in a few years symbolizes man and his illusions of perfection and greatness." This is making a good deal of

> Runners whom renown outran
> And the name died before the man,

but, even granting him the right to enlarge upon the status of these ancillary figures in the poem, we must conclude that they do not symbolize "man and his illusions of perfection and greatness." In the first place (and I dwell on this specific error because it resembles a thousand other errors of statement about so-called symbols), these runners cannot symbolize both man and his illusions. Men are one thing; illusions of perfection are of another order. What the student perhaps meant was that the relation of the runner to his fame symbolizes the relation of man to his illusions of perfection. But the runner's fame lives in the minds of others and "dies" when they forget; whereas a man's illusions of perfection are his own ideas, and they "die" when he is disappointed or disabused or just diverted. One cannot symbolize the other, for the jump from one logical pattern to another cannot be accommodated to the runner-as-symbol. There is nothing in the poem which directs the reader to see in the situation of the runners or in the word "renown" a symbol of illusions of perfection; and any brief discussion will make this fact clear.

Now (to proceed) perhaps what the student meant to mean was that, just as the loss of fame involves bitterness or disappointment, so the loss of illusions of perfection involves bitterness or disappointment. The two losses have in common that they cause, say, bitterness. This purely abstract remark—which is a simple classification, that is, the identification of a quality or aspect that is present in two items—is certainly true in so far as it shows a property common to loss of fame and loss of illusions (which is all many students require to make them cry havoc or "Symbol!"). But can the runner properly be said to symbolize "man and his illusions of perfection"? Loss of fame and loss of a new boat would cause bitterness; but this fact hardly makes the runner symbolize loss of a new boat. He might as well symbolize a nation past its glory, a garden that has withered, a wrecked airplane, or a thousand other items that partake of the same quality or somehow relate to it. Examination shows that the connection between "runners[449] whom renown outran" and "man and his illusions of perfection" is neither logical nor necessary nor particular nor (most important) exclusive.

Whenever we come upon the problem of symbolism, we are likely to be puzzled by a double-facedness that invites misinterpretations: There is the symbol which seems to "stand" for an institution or a situation or a problem. And then there is the accompanying fact that any situation or problem suggests dozens of similar or comparable problems which ring out around it like the ripples from a pebble dropped into a pond. When Robert Frost in "Stopping by Woods on a Snowy Evening" says, "But I have promises to keep / And miles to go before I sleep," he is suggesting the thousand obligations and duties which sometimes make life burdensome. They range from a call down the road, which the reader imagines, through some shopping he has promised to do for his wife, through his long-range plans for planting orchards and paying mortgages, out to the burden of life itself which man has perhaps promised his god that he will bear. These notions are suggested by the poem's "promises" and "miles to go"—but can we say they are definitely symbolized in the poem? I think not. I think the student must be shown that he is dealing with the examples or instances which any situation evokes through the imagination. A symbol must have a specific referent or a cluster of them to which it is somehow specifically attached. There may of course be ambiguities, but ambiguities are not the same as the countless examples of "promises" and "miles to go" that one could imagine. If these phrases can be said to symbolize anything, it must be the idea of duty or obligation—and nothing more specific.

If there is a symbol in Frost's poem, it is the woods—"lovely, dark and deep"—which are identified by the clause that follows them as symbolizing the impulse to escape. This is particular; it is specific; it is an idea carefully prepared for in the poem and then clearly evoked through its symbol. But, then, what about the last word in the poem? Is "sleep" a symbol of death? I should say that death is just one of many instances suggested by the tension of obligation-and-escape which gives the poem its life. Life makes us yearn for death: the thought of death makes us value life. Then can one say that the woods symbolize death, the final escape? Again, I think not, because the woods seem to me specifically to symbolize an impulse (the return to the womb, even?) but not a concept or a state like death. If we can define the specific intention of a symbol, we can then allow our imaginations to universalize the problem or situation in which it operates without losing sight of the symbol's specific reference. The important thing is to make clear the difference between a specific symbol and the general truth that any situation suggests a thousand other comparable and similar situations. Hedda Gabler's pistols are almost literally physical extensions of her personality. They are perfectly fashioned and beautiful, but precise, inflexible, hard, cold, deadly, and destructive. They are, thus, extraordinarily specific symbols of Hedda's personality and of her relation to the other characters.

Returning, now, to Housman's athlete, we find two other passages where the situation is different, where rich and precise symbols can be identified:

> And early though the laurel grows,
> It withers quicker than the rose.
>
> .   .   .   .   .   .   .   .   .   .   .   .
>
> And find unwithered on its curls
> The garland briefer than a girl's.[450]

The laurel is a definite symbol of victory. It is placed upon the winner as a sign of victory, and it has also come, in time, to symbolize victory in a way that a blue ribbon does not symbolize victory in a dog show. The distinction is that a sign points, whereas a symbol is. Except perhaps for the ardent dog-breeder, the blue ribbon merely indicates; yet, when the blue ribbon is used to decorate beer cans and beer advertising, we can see that it is on the way to becoming a general symbol—as the laurel has already done. It has become an emotional center and force. It evokes emotions directly, because of the meanings it has acquired; and this emotional force is more than the force of what it points to. The cross and the flag are outstanding symbols which plainly evoke direct responses, in contrast to such obvious signs as "W 26 STREET" or "LOGE" which do not have general direct emotional appeal (although they may have become symbols for certain individuals).

The rose, too, is a symbol. In this poem it can only be a symbol of beauty—because that is what it has generally been and that is what the poem makes it mean within its own structure. The fame that withers sooner even than beauty becomes an object of pathos, tenderness, and pitiful regret in a way that it can do only through the poet's juxtaposition of symbols both of which are possessed of their own magic. In the last two lines of the poem the same qualities of pathos and tenderness, fragile beauty and poignant regret, are evoked by the reappearance of the symbols in a setting. Before, they were presented as general symbols. Here they appear in a tableau—the strengthless dead gathered about the victorious garlanded youth, yearning toward the life which he reveals; the youth in his prime now in the place of shades; and the image too of a young girl, the rose of whose beauty has, in this place of shades, come to a pale, immobile, perfect stillness. She is there because the rose symbol evokes her; rose, laurel, girl, athlete, and shades make a very definite scene, a scene full of concrete particulars that not merely suggest but actually contain their universal meanings. It is not "reading into" the poem to see youth, beauty, and fame there immobilized before death; these universals must be felt by the responsible reader. Considerably more subtlety and discrimination are demanded of the student who will find that the young athlete has become identified both with and in the girl. Beauty fades, but in this poem it pathetically dies; the girl's qualities of fragility and perfection become assimilated into the image of the dead athlete.

Thus real symbols have magic and life, which they bring to a complex and subtle situation. Here the meaning glows in its own living form. It does not take us off into general ideas or remote and private applications of itself. Properly grasped, it is there to be felt rather than argued about. But argument is necessary and fruitful if it can be directed to show the follies of private improvisations as contrasted with the power of a symbol that has been apprehended as a living, incarnate idea. The nature of a symbol is the nature of poetry. The special quality of each is that it is powerfully concrete and yet suggests more than can be logically accounted for, because it enjoys a dimension of felt thought which cannot be reproduced by the phrases which attempt to describe it.[451]

The complexity of meanings that a poet can evoke with a rich symbol is little short of miraculous; and even more remarkable than the complexity is the clearness and precision of communication through symbols. Symbols are the artist's means of creating patterns of thought and emotion which did not previously exist and of communicating what had previously been ineffable. The challenge to the reader is to penetrate these symbols, to feel and think one's way into them, and so to participate in the artist's perception and creation. Above all, one must resist the temptation to overlay and smother the artist's creation with a creation of his own. The reader, too, must keep his eye steadily on the object.[454]

MARY McCARTHY

"Settling the Colonel's Hash." *Harper's Magazine*, CCVIII (February, 1954). Copyright, 1954, by Harper & Brothers. Reprinted by permission of the author.

Seven years ago, when I taught in a progressive college, I had a pretty girl student in one of my classes who wanted to be a short-story writer. She was not studying writing with me, but she knew that I sometimes wrote short stories, and one day, breathless and glowing, she came up to me in the hall, to tell me that she had just written a story that her writing teacher, a Mr. Converse, was terribly excited about.

"He thinks it's wonderful," she said, "and he's going to help me fix it up for publication."

I asked what the story was about; the girl was a rather simple being who loved clothes and dates. Her answer had a deprecating tone. It was just about a girl (herself) and some sailors she had met on the train. But then her face, which had looked perturbed for a moment, gladdened.

"Mr. Converse is going over it with me and we're going to put in the symbols."

Another girl in the same college, when asked by us in her sophomore orals why she read novels (one of the pseudo-profound questions that ought never to be put) answered in a defensive flurry: "Well, *of course*, I don't read them to find out what happens to the hero."

At the time, I thought these notions were peculiar to progressive education: it was old-fashioned or regressive to read a novel to find out what happens to the hero or to have a mere experience empty of symbolic pointers. But I now discover that this attitude is quite general, and that readers and students all over the country are in a state of apprehension, lest they read a book or story literally and miss the presence of a symbol. And like everything in America, this search for meanings has become a socially competitive enterprise; the best reader is the one who detects the most symbols in a given stretch of prose. And the benighted reader who fails to find any symbols humbly assents when they are pointed out to him; he accepts his mortification.

I had no idea how far this process had gone until last spring, when I began to get responses to a story I had published in *Harper's*. I say "story" because that was what it was called by *Harper's*. I myself would not know quite what to call it; it was a fragment of autobiography—an account of my meeting with an anti-Semitic army Colonel. It began in the club car of a train going to St. Louis; I was wearing an apple-green shirtwaist and a dark-green skirt and pink earrings; we got into an argument about the Jews. The Colonel was a rather dapper, flashy kind of Irish-American with a worldly blue eye; he took me, he said, for a sculptress, which made me feel, to my horror, that I looked Bohemian and therefore rather suspect. He was full of the usual profound clichés that anti-Semites air, like original epigrams, about the Jews: that he could tell a Jew, that they were different from other people, that you couldn't trust them in business, that some of his best friends were Jews, that he distinguished between[68] a Jew and a kike, and finally that, of course, he didn't agree with Hitler; Hitler went too far; the Jews were human beings.

All the time we talked, and I defended the Jews, he was trying to get my angle, as he called it; he thought it was abnormal for anybody who wasn't Jewish not to feel as he did. As a matter of fact, I have a Jewish grandmother, but I decided to keep this news to myself: I did not want the Colonel to think that I had any interested reason for speaking on behalf of the Jews, that is, that I was prejudiced. In the end, though, I got my come-uppance. Just as we were parting, the Colonel asked me my married name, which is Broadwater, and the whole mystery was cleared up for him, instantly; he supposed I was married to a Jew and that the name was spelled B-r-o-dwater. I did not try to enlighten him; I let him think what he wanted; in a certain sense, he was right; he had unearthed my Jewish grandmother or her equivalent. There were a few details that I must mention to make the next part clear: in my car, there were two nuns, whom I talked to as a distraction from the Colonel and the moral problems he raised. He and I finally had lunch together in the St. Louis railroad station, where we continued the discussion. It was a very hot day. I had a sandwich, he had roast-beef hash. We both had an old-fashioned.

The whole point of this "story" was that it really happened; it is written in the first person; I speak of myself in my own name, Mc-Carthy; at the end, I mention my husband's name, Broadwater. When I was thinking about writing the story, I decided not to treat it fictionally; the chief interest, I felt, lay in the fact that it happened, in real life, last summer, to the writer herself, who was a good deal at fault in the incident. I wanted to embarrass myself and, if possible, the reader too.

Yet, strangely enough, many of my readers preferred to think of this account as fiction. I still meet people who ask me, confidentially, "That story of yours about the colonel;—was it really true?" It seemed to them perfectly natural that I would write a fabrication, in which I figured under my own name, and sign it, though in my eyes this would be like perjuring yourself in court or forging checks. Shortly after the story was published, I got a kindly letter from a man in Mexico, in which he criticized the menu from an artistic point of view: he thought salads would be better for hot weather and it would be more in character for the narrator-heroine to have a martini. I did not answer the letter, though I was moved to, because I had the sense that he would not understand the distinction between what *ought* to have happened and what *did* happen.

Then in April I got another letter, from an English teacher in a small college in the Middle West, that reduced me to despair. I am going to cite it at length. "My students in freshmen English chose to analyze your story, 'Artists in Uniform,' from the March issue of *Harper's*. For a week I heard oral discussions on it and then the students wrote critical analyses. In so far as it is possible, I stayed out of their discussions, encouraging them to read the story closely with your intentions as a guide to their understanding. Although some of them insisted that the story has no other level than the realistic one, most of them decided it has symbolic overtones.

"The question is: how closely do you want the symbols labeled? They wrestled with the nuns, the author's two shades of green with pink accents, with the 'materialistic godlessness' of the Colonel. . . . A surprising number wanted exact symbols; for example, they searched for the significance of the Colonel's eating hash and the author eating a sandwich. . . . From my standpoint, the story was an entirely satisfactory springboard for understanding the various shades of prejudice, for seeing how much of the artist goes into his painting. If it is any satisfaction to you, our campus was alive with discussion about 'Artists in Uniform.' We liked the story and we thought it amazing that an author could succeed in making readers dislike the author—for a purpose, of course!"

I probably should have answered this letter, but I did not The gulf seemed to me too wide. I could not applaud the backward students who insisted that the story has no other level than the realistic one without giving offense to their teacher, who was evidently a well-meaning person. But I shall[69] try now to address a reply, not to this teacher and her unfortunate class, but to a whole school of misunderstanding. There were no symbols in this story; there was no deeper level. The nuns were in the story because they were on the train; the contrasting greens were the dress I happened to be wearing; the Colonel had hash because he had hash, materialistic godlessness meant just what it means when a priest thunders it from the pulpit—the phrase, for the first time, had meaning for me as I watched and listened to the Colonel.

But to clarify the misunderstanding, one must go a little further and try to see what a literary symbol is. Now in one sense, the Colonel's hash and my sandwich can be regarded as symbols; that is, they typify the Colonel's food tastes and mine. (The man in Mexico had different food tastes which he wished to interpose into our reality.) The hash and the sandwich might even be said to show something very obvious about our sexes; I was a woman, he was a man. And though on another day I might have ordered hash myself, that day I did not, because the Colonel and I, in our disagreement, were polarizing each other.

The hash and the sandwich, then, could be regarded as symbols of our disagreement, almost conscious symbols. And underneath our discussion of the Jews, there was a thin sexual current running, as there always is in such random encounters or pick-ups (for they have a strong suggestion of the illicit). The fact that I ordered something conventionally feminine and he ordered something conventionally masculine represented, no doubt, our awareness of a sexual possibility; even though I was not attracted to the Colonel, or he to me, the circumstances of our meeting made us define ourselves as a woman and a man.

The sandwich and the hash were our provisional, *ad hoc* symbols of ourselves. But in this sense all human actions are symbolic because they represent the person who does them. If the Colonel had ordered a fruit salad with whipped cream, this too would have represented him in some way; given his other traits, it would have pointed to a complexity in his character that the hash did not suggest.

In the same way, the contrasting greens of my dress were a symbol of my taste in clothes and hence representative of me—all too representative, I suddenly saw, in the club car, when I got an "artistic" image of myself flashed back at me from the men's eyes. I had no wish to stylize myself as an artist, that is, to parade about as a symbol of flamboyant unconventionality, but apparently I had done so unwittingly when I picked those colors off a rack, under the impression that they suited me or "expressed my personality" as salesladies say.

My dress, then, was a symbol of the perplexity I found myself in with the Colonel; I did not want to be categorized as a member of a peculiar minority—an artist or a Jew; but brute fate and the Colonel kept resolutely cramming me into both those uncomfortable pigeonholes. I wished to be regarded as ordinary or rather as universal, to be anybody and therefore everybody (that is, in one sense, I wanted to be on the Colonel's side, majestically above minorities); but every time the Colonel looked at my dress and me in it with my pink earrings I shrank to minority status, and felt the dress in the heat shriveling me, like the shirt of Nessus, the centaur, that consumed Hercules.

But this is not what the students meant when they wanted the symbols "labeled." They were searching for a more recondite significance than that afforded by the trite symbolism of ordinary life, in which a dress is a social badge. They supposed that I was engaging in literary or artificial symbolism, which would lead the reader out of the confines of reality into the vast fairy tale of myth, in which the color green would have an emblematic meaning (or did the two greens signify for them what the teacher calls "shades" of prejudice), and the Colonel's hash, I imagine, would be some sort of Eucharistic mince-meat.

Apparently, the presence of the nuns assured them there were overtones of theology; it did not occur to them (a) that the nuns were there because pairs of nuns are a standardized feature of summer Pullman travel, like crying babies, and perspiring business men in the club car, and (b) that if I thought the nuns worth mentioning, it was also because [70] of something very simple and directly relevant; the nuns and the Colonel and I all had something in common—we had all at one time been Catholics—and I was seeking common ground with the Colonel, from which to turn and attack his position.

In any account of reality, even a televised one, which comes closest to being a literal transcript or replay, some details are left out as irrelevant (though nothing is really irrelevant). The details that are not eliminated have to stand as symbols of the whole, like stenographic signs, and of course there is an art of selection, even in a newspaper account: the writer, if he has any ability, is looking for the revealing detail that will sum up the picture for the reader in a flash of recognition.

But the art of abridgment and condensation, which is familiar to anybody who tries to relate an anecdote or give a direction—the art of natural symbolism, which is at the basis of speech and all representation—has at bottom a centripetal intention. It hovers over an object, an event, or series of events and tries to declare what it is. Analogy (that is, comparison to other objects) is inevitably one of its methods. "The weather was soupy," i.e., like soup. "He wedged his way in," i.e., he had to enter, thin edge first, as a wedge enters, and so on. All this is obvious. But these metaphorical aids to communication are a far cry from literary symbolism, as taught in the schools and practiced by certain fashionable writers. Literary symbolism is centrifugal and flees from the object, the event, into the incorporeal distance, where concepts are taken for substance and floating ideas and archetypes assume a hieratic authority.

In this dream-forest, symbols become arbitrary; all counters are interchangeable; anything can stand for anything else. The Colonel's hash can be a Eucharist or a cannibal feast or the banquet of Atreus, or all three, so long as the actual dish set before the actual man is disparaged. What is depressing about this insistent symbolization is the fact that while it claims to lead to the infinite, it quickly reaches very finite limits—there are only so many myths on record, and once you have got through Bulfinch, the Scandinavian, and the Indian, there is not much left. And if all stories reduce themselves to myth and symbol, qualitative differences vanish, and there is only a single, monotonous story.

American fiction of the symbolist school demonstrates this mournful truth, without precisely intending to. A few years ago, when the mode was at its height, chic novels and stories fell into three classes; those which had a Greek myth for their framework, which the reader was supposed to detect, like finding the faces in the clouds in old newspaper puzzle contests; those which had symbolic modern figures, dwarfs, hermaphrodites, and cripples, illustrating maiming and loneliness; and those which contained symbolic animals, cougars, wild cats, and monkeys. One young novelist, a product of the Princeton school of symbolism, had all three elements going at once, like the ringmaster of a three-ring circus, with the freaks, the animals, and the statues.

The quest for symbolic referents had, as its object, of course the deepening of the writer's subject and the reader's awareness. But the result was paradoxical. At the very moment when American writing was penetrated by the symbolic urge, it ceased to be able to create symbols of its own. Babbitt, I suppose, was the last important symbol to be created by an American writer; he gave his name to a type that henceforth would be recognizable to everybody. He passed into the language. The same thing could be said, perhaps though to a lesser degree, of Caldwell's Tobacco Road, Eliot's Prufrock, and possibly of Faulkner's Snopeses. The discovery of new symbols is not the only function of a writer, but the writer who cares about this must be fascinated by reality itself, as a butterfly collector is fascinated by the glimpse of a new specimen. Such a specimen was Mme. Bovary or M. Homais or M. de Charlus or Jupien; these specimens were precious to their discoverers, not because they repeated an age-old pattern but because their markings were new. Once the specimen has been described, the public instantly spots other examples of the kind, and the world seems suddenly full of Babbitts and Charlus, where none had been noted before.

A different matter was Joyce's Mr. Bloom. Mr. Bloom can be called a symbol of eternal recurrence—the wandering Jew, Ulysses the[71] voyager—but he is a symbol thickly incarnate, fleshed out in a Dublin advertising canvasser. He is not like Ulysses or vaguely suggestive of Ulysses; he is Ulysses, circa 1905. Joyce evidently believed in a cyclical theory of history, in which everything repeated itself; he also subscribed in youth to the doctrine of the Incarnation, which declares that the Host, a piece of bread, is also God's body and blood. How it can be both things at the same time, consubstantially, is a mystery, and Mr. Bloom is just such a mystery: Ulysses in the visible appearance of a Dublin advertising-canvasser.

Mr. Bloom is not a symbol of Ulysses, but Ulysses-Bloom together, one and indivisible, symbolize or rather demonstrate eternal recurrence. I hope I make myself clear. The point is consubstantiation: Bloom and Ulysses are transfused into each other and neither reality is diminished. Both realities are locked together, like the protons and neutrons of an atom. *Finnegans Wake* is a still more ambitious attempt to create a fusion, this time a myriad fusion, and to exemplify the mystery of how a thing can be itself and at the same time be something else. The world is many and it is also one.

But the clarity and tension of Joyce's thought brought him closer in a way to the strictness of allegory than to the diffuse practices of latter-day symbolists. In Joyce, the equivalences and analogies are very sharp and distinct and the real world is almost querulously audible, like the voices of the washer-women on the Liffey that come into Earwicker's dream. But this is not true of Joyce's imitators or of the imitators of his imitators, for whom reality is only a shadowy pretext for the introduction of a whole *corps de ballet* of dancing symbols in mythic draperies and animal skins.

Let me make a distinction. There are some great writers, like Joyce or Melville, who have consciously introduced symbolic elements into their work; and there are great writers who have written fables or allegories. In both cases, the writer makes it quite clear to the reader how he is to be read; only an idiot would take *Pilgrim's Progress* for a realistic story, and even a young boy, reading *Moby Dick*, realizes that there is something more than whale-fishing here, though he cannot be sure what it is. But the great body of fiction contains only what I have called natural symbolism, in which selected events represent or typify a problem, a kind of society or psychology, a philosophical theory, in the same way they do in real life. What happens to the hero becomes of the highest importance. This symbolism needs no abstruse interpretation and abstruse interpretation will only lead the reader away from the reality that the writer is trying to press on his attention.

I will give an example or two of what I mean by natural symbolism and I will begin with a rather florid one: Henry James's *The Golden Bowl*. This is the story of a rich American girl who collects European objects. One of these objects is a husband, a Prince Amerigo, who proves to be unfaithful. Early in the story, there is a visit to an antique shop in which the Prince picks out a gold bowl for his fiancée and finds, to his annoyance, that it is cracked. It is not hard to see that the cracked bowl is a symbol, both of the Prince himself, who is a valuable antique but a little flawed, morally, and also of the marriage, which represents an act of acquisition or purchase on the part of the heroine and her father. If the reader should fail to notice the analogy, James himself helps him out in the title.

I myself would not regard the introduction of this symbol as necessary to this particular history; it seems to me, rather, an ornament of the kind that was fashionable in the architecture and interior decoration of the period, like stylized sheaves of corn or wreaths on the façade of a house. Nevertheless, it is handsome and has an obvious appropriateness to the theme. It leads the reader into the gilded matter of the novel, rather than away from it. I think there is also a scriptural echo in the title that conveys the idea of punishment. But having seen and felt the weight of meaning that James put in this symbol, one must not be tempted to go further and look at the bowl as a female sex symbol, a chalice, the Holy Grail, and so on; a book is not a pious excuse for reciting a litany of associations.

My second example is from Tolstoy's *Anna Karenina*. At the beginning of the novel, Anna meets the man who will be her lover, Vronsky, on the Moscow-St. Petersburg[72] express; as they meet, there has been an accident; a workman has been killed by the train coming in to the station. This is the beginning of Anna's doom, which is completed when she throws herself under a train and is killed; and the last we see of Vronsky is in a train, with a toothache; he is being seen off by a friend to the wars. The train is necessary to the plot of the novel, and I believe it is also symbolic, both of the iron forces of material progress that Tolstoy hated so and that played a part in Anna's moral destruction, and also of those iron laws of necessity and consequence that govern human action when it remains on the sensual level.

One can read the whole novel, however, without being aware that the train is a symbol; we do not have to "interpret" to feel the import of doom and loneliness conveyed by the train's whistle—the same import we ourselves can feel when we hear a train go by in the country, even today. Tolstoy was a greater artist than James, and one cannot be certain that the train was a conscious device with him. The appropriateness to Anna's history may have been only a *felt* appropriateness; everything in Tolstoy has such a supreme naturalness that one shrinks from attributing contrivance to him, as if it were a sort of fraud. Yet he worked very hard on his novels—I forget how many times the Countess Tolstoy copied out *War and Peace* by hand.

The impression one gets from his diaries is that he wrote by ear; he speaks repeatedly, even as an old man, of having to start a story over again because he has the wrong tone, and I suspect that he did not think of the train as a symbol but that it sounded "right" to him, because it was, in that day, an almost fearsome emblem of ruthless and impersonal force, not only to a writer of genius but to the poorest peasant who watched it pass through the fields. And in Tolstoy's case, I think it would be impossible, even for the most fanciful critic, to extricate the train from the novel and try to make it bear a meaning that the novel itself does not proclaim, explicitly and tacitly, on every page. Every detail in Tolstoy has an almost cruel and vise-like meaningfulnes and truth to itself that makes it tautological_to talk of symbolism; he was a moralist and to him the tiniest action, even the curiosities of physical appearance, Vronsky's bald spot, the small white hands of Prince Andrei, told a moral tale.

It is now considered very old-fashioned and tasteless to speak of an author's "philosophy of life" as something that can be harvested from his work. Actually, most of the great authors did have a "philosophy of life" which they were eager to communicate to the public; this was one of their motives for writing. And to disentangle a moral philosophy from a work that evidently contains one is far less damaging to the author's purpose and the integrity of his art than to violate his imagery by symbol-hunting, as though reading a novel were a sort of paper chase.

The images of a novel or a story belong, as it were, to a family, very closely knit and inseparable from each other; the parent "idea" of a story or a novel generates events and images all bearing a strong family resemblance. And to understand a story or a novel, you must look for the parent "idea" which is usually in plain view, if you read quite carefully and literally what the author says.

I will go back, for a moment, to my own story, to show how this can be done. Clearly, it is about the Jewish question, for that is what the people are talking about. It also seems to be about artists, since the title is "Artists in Uniform." Then there must be some relation between artists and Jews. What is it? They are both minorities that other people claim to be able to recognize by their appearance. But artists and Jews do not care for this categorization; they want to be universal, that is, like everybody else. But this aim is really hopeless, for life has formed them as Jews or artists, in a way that immediately betrays them to the majority they are trying to melt into. In my conversation with the Colonel, I was endeavoring to play a double game. I was trying to force him into a minority by treating anti-Semitism as an aberration, which, in fact, I believe it is. On his side, the Colonel resisted this attempt and tried to show that anti-Semitism was normal, and he was normal, while I was the queer one.

He declined to be categorized as an anti-Semite; he regarded himself as an independent[73] thinker, who by a happy chance thought 'the same as everybody else.

I imagined I had a card up my sleeve; I had guessed that the colonel was Irish (*i.e.*, that he belonged to a minority) and presumed that he was a Catholic. I did not see how he could possibly guess that I, with my Irish name and Irish appearance, had a Jewish grandmother in the background. Therefore when I found I had not convinced him by reasoning, I played my last card; I told him that the Church, his Church, forbade anti-Semitism. I went even further; I implied that God forbade it, though I had no right to do this, since I did not believe in God, but was only using Him as a whip to crack over the Colonel, to make him feel humble and inferior, a raw Irish Catholic lad under discipline. But the Colonel, it turned out, did not believe in God, either, and I lost. And since, in a sense, I had been cheating all along in this game we were playing, I had to concede the Colonel a sort of moral victory in the end; I let him think that my husband was Jewish and that that "explained" everything satisfactorily.

Now there are a number of morals or meanings in this little tale, starting with the simple one: don't talk to strangers on a train. The chief moral or meaning (what I learned, in other words, from this experience) was this: you cannot be a universal unless you accept the fact that you are a singular, that is, a Jew or an artist or what-have-you. What the Colonel and I were discussing, and at the same time illustrating and enacting, was the definition of a human being. I was trying to be something better than a human being; I was trying to be the voice of pure reason; and pride went before a fall. The Colonel, without trying, was being something worse than a human being, and somehow we found ourselves on the same plane—facing each other, like mutually repellent twins. Or, put it another way: it is dangerous to be drawn into discussions of the Jews with anti-Semites: you delude yourself that you are spreading light, but you are really sinking into muck; if you endeavor to be dispassionate, you are really claiming for yourself a privileged position, a little mountain top, from which you look down, impartially, on both the Jews and the Colonel.

Anti-Semitism is a horrible disease from which nobody is immune, and it has a kind of evil fascination that makes an enlightened person draw near the source of infection, supposedly in a scientific spirit, but really to sniff the vapors and dally with the possibility. The enlightened person who lunches with the Colonel in order, as she tells herself, to improve him, is cheating herself, having her cake and eating it. This attempted cheat, on my part, was related to the question of the artist and the green dress; I wanted to be an artist but not to pay the price of looking like one, just as I was willing to have Jewish blood but not willing to show it, where it would cost me something— the loss of superiority in an argument.

These meanings are all there, quite patent, to anyone who consents to look *into* the story. They were *in* the experience itself, waiting to be found and considered. I did not perceive them all at the time the experience was happening; otherwise, it would not have taken place, in all probability—I should have given the Colonel a wide berth. But when I went back over the experience, in order to write it, I came upon these meanings, protruding at me, as it were, from the details of the occasion. I put in the green dress and my mortification over it because they were part of the truth, just as it had occurred, but I did not see how they were related to the general question of anti-Semitism and my grandmother until they *showed* me their relation in the course of writing.

Every short story, at least for me, is a little act of discovery. A cluster of details presents itself to my scrutiny, like a mystery that I will understand in the course of writing or sometimes not fully until afterward, when, if I have been honest and listened to these details carefully, I will find that they are connected and that there is a coherent pattern. This pattern is *in* experience itself; you do not impose it from the outside and if you try to, you will find that the story is taking the wrong tack, dribbling away from you into artificiality or inconsequence. A story that you do not learn something from while you are writing it, that does not illuminate something for you, is dead, finished before you[74] started it. The "idea" of a story is implicit in it, on the one hand; on the other hand, it is always ahead of the writer, like a form dimly discerned in the distance; he is working *toward* the "idea."

It can sometimes happen that you begin a story thinking that you know the "idea" of it and find, when you are finished, that you have said something quite different and utterly unexpected to you. Most writers have been haunted all their lives by the "idea" of a story or a novel that they think they want to write and see very clearly: Tolstoy always wanted to write a novel about the Decembrists and instead, almost against his will, wrote *War and Peace;* Henry James thought he wanted to write a novel about Napoleon. Probably these ideas for novels were too set in their creators' minds to inspire creative discovery.

In any work that is truly creative, I believe, the writer cannot be omniscient in advance about the effects that he proposes to produce. The suspense in a novel is not only in the reader, but in the novelist himself, who is intensely curious too about what will happen to the hero. Jane Austen may know in a general way that Emma will marry Mr. Knightley in the end (the reader knows this too, as a matter of fact); the suspense for the author lies in the how, in the twists and turns of circumstance, waiting but as yet unknown, that will bring the consummation about. Hence, I would say to the student of writing that outlines, patterns, arrangements of symbols may have a certain usefulness at the outset for some kinds of minds, but in the end they will have to be scrapped. If the story does not contradict the outline, overrun the pattern, break the symbols, like an insurrection against authority, it is surely a stillbirth. The natural symbolism of reality has more messages to communicate than the dry Morse code of the disengaged mind.

The tree of life, said Hegel, is greener than the tree of thought; I have quoted this before but I cannot forbear from citing it again in this context. This is not an incitement to mindlessness or an endorsement of realism in the short story (there are several kinds of reality, including interior reality); it means only that the writer must be, first of all, a listener and observer, who can pay attention to reality, like an obedient pupil, and who is willing, always, to be surprised by the messages reality is sending through to him. And if he gets the messages correctly he will not have to go back and put in the symbols; he will find that the symbols are there, staring at him significantly from the commonplace.[75]

# 1. HUMPTY DUMPTY

Humpty Dumpty sat on a wall.
Humpty Dumpty had a great fall.
  All the king's horses,
  And all the king's men
Couldn't put Humpty together again.

*—Traditional nursery rhyme*

BERNARD M. KNIEGER

"Humpty Dumpty and Symbolism." *College English*, XX (February, 1959). Reprinted by permission of the author and the publisher.

When is an egg not an egg? When the egg is Humpty Dumpty —that is, primarily a literary symbol, might be one answer. Certainly, nothing in the poem specifically identifies Humpty Dumpty as an egg, as a member of the anti-egg faction of my sophomore literature class immediately pointed out. Furthermore, Humpty Dumpty's behavior is most unegglike. "How can an egg sit on a wall?" added a supporting dissident. "It might just as well be a glass jar." But through a thorough-going analysis of "Humpty Dumpty," even an anti-eggian may come to see that the reader must bring cultural knowledge to the reading of a literary work (particularly of a poem), that a work may be powerful to the degree that it departs from realism, that the meanings of a symbol cannot be exhausted, that a poem may be enjoyed for many reasons—its sound, organization, dramatic situation, humor, ethical content, and use of symbolism.

Class response to an analysis of "Humpty Dumpty" is guaranteed: the very idea of analyzing so simple a poem is amusing. Furthermore, the poem encourages a conflict of initial interpretations: in a class of thirty-five, twenty-five were pro-eggians, five anti-eggians and five were undecided.

How do the pro-eggians know that Humpty Dumpty is an egg? Of course, they've seen illustrations from Mother Goose. "But can't the portrait," asks an anti-eggian, "represent an artist's mistaken interpretation of the nursery rhyme?" "Be that as it may, and how could that question ever be answered," is the reply, "Humpty Dumpty is a traditional figure in our culture, always identified as an egg. So Humpty Dumpty's eggness cannot be disputed; the question is, rather, of what is Humpty Dumpty a symbol, and how successfully?"

First, however, the pro-eggian must concede that Humpty Dumpty's behavior is truly most unegglike: eggs do not sit on walls. Moreover, no monarch would be so foolish as to try to put a broken egg together again, or rather expect his horses and men to achieve this goal. In other words, "Humpty Dumpty" is a fantasy in which—surprisingly enough to both anti- and pro-eggian students, weaned on realism,[244] they think—the effectiveness of the communication of the theme is in direct relationship to the fantasy of the dramatic situation. The poem's fantasy achieves two results: the poem is funny; attention is focused on the theme.

An egg sitting on a wall is an amusing concept to the child, and perhaps to the adult. Expecting fierce, warlike horses (source of the king's power) and an army of men to put together the fragile, broken egg is an even more amusing visual image. But how better dramatize the universal desire to undo what has been done? Thus, the poet brings home through this picturesque example based on homely experience —we've all broken eggs and wanted to put them together again—the futility of trying to undo certain actions.

Not only the concluding couplet, but also the poem as a whole dramatizes the limits of temporal power: certain actions cannot be done; others should not be. Thus eggs which sit on walls risk almost certain destruction. As an egg, Humpty Dumpty is a symbol of fragility; as an egg sitting on a wall, he is a symbol of aspiring pride. Pride, however, is a human trait; so Humpty Dumpty emerges as a symbol of sinful man.

"Humpty Dumpty," in its fullest implications, is definitely a religious poem, an example of how folk wisdom, if you will, justifies the ways of God to man in four lines. Eggs have a seemingly hard exterior but a ridiculously flabby interior—they are not equipped to sit on walls. This prohibition is not arbitrary any more than God's prohibitions against a sinful action are arbitrary. Rather, these prohibitions are a manifestation of God's wisdom, of the infinite power of God contrasted with the finite powers of man, of a recognition that in an ordered universe there can be no trespassing beyond prescribed limits. And "a great fall" certainly has specific theological and mythic connotations: one thinks of the fall of Adam, of Satan, of Icarus, of Phaethon.

"What if instead of Humpty Dumpty the poem had Adolph Hitler; would the poem be better, or worse, or what?" I ask. By now, a convinced class will agree that the poem is better as it is since Humpty Dumpty is a more universal symbol of pride and of an utter fall because free from a specific historical context. "Humpty Dumpty makes a better rhyme," adds one formalist. . . .[245]

## 2. HENRY DAVID THOREAU — A Hound, a Bay Horse, and a Turtledove

From *Walden; or, Life in the Woods* [1854], edited by Norman Holmes Pearson. New York: Rinehart, 1948.

I long ago lost a hound, a bay horse, and a turtledove, and am still on their trail. Many are the travellers I have spoken concerning them, describing their tracks and what calls they answered to. I have met one or two who had heard the hound, and the[12] tramp of the horse, and even seen the dove disappear behind a cloud, and they seemed as anxious to recover them as if they had lost them themselves.[13]

WALTER HARDING

"Hound, Bay Horse, and Turtledove." From the notes of a projected annotated edition of *Walden*. Used by kind permission of the author.

This cryptic passage is one of the most discussed in *Walden*. At least three different people attempted to learn Thoreau's own interpretation directly from him:

(1) Miss Ellen Watson, in "Thoreau Visits Plymouth" (*Thoreau Society Bulletin* No. 21, October, 1947), reports that when Thoreau visited Plymouth, Massachusetts, a year or two after the publication of *Walden*, he there met "Uncle Ed" Watson, who asked him what he meant when he said he lost a hound, a horse, and a dove. Thoreau replied, "Well, Sir, I suppose we have all had our losses." "That's a pretty way to answer a fellow," replied Uncle Ed.

(2) When Thoreau's friend B. B. Wiley wrote from Chicago inquiring as to the meaning of the symbols, Thoreau replied in a letter of April 26, 1857: "How shall we account for our pursuits, if they are original? We get the language with which to describe our various lives

out of a common mint. If others have their losses which they are busy
repairing, so have I *mine,* and their hound and horse may *perhaps* be
the symbols of some of them. But also I have lost, or am in danger of
losing, a far finer and more ethereal treasure which commonly no loss,
of which they are conscious, will symbolize. This I answer hastily and
with some hesitation, according as I now understand my words" (*Writings,* [Boston: Houghton Mifflin, 1894] VI, 301-302).

(3) T. M. Raysor, speaking of Thoreau's love for Ellen Sewall,
says, "When Thoreau discovered Miss Ward's knowledge of the affair,
he told her that the references in the first chapter of *Walden* to 'a
hound, a bay horse, and a turtledove' which he had lost long ago were
allusions to the boy Edmund Sewall, to John Thoreau, and to Ellen
Sewall."—"The Love Story of Thoreau," *Studies in Philology,* XXIII
(October, 1926), 460, which also contains further information on
Thoreau's relationships with the Sewall family. For further details of
this interpretation, see Raymond Adams, "Thoreau's Growth at
Walden," *Christian Register,* CCXXIV (1945), 268-270. It is only fair
to state, however, that virtually none of the major biographers of
Thoreau have accepted this story as fact.

Among the many interpretations offered by various critics are
these:

Ralph Waldo Emerson, in his biographical sketch of Thoreau
(Centenary Edition, X, 476), says, "He had many reserves, an unwill-
ingness to exhibit to profane eyes what was still sacred in his own, and
knew well how to throw a poetic veil over his experience. All readers
of *Walden* will remember his mythical record of his disappointments:—

[He then quotes the passage.]

"His riddles are worth the reading, and I confide that if at any
time I do not understand the expression, it is yet just. Such was the
wealth of his truth that it was not worth his while to use words in
vain."

Vivian Hopkins, in *Spires of Form* (Cambridge, 1951, p. 243n),
tells us that, "In a late manuscript fragment, Notes on Thoreau,
Emerson records Thoreau's own statement from his journal, 1840, on
'the hound': 'A good book will not be dropped by its author but
thrown up. It will be so long a promise that he will not overtake it
soon. He will have slipped the leash of a fleet hound.' Emerson adds:
'The bay horse might be such command of property as he desired,
and the turtle dove might be the wife of his dream.' "

John Burroughs, in "Henry D. Thoreau," *Century Magazine,*
II (July, 1882), 377, says that Thoreau states in his Journal, " 'The
ultimate expression or fruit of any created thing is a fine effluence,
which only the most ingenuous worshipper perceives at a reverent dis-

tance from its surface even.' This 'fine effluence' he was always reaching after, and often grasping or inhaling. This is the mythical hound and horse and turtle-dove which he says in 'Walden' he long ago lost, and has been on their trail ever since. He never abandons the search, and in every woodchuck-hole or musk-rat-den, in retreat of bird, or squirrel, or mouse, or fox that he pries into, in every walk and expedition to the fields or swamps, or to distant woods, in every spring note and call that he listens to so patiently, he hopes to get some clew to his lost treasures, to the effluence that so provokingly eludes him."

Samuel Arthur Jones says, "To this man Thoreau every created thing was a divine message from its Maker and his. Oh, if he could but catch the meaning of the message or of the messenger. . . . Alas for us all! they had lost them, even as we have: for what is the hound but the divine scent that finds the trail: what the bay horse but sagacity and strength to carry us in pursuit; what the turtle-dove but innocence to secure us the Divine protection? And we have lost them all."— *Thoreau: A Glimpse* (Concord: Erudite, 1903), pp. 19-20.

Mark Van Doren says: "The parable of the hound, the bay horse, and the turtle-dove is plainly a 'mythical record of disappointments.' . . . It is clear enough that Thoreau's quest was not for any metaphysical entity, because he wore his metaphysics as comfortably as any one. It is clear enough that this single disappointment of his life was not an intellectual but an emotional one, and that it arose in the domain of the human relations. His ideal was perfection in human intercourse, and his quest was for an absolutely satisfactory condition of friendship."—*Henry David Thoreau: A Critical Study* (Boston: Houghton Mifflin, 1916), pp. 16-17.

Mr. John Girdler presents a 118 page analysis of this allusion in his unpublished master's thesis, *A Study of the Hound, Bay Horse, and Turtle-dove Allusion in Thoreau's Walden* (University of Southern California, 1935). But he sheds little light on the problem. Most of his space is devoted to a refutation of Mark Van Doren's interpretation. In conclusion he states that Thoreau "is an idealist. He is searching for the thing which he thinks will most benefit man, and he is using the methods that he believes best suit his genius. Consequently, his fables must, in his own words, be given the 'most generous interpretation.' It is not enough to seek a narrow and personal interpretation of the hound and bay horse allegory for, to quote him again, those thoughts which are 'contemporaneous with social and personal connections, though they may be humane and tender, are not the wisest and most universal' " (p. 110).

Miss Edith Peairs, in "The Hound, the Bay Horse, and the Turtledove: A Study of Thoreau and Voltaire," *PMLA*, LII (September, 1937), attempts to prove that Thoreau's source for these symbols was Voltaire's *Zadig* and to interpret them in terms of Thoreau's biography. This editor, at least, remains unconvinced.

Frank Davidson interprets the passage in light of other hound, horse, and bird imagery in *Walden* and suggests that "The hound, the bay horse, and the turtle-dove seem to be respectively for Thoreau symbols of a wildness that keeps man in touch with nature, intellectual stimulus, and purification of spirit."—"Thoreau's Hound, Bay Horse, and Turtle-Dove," *New England Quarterly*, XXVII (December, 1954), 521-524.

Henry Seidel Canby states, "In the symbolic language of the Persian poets which he [Thoreau] so often read, he is clearly describing a search for no lost maid or boy, but for that sense of the spiritual reality behind nature, which again and again in his Journal he deplores as something felt in youth, but never quite regained."—*Thoreau* (Boston: Houghton Mifflin, 1939), p. 294.

Among other possible sources for Thoreau's symbols are these:

In 1843, Thoreau edited passages from the "Chinese Four Books" for the *Dial* (IV, 206), and one passage there, which Thoreau later included in *A Week* (*Writings*, I, 208), resembles Thoreau's parable remarkably: "Benevolence is man's heart, and justice is man's path. If a man lose his fowls or his dogs, he knows how to seek them. There are those who lose their hearts and know not how to seek them. The duty of the student is no other than to seek his lost heart."

It might also be noted that many of the old ballads such as "The Twa Corbies" associate together a hound, a horse, and a bird—although the bird is usually a falcon rather than a turtle-dove.

William Bysshe Stein, in "Thoreau's Hound, Bay Horse, and Turtledove" (*Thoreau Society Bulletin* No. 67, Spring, 1959), suggests "The Story of Conn-eda; or the Golden Apples of Lough Erne," an old Irish folk tale, as a specific source for the images.

Emerson's poem "Forerunners" (Centennial Edition, IX, 85-86) also hints of the combination of hound, horse, and dove.

In conclusion, however, it should be pointed out that there is no unanimity on interpretation of these symbols and the individual critic is left free to interpret as he wishes.

## 3. ROBERT FROST — "Stopping by Woods on a Snowy Evening"

Whose woods these are I think I know.
His house is in the village though;
He will not see me stopping here
To watch his woods fill up with snow.

My little horse must think it queer
To stop without a farmhouse near
Between the woods and frozen lake
The darkest evening of the year.

He gives his harness bells a shake
To ask if there is some mistake.
The only other sound's the sweep
Of easy wind and downy flake.

The woods are lovely, dark and deep.
But I have promises to keep,
And miles to go before I sleep,
And miles to go before I sleep. [275]

EARL DANIELS

From *The Art of Reading Poetry*. New York: Farrar and Rinehart, 1941. Copyright 1941 by Earl Daniels. Reprinted by permission of Rinehart & Company, Inc., publishers.

If you are one of those taught to approach the presence of the poem in quest of vital lesson, of profound comment on man and the universe, the answer is, *Don't.* Here should be no halfway measures, no reducing the urge to philosophy by half, no gradual tapering-off. You may, after all, rest comfortable in the assurance that if philosophy and morals are present in any vital way, they will make themselves felt without your conscious searching for them, insistent on their share in your awareness of the complete poem.

The way of a group of college freshmen with a poem of Robert Frost ["Stopping by Woods on a Snowy Evening"] illustrates how deadly this concern about morals may be. . . .[16]

Here are some interpretations by freshmen who were supposed to be better-than-average students:

a) In this poem the underlying thought seems to be that of suicide. . . . The last four lines of the poem indicate that the person decides he has more work to do on earth before he dies in order to fulfill a promise of some kind.

b) A man who has promised to leave town after committing some crime, and has been told "to get going and don't stop." The line, "The darkest evening of the year," might mean the disgrace he has brought on himself; and, "I have promises to keep," may mean he has promised to get out of the country.

c) If he didn't mention that the owner of the woods lived in the village, I would say he was talking about the life he has yet to live before he meets his Maker.

d) It deals with the thought of eternal rest. . . . But then the subject is brought back to reality with the thought of the things he has yet to do, and the rest of his life he has yet to spend.

e) It may represent one who is tired of life's hardships, and is tempted to drop by the wayside in some secluded retreat, but who must press on since he has many years of work ahead and many obligations to fulfill before such rest may be his.

f) Almost every day we find ourselves faced with the lures of temptation. We realize that we ought to keep on our way, yet the temptation to stay
where all is peaceful and quiet is often too great for us to resist. While we
are here in college we are often tempted to do the easiest thing. That is, to
neglect our studies and to run around and have a good time. However we
know that there are promises to be kept and obligations to be filled. We
have been sent here by our parents for the purpose of receiving an education,
and there is no doubt that our duty is to do all in our power to take advantage of this opportunity.

g) I am a college man. I am taking a pre-med course. I am away from
home. I am open to temptations that college may offer me. Am I to take advantage of their owner's absence to sit and gaze in his woods—to take advantage of being away from my parents to stop by the wayside and admire
the beautiful sirens? Or, am I to be a second Ulysses and have sufficient will
power to overcome these temptations? Am I to stop where there is "easy
wind and downy flake"—to sit back in my chair, just to dream and forget all
hardships? Or am I to heed the impatience of the horse and the warning
of the harness bell—to awaken to my will calling for me to go on? True, it is
dark now, and I cannot see well, but do I not remember the vows that I
have made—to go through at all costs? Yes, I must go through those long
miles of roads rougher than *I* can imagine, before *I* call for time out.

Comments *f* and *g* are especially nauseous misunderstandings,
and they represent the cardinal sin of personal application. To make a
poem mean privately, to ourselves alone, to look first for directions
about[17] *our* life and *our* problems—no going wrong can be more
abysmally bad. Like the old hocus-pocus magic-formula way in which
the Bible used to be consulted, you put your question, open the book
at random, drop an equally random finger on the page, and there you
are—provided you are ingenious enough in twisting words to meet
special situations and personal needs. The method is equally unintel-
ligent with the Bible and with poetry, and to resort to it is to proclaim
oneself part of an intellectual underworld of superstition and igno-
rance. The poet's message, so far as he has a message for the individual,
is a message to the individual not in his private and peculiar selfhood,
but in his representative capacity as a normal human being, as a man;
it is part of the universality of the poet's speaking.[18]

LEONARD UNGER and WILLIAM VAN O'CONNOR

From *Poems for Study*. New York: Rinehart, 1953. Copyright 1953 by Leonard Unger and William Van O'Connor. Reprinted by permission of Rinehart & Company, Inc., publishers.

Frost's poem obviously contains no explicit interpretation. It may, nonetheless, be found significant beyond the scene and situation which it presents—that is, the poem is its own interpretation in that it implies some meanings in addition to those which are directly stated. We have already noticed that the poem has a particular kind of development. The scene is presented with some indirection. It is considered as someone's property and from the playfully imagined point of view of the little horse. That is, the speaker is not utterly absorbed in the scene. Although he responds to its loveliness, he is not so possessed by it that other thoughts, casual and whimsical, may not enter his mind. The implication is that the speaker does not forsake or forget all his other attitudes while he experiences the loveliness of the woods. His sensibility and appreciation exist among other attitudes and habits of mind, and they are therefore not put in the foreground of the poem.

These implications, which follow from the development of the poem, may be called immediate implications, for there are others less immediate. While the implications already mentioned qualify the speaker's act of contemplating the woods, there are implications which differentiate the several attitudes from which the woods may be regarded. From the first stanza we learn that they are the property of a man who lives in the village. The implication is that they represent an economic value and a practical purpose, as distinguished from their aspect as a lovely object to be watched, to be contemplated. In the second and third stanzas the playful remarks about the horse indicate that he is an animal that has been conditioned to a routine of purposeful behavior, and they thus imply that the speaker's behavior is not, in a sense, purposeful. He has stopped in order to watch the woods and the snow, and he watches toward no other end, but just for watching, for contemplating, for appreciating.

This implication is even clearer in the last stanza. The woods are unusually lovely, but the speaker must eventually be about his business and his responsibilities. There are still other implications in this stanza. The woods are symbolic of beauty in general, of esthetic value. This[599] symbolism is enforced by the word *"but"* in the second line. If it were not for the promises and the miles, what would the speaker do? He might watch the woods indefinitely—he might devote his life to the experience of esthetic value. Or he might enter the woods, for it is their interior, their darkness and depth, which is lovely, and which thus suggests the peacefulness of death. In their fullest symbolic potentiality, then, the woods equate death with an exclusive commitment to esthetic value. The final lines of the poem have implications which are in accord with this interpretation. The speaker feels the urge to escape into loveliness, into the peacefulness of death, but he also acknowledges the fact that there are other values and other urges. He is committed to life, in all its diversity and complexity, and he wants to go on living, to fulfill that commitment, for death will come in time—"And miles to go before I sleep." The repetition of this last line, while it successfully closes the formal pattern of the poem, also emphasizes the symbolic function of the statement.

Considerable interpretive pressure has been put upon Frost's poem, but the poem can withstand this pressure. The ultimate meanings that are found, the less immediate implications, fit nicely with those which are more immediate and obvious. For example, the life-death tension (or dilemma) which is both raised and resolved in the last stanza is logically related to earlier parts of the poem—to the tension between the speaker's contemplation of the woods and his passing thoughts about their owner and the little horse. In its ultimate implication, the last stanza summarizes and generalizes some of the meanings of the foregoing stanzas. This development is marked also by the slight shift of tone which occurs with the last stanza, for the whimsy and playfulness of the earlier stanzas do not continue in the last.[600]

JOHN CIARDI

From "Robert Frost: The Way to the Poem." *Saturday Review*, XLII (April 12, 1958), 13-15, 65. Reprinted by permission of the author and the publisher.

. . . .

Many readers are forever unable to accept the poet's essential duplicity. It is almost safe to say that a poem is never about what it

seems to be about. As much could be said of the proverb. The bird
in the hand, the rolling stone, the stitch in time never (except by an
artful double-deception) intend any sort of statement about birds,
stones, or sewing. The incident of this poem ["Stopping by Woods on
a Snowy Evening"], one must conclude, is at root a metaphor.

Duplicity aside, this poem's movement from the specific to the
general illustrates one of the basic formulas[13] of all poetry. Such a
grand poem as Arnold's "Dover Beach" and such lesser, though unfortunately better known, poems as Longfellow's "The Village Black-
smith" and Holmes's "The Chambered Nautilus" are built on the
same progression. In these three poems, however, the generalization
is markedly set apart from the specific narration, and even seems additional to the telling rather than intrinsic to it. It is this sense of divi-
sion one has in mind in speaking of "a tacked-on moral."

There is nothing wrong-in-itself with a tacked-on moral. Frost,
in fact, makes excellent use of the device at times. In this poem, however, Frost is careful to let the whatever-the-moral-is grow out of the
poem itself. When the action ends the poem ends. There is no epi-
logue and no explanation. Everything pretends to be about the nar-
rated incident. And that pretense sets the basic tone of the poem's
performance of itself.

The dramatic force of that performance is best observable, I
believe, as a progression in three scenes.

In scene one, which coincides with stanza one, a man—a New
England man—is driving his sleigh somewhere at night. It is snowing,
and as the man passes a dark patch of woods he stops to watch the
snow descend into the darkness. We know, moreover, that the man is
familiar with these parts (he knows who owns the woods and where
the owner lives), and we know that no one has seen him stop. As scene
one forms itself in the theatre of the mind's-eye, therefore, it serves to
establish some as yet unspecified relation between the man and the
woods.

It is necessary, however, to stop here for a long parenthesis:
Even so simple an opening statement raises any number of questions.
It is impossible to address all the questions that rise from the poem
stanza by stanza, but two that arise from stanza one illustrate the sort
of thing one might well ask of the poem detail by detail.

Why, for example, does the man not say what errand he is on?
What is the force of leaving the errand generalized? He might just as
well have told us that he was going to the general store, or returning
from it with a jug of molasses he had promised to bring Aunt Harriet
and two suits of long underwear he had promised to bring the hired
man. Frost, moreover, can handle homely detail to great effect. He
preferred to leave his motive generalized. Why?

And why, on the other hand, does he say so much about knowing the absent owner of the woods and where he lives? Is it simply
that one set of details happened-in whereas another did not? To speak
of things "happening-in" is to assault the integrity of a poem. Poetry
cannot be discussed meaningfully unless one can assume that everything in the poem—every last comma and variant spelling—is in it by
the poet's specific act of choice. Only bad poets allow into their poems
what is haphazard or cheaply chosen.

The errand, I will venture a bit brashly for lack of space, is left
generalized in order the more aptly to suggest *any* errand in life and,
therefore, life itself. The owner is there because he is one of the forces
of the poem. Let it do to say that the force he represents is the village
of mankind (that village at the edge of winter) from which the poet
finds himself separated (has separated himself?) in his moment by the
woods (and to which, he recalls finally, he has promises to keep). The
owner is he-who-lives-in-his-village-house, thereby locked away from
the poet's awareness of the-time-the-snow-tells as it engulfs and obliter-
ates the world the village man allows himself to believe he "owns."
Thus, the owner is a representative of an order of reality from which
the poet has divided himself for the moment, though to a certain
extent he ends by reuniting with it. Scene one, therefore, establishes
not only a relation between the man and the woods, but the fact that
the man's relation begins with his separation (though momentarily)
from mankind.

End parenthesis one, begin parenthesis two.

Still considering the first scene as a kind of dramatic performance of forces, one must note that the poet has meticulously matched
the simplicity of his language to the pretended simplicity of the narrative. Clearly, the man stopped because the beauty of the scene moved
him, but he neither tells us that the scene is beautiful nor that he is
moved. A bad writer, always ready to overdo, might have written:
"The vastness gripped me, filling my spirit with the slow steady sinking of the snow's crystalline perfection into the glimmerless profundi-
ties of the hushed primeval wood." Frost's avoidance of such a spate
illustrates two principles of good writing. The first, he has stated himself in "The Mowing": "Anything *more* than the truth would have
seemed too weak" (italics mine). Understatement is one of the basic
sources of power in English poetry. The second principle is to let the
action speak for itself. A good novelist does not tell us that a given
character is good or bad (at least not since the passing of the Dickens
tradition): he shows us the character in action and then, watching
him, we know. Poetry, too, has fictional obligations: even when the
characters are ideas and metaphors rather than people, they must be
*characterized in action*. A poem does not *talk about* ideas; it *enacts*
them. The force of the poem's performance, in fact, is precisely to act

out (and thereby to make us act out empathically that is, to *feel out*, that is, *to identify with*) the speaker and why he stopped. The man is the principal actor in this little "drama of why" and in scene one he is the only character, though as noted, he is somehow related to the absent owner.

End second parenthesis.

In scene two (stanzas two and three) a *foil* is introduced. In fiction and drama, a foil is a character who "plays against" a more important character. By presenting a different point of view or an opposed set of motives, the foil moves the more important character to react in ways that might not have found expression without such opposition. The more important character is thus more fully revealed—to the reader and to himself. The foil here is the horse.

The horse forces the question. Why did the man stop? Until it occurs to him that his "little horse must think it queer" he had not asked himself for reasons. He had simply stopped. But the man finds himself faced with the question he imagines the horse to be asking: what *is* there to stop for out there in the cold, away from bin and stall (house and village and mankind?) and all that any self-respecting beast could value on such a night? In sensing that other view, the man is forced to examine his own more deeply.

In stanza two the question arises only as a feeling within the man. In stanza three, however (still scene two), the horse acts. He gives his harness bells a shake. "What's wrong?" he seems to say. "What are we waiting for?"

By now, obviously, the horse—without[14] losing its identity as horse—has also become a symbol. A symbol is something that stands for something else. Whatever that something else may be, it certainly begins as that order of life that does not understand why a man stops in the wintry middle of nowhere to watch the snow come down. (Can one fail to sense by now that the dark and the snowfall symbolize a death-wish, however momentary, *i.e.*, that hunger for final rest and surrender that a man may feel, but not a beast?)

So by the end of scene two the performance has given dramatic force to three elements that work upon the man. There is his relation to the world of the owner. There is his relation to the brute world of the horse. And there is that third presence of the unownable world, the movement of the all-engulfing snow across all the orders of life, the man's, the owner's, and the horse's—with the difference that the man knows of that second dark-within-the-dark of which the horse cannot, and the owner will not, know.

The man ends scene two with all these forces working upon him simultaneously. He feels himself moved to a decision. And he feels a last call from the darkness: "the sweep / Of easy wind and downy flake." It would be so easy and so downy to go into the woods and let himself be covered over.

But scene three (stanza four) produces a fourth force. This fourth force can be given many names. It is certainly better, in fact, to give it many names than to attempt to limit it to one. It is social obligation, or personal commitment, or duty, or just the realization that a man cannot indulge a mood forever. All of these and more. But, finally, he has a simple decision to make. He may go into the woods and let the darkness and the snow swallow him from the world of beast and man. Or he must move on. And unless he is going to stop here forever, it is time to remember that he has a long way to go and that he had best be getting there. (So there is something to be said for the horse, too.)

Then and only then, his question driven more and more deeply into himself by these cross-forces, does the man venture a comment on what attracted him "The woods are lovely, dark and deep." His mood lingers over the thought of that lovely dark-and-deep (as do the very syllables in which he phrases the thought), but the final decision is to put off the mood and move on. He has his man's way to go and his man's obligations to tend to before he can yield. He has miles to go before his sleep. He repeats that thought and the performance ends.

But why the repetition? The first time Frost says "And miles to go before I sleep," there can be little doubt that the primary meaning is: "I have a long way to go before I get to bed tonight." The second time he says it, however, "miles to go" and "sleep" are suddenly transformed into symbols. What are those "something-elses" the symbols stand for? Hundreds of people have tried to ask Mr. Frost that question and he has always turned it away. He has turned it away *because, he cannot answer it.* He could answer some part of it. But some part is not enough.

For a symbol is like a rock dropped into a pool: it sends out ripples in all directions, and the ripples are in motion. Who can say where the last ripple disappears? One may have a sense that he knows the approximate center point of the ripples, the point at which the stone struck the water. Yet even then he has trouble marking it surely. How does one make a mark on water? Oh very well—the center point of that second "miles to go" is probably approximately in the neighborhood of being close to meaning, perhaps, "the road of life"; and the second "before I sleep" is maybe that close to meaning "before I take my final rest," the rest in darkness that seemed so temptingly dark-and-deep for the moment of the mood. But the ripples continue to move and the light to change on the water, and the longer one watches the more changes he sees. Such shifting-and-being-at-the-same-instant is of the very sparkle and life of poetry. One experiences it as one experiences life, for everytime he looks at an experience he sees something new, and he sees it change as he watches it. And that sense of continuity in fluidity is one of the primary kinds of knowledge, one of man's basic ways of knowing, and one that only the arts can teach, poetry foremost among them.

Frost himself certainly did not ask what that repeated last line meant. It came to him and he received it. He "felt right" about it. And what he "felt right" about was in no sense a "meaning" that, say, an essay could apprehend, but an act of experience that could be fully presented only by the dramatic enactment of forces which is the performance of the poem.[15] . . .

# 4. JONAH AND THE WHALE

THE BOOK OF JONAH

From the Authorized (King James) Version of
*The Holy Bible.*

Now the word of the LORD came unto Jonah the son of Amittai, saying, Arise, go to Nineveh, that great city, and cry against it; for their wickedness is come up before me. But Jonah rose up to flee unto Tarshish from the presence of the LORD, and went down to Joppa; and he found a ship going to Tarshish: so he paid the fare thereof, and went down into it, to go with them unto Tarshish from the presence of the LORD.

But the LORD sent out a great wind into the sea, and there was a mighty tempest in the sea, so that the ship was like to be broken. Then the mariners were afraid, and cried every man unto his god, and cast forth the wares that were in the ship into the sea, to lighten it of them. But Jonah was gone down into the sides of the ship; and he lay, and was fast asleep. So the shipmaster came to him, and said unto him, What meanest thou, O sleeper? arise, call upon thy God, if so be that God will think upon us, that we perish not. And they said every one to his fellow, Come, and let us cast lots, that we may know for whose cause this evil is upon us. So they cast lots, and the lot fell upon Jonah. Then said they unto him, Tell us, we pray thee, for whose cause this evil is upon us; What is thine occupation? and whence comest thou? what is thy country? and of what people art thou? And he said unto them, I am a Hebrew; and I fear the LORD, the God of heaven, which hath made the sea and the dry land. Then were the men exceedingly afraid, and said unto him, Why hast thou done this? For the men knew that he fled from the presence of the LORD, because he had told them.

Then said they unto him, What shall we do unto thee, that the sea may be calm unto us? for the sea wrought, and was tempestuous. And he said unto them, Take me up, and cast me forth into the sea; so shall the sea be calm unto you: for I know that for my sake this great tempest is upon you. Nevertheless the men rowed hard to bring it to the land; but they could not: for the sea wrought, and was tempestuous against them. Wherefore they cried unto the LORD, and said, We beseech thee, o LORD, we beseech thee, let us not perish for this man's life, and lay not upon us innocent blood: for thou, o LORD, hast done as it pleased thee. So they took up Jonah, and cast him forth into the sea: and the sea ceased from her raging. Then the men feared the LORD exceedingly, and offered a sacrifice unto the LORD, and made vows.

Now the LORD had prepared a great fish to swallow up Jonah. And Jonah was in the belly of the fish three days and three nights.

## Chapter Two

Then Jonah prayed unto the LORD his God out of the fish's belly, And said,

> I cried by reason of mine affliction
> Unto the LORD, and he heard me;
> Out of the belly of hell cried I,
> And thou heardest my voice.
> For thou hadst cast me into the deep,
> In the midst of the seas;
> And the floods compassed me about:
> All thy billows and thy waves passed over me.
> Then I said, I am cast out of thy sight;
> Yet I will look again toward thy holy temple.
> The waters compassed me about, even to the soul:
> The depth closed me round about,
> The weeds were wrapped about my head.
> I went down to the bottoms of the mountains;
> The earth with her bars was about me for ever:
> Yet hast thou brought up my life from corruption,
> o LORD my God.
> When my soul fainted within me
> I remembered the LORD:
> And my prayer came in unto thee,
> Into thine holy temple.,
> They that observe lying vanities
> Forsake their own mercy.
> But I will sacrifice unto thee
> With the voice of thanksgiving;
> I will pay that that I have vowed.
> Salvation is of the LORD.

And the LORD spake unto the fish, and it vomited out Jonah upon the dry land.

## Chapter Three

And the word of the LORD came unto Jonah the second time, saying, Arise, go unto Nineveh, that great city, and preach unto it the preaching that I bid thee. So Jonah arose, and went unto Nineveh, according to the word of the LORD. Now Nineveh was an exceeding great city of three days' journey. And Jonah began to enter into the city a day's journey, and he cried, and said, Yet forty days, and Nineveh shall be overthrown.

So the people of Nineveh believed God, and proclaimed a fast, and put on sackcloth, from the greatest of them even to the least of them. For word came unto the king of Nineveh, and he arose from his throne, and he laid his robe from him, and covered him with sackcloth, and sat in ashes. And he caused it to be proclaimed and published through Nineveh by the decree of the king and his nobles, saying, Let neither man nor beast, herd nor flock, taste anything: let them not feed, nor drink water: But let man and beast be covered with sackcloth, and cry mightily unto God: yea, let them turn every one from his evil way, and from the violence that is in their hands. Who can tell if God will turn and repent, and turn away from his fierce anger, that we perish not?

And God saw their works, that they turned from their evil way; and God repented of the evil, that he had said that he would do unto them; and he did it not.

## Chapter Four

But it displeased Jonah exceedingly, and he was very angry. And he prayed unto the LORD, and said, I pray thee, O LORD, was not this my saying, when I was yet in my country? Therefore I fled before unto Tarshish: for I knew that thou art a gracious God, and merciful, slow to anger, and of great kindness, and repentest thee of the evil. Therefore now, O LORD, take, I beseech thee, my life from me; for it is better for me to die than to live. Then said the LORD, Doest thou well to be angry?

So Jonah went out of the city, and sat on the east side of the city, and there made him a booth, and sat under it in the shadow, till he might see what would become of the city. And the LORD God prepared a gourd, and made it to come up over Jonah, that it might be a shadow over his head, to deliver him from his grief. So Jonah was exceedingly glad of the gourd. But God prepared a worm when the morning rose the next day, and it smote the gourd that it withered. And it came to pass, when the sun did arise, that God prepared a vehement east wind; and the sun beat upon the head of Jonah, that he fainted, and wished in himself to die, and said, It is better for me to die than to live. And God said to Jonah, Doest thou well to be angry for the gourd? And he said, I do well to be angry, even unto death. Then said the LORD, Thou hast had pity on the gourd, for the which thou hast not labored, neither madest it grow; which came up in a night, and perished in a night. And should not I spare Nineveh, that great city, wherein are more than sixscore thousand persons that cannot discern between their right hand and their left hand; and also much cattle?

## TRADITIONAL JEWISH FOLKLORE

From Joseph Gaer, *The Lore of the Old Testament*. Boston: Little, Brown and Company, 1952. Copyright, 1951, by Joseph Gaer. Reprinted by permission of the publisher.

. . . .
Jonah fled to the seaport of Joppa and boarded a ship leaving for Tarshish. When the boat was far out at sea a storm arose, and it seemed as if the ship would break in two.

There were passengers on the boat from seventy different nations, and they began to pray in seventy languages to seventy different gods. Only Jonah did not pray. He slept a sound sleep in the midst of the storm.

When the captain of the ship found Jonah fast asleep he woke him in anger: "We toss between life and death, and you sleep! Pray to your God or we will throw you overboard."

All the people on the ship prayed, but the fury of the storm did not diminish.

"There is one among us whom his God wishes to destroy," said the passengers. "Let us cast lots to find the culprit and throw him overboard."

"I am the culprit," said Jonah. "Throw me into the sea and you will all be saved."

The passengers would not believe him.

"Lower me into the water," said Jonah, "and you will be convinced."

They lowered Jonah until the water rose to his waist, and the storm ceased. They raised him out of the water, and the storm redoubled its fury. They lowered him several times, and each time the same thing happened.

The passengers then said to God: "He is Your prophet and You must know why You want him thrown into the sea." And they cast Jonah overboard.

But that was not the end of Jonah. When the passengers let go of him he fell, not into the waters, but into the mouth of a mammoth[270] whale. This was the whale especially created on the Fifth Day of Creation to serve the Prophet Jonah. Its mouth was like a gate, its tongue like a carpet; a precious stone lit up every part inside the fish; and walks led from part to part. If he wished, Jonah could walk into its eye and look out into the ocean.

"Today is the day," said the whale sadly, "when the Leviathan will devour me."

"Take me to him," said Jonah, "and I will rescue you."

When they came near the Leviathan, Jonah said: "I have come to see you, King of the Fish, for when the Messiah comes you will be served at the great feast."

The Leviathan turned and raced away.

"I have saved your life," said Jonah to the whale. "Now take me to see all the wonders of the deep."

The whale took Jonah to see everything in the Great Okeanus that surrounds the earth. He showed him where Korah and his followers sank; where the Jews crossed the Red Sea; the underwater entrance to *Gehinnom;* the mouth of the river from which all the oceans flow; and the River of Youth at the gates of the Garden of Eden.

For three days Jonah traveled in the whale to see the wonders of the sea and they so engrossed him that he forgot his daily prayers.

"He is too comfortable where he is," said God.

Instantly another and even larger whale appeared and called: "In the name of God, give up the prophet you harbor. If you fail to obey, I shall devour you."

The whale spat Jonah out and the female whale swallowed him. Here Jonah was crowded. It was dark inside. And he could not see through the whale's eyes.

Jonah prayed: "Creator of the World, how foolish was I to think that I could escape You. Heaven is Your seat and the earth is Your footstool. Not a deed nor a thought escapes You. Your abode is not Israel but the Universe. Help me, O Lord, and deliver me[271] from my prison in the deep. You can mete out death to the living and life to the dead, help me!"

God commanded the whale to spit Jonah out. This she did with such force that he landed nine hundred and fifty-six miles inland from the nearest shore.

"Now," said God, "go to Nineveh and warn the people to repent."[272]

. . . .

HERMAN MELVILLE

"The Sermon." Chapter 9 of *Moby-Dick; or,
the Whale* [1851], ed. Luther S. Mansfield and
Howard P. Vincent. New York: Hendricks
House, 1952.

Father Mapple rose, and in a mild voice of unassuming authority ordered the scattered people to condense. "Starboard gangway, there! side away to larboard—larboard gangway to starboard! Midships! midships!"

There was a low rumbling of heavy sea-boots among the benches, and a still slighter shuffling of women's shoes, and all was quiet again, and every eye on the preacher.

He paused a little; then kneeling in the pulpit's bows, folded his large brown hands across his chest, uplifted his closed eyes,[39] and offered a prayer so deeply devout that he seemed kneeling and praying at the bottom of the sea.

This ended, in prolonged solemn tones, like the continual tolling of a bell in a ship that is foundering at sea in a fog—in such tones he commenced reading the following hymn; but changing his manner towards the concluding stanzas, burst forth with a pealing exultation and joy—

> "The ribs and terrors in the whale,
>     Arched over me a dismal gloom,
> While all God's sun-lit waves rolled by,
>     And left me deepening down to doom.
>
> "I saw the opening maw of hell,
>     With endless pains and sorrows there;
> Which none but they that feel can tell—
>     Oh, I was plunging to despair.
>
> "In black distress, I called my God,
>     When I could scarce believe him mine,
> He bowed his ear to my complaints—
>     No more the whale did me confine.
>
> "With speed he flew to my relief,
>     As on a radiant dolphin borne;
> Awful, yet bright, as lightning shone
>     The face of my Deliverer God.

"My song for ever shall record
    That terrible, that joyful hour;
I give the glory to my God,
    His all the mercy and the power."

Nearly all joined in singing this hymn, which swelled high above the howling of the storm. A brief pause ensued; the preacher slowly turned over the leaves of the Bible, and at last, folding his hand down upon the proper page, said: "Beloved shipmates, clinch the last verse of the first chapter of Jonah—"And God had prepared a great fish to swallow up Jonah."

"Shipmates, this book, containing only four chapters—four yarns—is one of the smallest strands in the mighty cable of the Scriptures. Yet what depths of the soul does Jonah's deep sealine sound! what a pregnant lesson to us is this prophet! What[40] a noble thing is that canticle in the fish's belly! How billow-like and boisterously grand! We feel the floods surging over us; we sound with him to the kelpy bottom of the waters; sea-weed and all the slime of the sea is about us! But *what* is this lesson that the book of Jonah teaches? Shipmates, it is a two-stranded lesson; a lesson to us all as sinful men, and a lesson to me as a pilot of the living God. As sinful men, it is a lesson to us all, because it is a story of the sin, hard-heartedness, suddenly awakened fears, the swift punishment, repentance, prayers and finally the deliverance and joy of Jonah. As with all sinners among men, the sin of this son of Amittai was in his wilful disobedience of the command of God—never mind now what that command was, or how conveyed—which he found a hard command. But all the things that God would have us do are hard for us to do—remember that—and hence, he oftener commands us than endeavors to persuade. And if we obey God, we must disobey ourselves; and it is in this disobeying ourselves, wherein the hardness of obeying God consists.

"With this sin of disobedience in him, Jonah still further flouts at God, by seeking to flee from Him. He thinks that a ship made by men, will carry him into countries where God does not reign, but only the Captains of this earth. He skulks about the wharves of Joppa, and seeks a ship that's bound for Tarshish. There lurks, perhaps, a hitherto unheeded meaning here. By all accounts Tarshish could have been no other city than the modern Cadiz. That's the opinion of learned men. And where is Cadiz, shipmates? Cadiz is in Spain; as far by water, from Joppa, as Jonah could possibly have sailed in those ancient days, when the Atlantic was an almost unknown sea. Because Joppa, the modern Jaffa, shipmates, is on the most easterly coast of the Mediterranean, the Syrian; and Tarshish or Cadiz more than two thousand miles to the westward from that, just outside the Straits of Gibraltar. See ye not then, shipmates, that Jonah sought to flee world-wide from God? Miserable man! Oh! most contemptible and worthy of all scorn;

with slouched hat and guilty eye, skulking from his God; prowling among the shipping like a vile burglar hastening to cross the seas. So disordered, self-condemning is his look, that had there been policemen in[41] those days, Jonah, on the mere suspicion of something wrong, had been arrested ere he touched a deck. How plainly he's a fugitive! no baggage, not a hat-box, valise, or carpet-bag,—no friends accompany him to the wharf with their adieux. At last, after much dodging search, he finds the Tarshish ship receiving the last items of her cargo; and as he steps on board to see its Captain in the cabin, all the sailors for the moment desist from hoisting in the goods, to mark the stranger's evil eye. Jonah sees this; but in vain he tries to look all ease and confidence; in vain essays his wretched smile. Strong intuitions of the man assure the mariners he can be no innocent. In their gamesome but still serious way, one whispers to the other—'Jack, he's robbed a widow;' or, 'Joe, do you mark him; he's a bigamist;' or, 'Harry lad, I guess he's the adulterer that broke jail in old Gomorrah, or belike, one of the missing murderers from Sodom.' Another runs to read the bill that's stuck against the spile upon the wharf to which the ship is moored, offering five hundred gold coins for the apprehension of a parricide, and containing a description of his person. He reads, and looks from Jonah to the bill; while all his sympathetic shipmates now crowd round Jonah, prepared to lay their hands upon him. Frighted Jonah trembles, and summoning all his boldness to his face, only looks so much the more a coward. He will not confess himself suspected; but that itself is strong suspicion. So he makes the best of it; and when the sailors find him not to be the man that is advertised, they let him pass, and he descends into the cabin.

'Who's there?' cries the Captain at his busy desk, hurriedly making out his papers for the Customs—'Who's there?' Oh! how that harmless question mangles Jonah! For the instant he almost turns to flee again. But he rallies. 'I seek a passage in this ship to Tarshish; how soon sail ye, sir?' Thus far the busy Captain had not looked up to Jonah, though the man now stands before him; but no sooner does he hear that hollow voice, than he darts a scrutinizing glance. 'We sail with the next coming tide,' at last he slowly answered, still intently eyeing him. 'No sooner, sir?'—'Soon enough for any honest man that goes a passenger.' Ha! Jonah, that's another stab. But he swiftly calls away the Captain from that scent. 'I'll sail with ye,'—he says,—'the passage[42] money, how much is that?—I'll pay now.' For it is particularly written, shipmates, as if it were a thing not to be overlooked in this history, 'that he paid the fare thereof' ere the craft did sail. And taken with the context, this is full of meaning.

Now Jonah's Captain, shipmates, was one whose discernment detects crime in any, but whose cupidity exposes it only in the penniless. In this world, shipmates, sin that pays its way can travel freely, and without a passport; whereas Virtue, if a pauper, is stopped at all frontiers. So Jonah's Captain prepares to test the length of Jonah's purse, ere he judge him openly. He charges him thrice the usual sum; and it's assented to. Then the Captain knows that Jonah is a fugitive; but at the same time resolves to help a flight that paves its rear with gold. Yet when Jonah fairly takes out his purse, prudent suspicions still molest the Captain. He rings every coin to find a counterfeit. Not a forger, any way, he mutters; and Jonah is put down for his passage. 'Point out my state-room, Sir,' says Jonah now, 'I'm travel-weary; I need sleep.' 'Thou look'st like it,' says the Captain, 'there's thy room.' Jonah enters, and would lock the door, but the lock contains no key. Hearing him foolishly fumbling there, the Captain laughs lowly to himself, and mutters something about the doors of convicts' cells being never allowed to be locked within. All dressed and dusty as he is, Jonah throws himself into his berth, and finds the little state-room ceiling almost resting on his forehead. The air is close, and Jonah gasps. Then, in that contracted hole, sunk, too, beneath the ship's water-line, Jonah feels the heralding presentiment of that stifling hour, when the whale shall hold him in the smallest of his bowel's wards.

"Screwed at its axis against the side, a swinging lamp slightly oscillates in Jonah's room; and the ship, heeling over towards the wharf with the weight of the last bales received, the lamp, flame and all, though in slight motion, still maintains a permanent obliquity with reference to the room; though, in truth, infallibly straight itself, it but made obvious the false, lying levels among which it hung. The lamp alarms and frightens Jonah; as lying in his berth his tormented eyes roll round the place, and this thus far successful fugitive finds no refuge for his restless glance. But that contradiction in the lamp more and[43] more appals him. The floor, the ceiling, and the side, are all awry. 'Oh! so my conscience hangs in me!' he groans, 'straight upward, so it burns; but the chambers of my soul are all in crookedness!'

"Like one who after a night of drunken revelry hies to his bed, still reeling, but with conscience yet pricking him, as the plungings of the Roman race-horse but so much the more strike his steel tags into him; as one who in that miserable plight still turns and turns in giddy anguish, praying God for annihilation until the fit be passed; and at last amid the whirl of woe he feels, a deep stupor steals over him, as over the man who bleeds to death, for conscience is the wound, and there's naught to staunch it; so, after sore wrestlings in his berth, Jonah's prodigy of ponderous misery drags him drowning down to sleep.

"And now the time of tide has come; the ship casts off her cables; and from the deserted wharf the uncheered ship for Tarshish, all careening, glides to sea. That ship, my friends, was the first of re-corded smugglers! the contraband was Jonah. But the sea rebels; he will not bear the wicked burden. A dreadful storm comes on, the ship is like to break. But now when the boatswain calls all hands to lighten her; when boxes, bales, and jars are clattering overboard; when the wind is shrieking, and the men are yelling, and every plank thunders with trampling feet right over Jonah's head; in all this raging tumult, Jonah sleeps his hideous sleep. He sees no black sky and raging sea, feels not the reeling timbers, and little hears he or heeds he the far rush of the mighty whale, which even now with open mouth is cleaving the seas after him. Aye, shipmates, Jonah was gone down into the sides of the ship—a berth in the cabin as I have taken it, and was fast asleep. But the frightened master comes to him, and shrieks in his dead ear, 'What meanest thou, O sleeper! arise!' Startled from his lethargy by that direful cry, Jonah staggers to his feet, and stumbling to the deck, grasps a shroud, to look out upon the sea. But at that moment he is sprung upon by a panther billow leaping over the bulwarks. Wave after wave thus leaps into the ship, and finding no speedy vent runs roaring fore and aft, till the mariners come nigh to drowning while yet afloat. And ever, as the white moon shows[44] her affrighted face from the steep gullies in the blackness overhead, aghast Jonah sees the rearing bowsprit pointing high upward, but soon beat downward again towards the tormented deep.

"Terrors upon terrors run shouting through his soul. In all his cringing attitudes, the God-fugitive is now too plainly known. The sailors mark him; more and more certain grow their suspicions of him, and at last, fully to test the truth, by referring the whole matter to high Heaven, they fall to casting lots, to see for whose cause this great tempest was upon them. The lot is Jonah's; that discovered, then how furiously they mob him with their questions. 'What is thine occupation? Whence comest thou? Thy country? What people?' But mark now, my shipmates, the behavior of poor Jonah. The eager mariners but ask him who he is, and where from; whereas, they not only receive an answer to those questions, but likewise another answer to a question not put by them, but the unsolicited answer is forced from Jonah by the hard hand of God that is upon him.

" 'I am a Hebrew,' he cries—and then—'I fear the Lord the God of Heaven who hath made the sea and the dry land!' Fear him, O Jonah? Aye, well mightest thou fear the Lord God *then!* Straightway, he now goes on to make a full confession; whereupon the mariners became more and more appalled, but still are pitiful. For when Jonah, not yet supplicating God for mercy, since he but too well knew the darkness of his deserts,—when wretched Jonah cries out to them to take him and cast him forth into the sea, for he knew that for *his* sake this great tempest was upon them; they mercifully turn from him, and seek by other means to save the ship. But all in vain; the indignant gale howls louder; then, with one hand raised invokingly to God, with the other they not unreluctantly lay hold of Jonah.

"And now behold Jonah taken up as an anchor and dropped into the sea; when instantly an oily calmness floats out from the east, and the sea is still, as Jonah carries down the gale with him, leaving smooth water behind. He goes down in the whirling heart of such a masterless commotion that he scarce heeds the moment when he drops seething into the yawning jaws[45] awaiting him; and the whale shoots-to all his ivory teeth, like so many white bolts, upon his prison. Then Jonah prayed unto the Lord out of the fish's belly. But observe his prayer, and learn a weighty lesson. For sinful as he is, Jonah does not weep and wail for direct deliverance. He feels that his dreadful punishment is just. He leaves all his deliverance to God, contenting himself with this, that spite of all his pains and pangs, he will still look towards His holy temple. And here, shipmates, is true and faithful repentance; not clamorous for pardon, but grateful for punishment. And how pleasing to God was this conduct in Jonah, is shown in the eventual deliverance of him from the sea and the whale. Shipmates, I do not place Jonah before you to be copied for his sin but I do place him before you as a model for repentance. Sin not; but if you do, take heed to repent of it like Jonah."

While he was speaking these words, the howling of the shrieking, slanting storm without seemed to add new power to the preacher, who, when describing Jonah's sea-storm, seemed tossed by a storm himself. His deep chest heaved as with a ground-swell; his tossed arms seemed the warring elements at work; and the thunders that rolled away from off his swarthy brow, and the light leaping from his eye, made all his simple hearers look on him with a quick fear that was strange to them.

There now came a lull in his look, as he silently turned over the leaves of the Book once more; and, at last, standing motionless, with closed eyes, for the moment, seemed communing with God and himself.

But again he leaned over towards the people, and bowing his head lowly, with an aspect of the deepest yet manliest humility, he spake these words:

"Shipmates, God has laid but one hand upon you; both his hands press upon me. I have read ye by what murky light may be mine the lesson that Jonah teaches to all sinners; and therefore to ye, and still more to me, for I am a greater sinner than ye. And now how gladly would I come down from this masthead and sit on the hatches there where you sit, and listen as you listen, while some one of you reads *me* that other and more awful lesson which Jonah teaches to *me*, as a pilot of[46] the living God. How being an anointed pilot-prophet, or speaker of true things, and bidden by the Lord to sound those unwelcome truths in the ears of a wicked Nineveh, Jonah, appalled at the hostility he should raise, fled from his mission, and sought to escape his duty and his God by taking ship at Joppa. But God is everywhere; Tarshish he never reached. As we have seen, God came upon him in the whale, and swallowed him down to living gulfs of doom, and with swift slantings tore him along 'into the midst of the seas,' where the eddying depths sucked him ten thousand fathoms down, and 'the weeds were wrapped about his head,' and all the watery world of woe bowled over him. Yet even then beyond the reach of any plummet—'out of the belly of hell'—when the whale grounded upon the ocean's utmost bones, even then, God heard the engulphed, repenting prophet when he cried. Then God spake unto the fish; and from the shuddering cold and blackness of the sea, the whale came breeching up towards the warm and pleasant sun, and all the delights of air and earth; and 'vomited out Jonah upon the dry land'; when the word of the Lord came a second time; and Jonah, bruised and beaten—his ears, like two sea-shells, still multitudinously murmuring of the ocean—Jonah did the Almighty's bidding. And what was that, shipmates? To preach the Truth to the face of Falsehood! That was it!

"This, shipmates, this is that other lesson; and woe to that pilot of the living God who slights it. Woe to him whom this world charms from Gospel duty! Woe to him who seeks to pour oil upon the waters when God has brewed them into a gale! Woe to him who seeks to please rather than to appal! Woe to him whose good name is more to him than goodness! Woe to him who, in this world, courts not dishonor! Woe to him who would not be true, even though to be false were salvation! Yea, woe to him who, as the great Pilot Paul has it, while preaching to others is himself a castaway!"

He drooped and fell away from himself for a moment; then lifting his face to them again, showed a deep joy in his eyes, as he cried out with a heavenly enthusiasm,—"But oh! shipmates! on the starboard hand of every woe, there is a sure delight; and higher the top of that delight, than the bottom of the woe is[47] deep. Is not the main-truck higher than the kelson is low? Delight is to him—a far, far upward, and inward delight—who against the proud gods and commodores of this earth, ever stands forth his own inexorable self. Delight is to him whose strong arms yet support him, when the ship of this base treacherous world has gone down beneath him. Delight is to him, who gives no quarter in the truth, and kills, burns, and destroys all sin though he pluck it out from under the robes of Senators and Judges. Delight,—top-gallant delight is to him, who acknowledges no law or lord, but the Lord his God, and is only a patriot to heaven. Delight is to him, whom all the waves of the billows of the seas of the boisterous mob can never shake from this sure Keel of the Ages. And eternal delight and deliciousness will be his, who coming to lay him down, can say with his final breath—O Father!—chiefly known to me by Thy rod—mortal or immortal, here I die. I have striven to be Thine, more than to be this world's, or mine own. Yet this is nothing; I leave eternity to Thee; for what is man that he should live out the lifetime of his God?"

He said no more, but slowly waving a benediction, covered his face with his hands, and so remained kneeling, till all the people had departed, and he was left alone in the place.[48]

"Jonah Historically Regarded." Chapter 83
of *Moby-Dick; or, the Whale,* ed. Luther S.
Mansfield and Howard P. Vincent. New York:
Hendricks House, 1952.

Reference was made to the historical story of Jonah and the
whale in the preceding chapter. Now some Nantucketers rather dis-
trust this historical story of Jonah and the whale. But then there were
some sceptical Greeks and Romans, who, standing out from the ortho-
dox pagans of their times, equally doubted the story of Hercules and
the whale, and Arion and the dolphin; [362] and yet their doubting
those traditions did not make those traditions one whit the less facts,
for all that.

One old Sag-Harbor whaleman's chief reason for questioning
the Hebrew story was this:—He had one of those quaint old-fashioned
Bibles, embellished with curious, unscientific plates; one of which
represented Jonah's whale with two spouts in his head—a peculiarity
only true with respect to a species of the Leviathan (the Right Whale,
and the varieties of that order), concerning which the fishermen have
this saying, "A penny roll would choke him;" his swallow is so very
small. But, to this, Bishop Jebb's anticipative answer is ready. It is not
necessary, hints the Bishop, that we consider Jonah as tombed in the
whale's belly, but as temporarily lodged in some part of his mouth.
And this seems reasonable enough in the good Bishop. For truly, the
Right Whale's mouth would accommodate a couple of whist-tables,
and comfortably seat all the players. Possibly, too, Jonah might have
ensconced himself in a hollow tooth; but, on second thoughts, the
Right Whale is toothless.

Another reason which Sag-Harbor (he went by that name) urged
for his want of faith in this matter of the prophet, was something
obscurely in reference to his incarcerated body and the whale's gastric
juices. But this objection likewise falls to the ground, because a Ger-
man exegetist supposes that Jonah must have taken refuge in the
floating body of a *dead* whale—even as the French soldiers in the Rus-
sian campaign turned their dead horses into tents, and crawled into
them. Besides, it has been divined by other continental commentators,
that when Jonah was thrown overboard from the Joppa ship, he
straightway effected his escape to another vessel near by, some vessel
with a whale for a figure-head; and, I would add, possibly called "The
Whale," as some craft are nowadays christened the "Shark," the
"Gull," the "Eagle." Nor have there been wanting learned exegetists
who have opined that the whale mentioned in the book of Jonah
merely meant a life-preserver—an inflated bag of wind—which the

endangered prophet swam to, and so was saved from a watery doom. Poor Sag-Harbor, therefore, seems worsted all round. But he had still another reason for his want of faith. It was this, if I remember right: Jonah was[363] swallowed by the whale in the Mediterranean Sea, and after three days he was vomited up somewhere within three days' journey of Nineveh, a city on the Tigris, very much more than three · days' journey across from the nearest point of the Mediterranean coast. How is that?

But was there no other way for the whale to land the prophet within that short distance of Nineveh? Yes. He might have carried him round by the way of the Cape of Good Hope. But not to speak of the passage through the whole length of the Mediterranean, and another passage up the Persian Gulf and Red Sea, such a supposition would involve the complete circumnavigation of all Africa in three days, not to speak of the Tigris waters, near the site of Nineveh, being too shallow for any whale to swim in. Besides, this idea of Jonah's weathering the Cape of Good Hope at so early a day would wrest the honor of the discovery of that great headland from Bartholomew Diaz, its reputed discoverer, and so make modern history a liar.

But all these foolish arguments of old Sag-Harbor only evinced his foolish pride of reason—a thing still more reprehensible in him, seeing that he had but little learning except what he had picked up from the sun and the sea. I say it only shows his foolish, impious pride, and abominable, devilish rebellion against the reverend clergy. For by a Portuguese Catholic priest, this very idea of Jonah's going to Nineveh viâ the Cape of Good Hope was advanced as a signal magnification of the general miracle. And so it was. Besides, to this day, the highly enlightened Turks devoutly believe in the historical story of Jonah. And some three centuries ago, an English traveller in old Harris's Voyages, speaks of a Turkish Mosque built in honor of Jonah, in which mosque was a miraculous lamp that burnt without any oil.[364]

## HAROLD H. WATTS

From *The Modern Reader's Guide to the Bible*. New York: Harper & Brothers, 1949. Reprinted by permission of the author and the publisher.

The story of *Jonah* concerns a prophet who is supposedly a contemporary of the Assyrian empire, an empire—as the books of *Kings* tell us—little likely to respond favorably to missionary effort on behalf of the one true God. Actually, *Jonah*, like *Ruth*, is a manipulation of historical details to drive home a point[165] cogent to a later age. The point is that the Ninevites (who stand for the impure peoples round about the Jewish theocratic state set up after the return from exile in 538 B C.) are as worthy of salvation—and as eager for it—as is the self-righteous Jonah, who is unwilling to carry the Lord's message. The eager conversion of Nineveh is analogous to the simple if crude trust in God to be found among the "impure" Hebrews; and the churlish Jonah, unwilling to take God's message to outsiders and angry when they respond to it, stands for the group in Israel that on trivial or legalistic ground wishes to exclude large numbers from the community.

So viewed, the story has point if not artistic finish. It can indeed be regarded as employing a method similar to that of the modern political cartoon wherein crude figures of donkey and elephant stand as intelligible symbols for abstract political entities. In such a light the whale's function in the tale would not be misunderstood by those who had the key to the entire tale. The whale is but another item in the story that has been schematized to drive home a doctrinal point. We who have to fumble for the clue can but guess at the symbolic meaning. Does the whale stand for the great exile in Babylon—an exile that was a punishment for past Hebrew misdeeds but from which too many Hebrews returned not in humility but with the sense of self-righteousness and apartness that Jonah displays? Or, more simply, is the whale the wrath of a god whose plain instructions have been ignored? Whatever our answer here, the point to be perceived is that the whale in this story . . . was to its audience an understood gambit, an "opening" full of meaning to the initiate. To the initiate, the importance of the whale was not literal but allegorical. Those who allow their energies to be trapped in an argument as to the possibility of the whale episode perhaps resemble the child of today who looks at a political cartoon and judges it a precise picture of something that has actually happened.

## ERICH FROMM

From *Man for Himself: An Inquiry into the Psychology of Ethics*. New York: Rinehart, 1947. Reprinted by permission of the publisher.

Care and responsibility denote that love is an activity and not a passion by which one is overcome, nor an affect which one is "affected by." The element of care and responsibility in productive love has been admirably described in the book of Jonah. God has told Jonah to go to Nineveh to warn its inhabitants that they will be punished unless they mend their evil ways. Jonah runs away from his mission because he is afraid that the people in Nineveh will repent and that God will forgive them. He is a man with a strong sense of order and law, but without love. However, in his attempt to escape he finds himself in the belly of a whale, symbolizing the state of isolation and imprisonment which his lack of love and solidarity has brought upon him. God saves him, and Jonah goes to Nineveh. He preaches to the inhabitants as God has told him, and the very thing[98] he was afraid of happens. The men of Nineveh repent their sins, mend their ways, and God forgives them and decides not to destroy the city. Jonah is intensely angry and disappointed; he wanted "justice" to be done, not mercy. At last he finds some comfort by the shade of a tree which God had made to grow for him to protect him from the sun. But when God makes the tree wilt Jonah is depressed and angrily complains to God. God answers: "Thou hast had pity on the gourd for the which thou has not labored neither madest it grow; which came up in a night, and perished in a night. And should I not spare Nineveh, that great city, wherein are more than sixscore thousand people that cannot discern between their right hand and their left hand; and also much cattle?" God's answer to Jonah is to be understood symbolically. God explains to Jonah that the essence of love is to "labor" for something and "to make something grow," that love and labor are inseparable. One loves that for which one labors, and one labors for that which one loves.

The story of Jonah implies that love cannot be divorced from *responsibility*. Jonah does not feel responsible for the life of his brothers. He, like Cain, could ask, "Am I my brother's keeper?" Responsibility is not a duty imposed upon one from the outside, but is my response to a request which I feel to be my concern. Responsibility and response have the same root, *respondere* = "to answer"; to be responsible means to be ready to respond.[99]

From *The Forgotten Language: An Introduction to the Understanding of Dreams, Fairy Tales and Myths.* New York: Rinehart, 1951. Reprinted by permission of the publisher.

A good illustration of the function of the universal symbol is a story, written in symbolic language, which is known to almost everyone in Western culture: the Book of Jonah. Jonah has heard God's voice telling him to go to Nineveh and preach to its inhabitants to give up their evil ways lest they be destroyed. Jonah cannot[20] help hearing God's voice and that is why he is a prophet. But he is an unwilling prophet, who, though knowing what he should do, tries to run away from the command of God (or, as we may say, the voice of his conscience). He is a man who does not care for other human beings. He is a man with a strong sense of law and order, but without love.

How does the story express the inner processes in Jonah?

We are told that Jonah went down to Joppa and found a ship which should bring him to Tarshish. In mid-ocean a storm rises and, while everyone else is excited and afraid, Jonah goes into the ship's belly and falls into a deep sleep. The sailors, believing that God must have sent the storm because someone on the ship is to be punished, wake Jonah, who had told them he was trying to flee from God's command. He tells them to take him and cast him forth into the sea and that the sea would then become calm. The sailors (betraying a remarkable sense of humanity by first trying everything else before following his advice) eventually take Jonah and cast him into the sea, which immediately stops raging. Jonah is swallowed by a big fish and stays in the fish's belly three days and three nights. He prays to God to free him from this prison. God makes the fish vomit out Jonah unto the dry land and Jonah goes to Nineveh, fulfills God's command, and thus saves the inhabitants of the city.[21]

The story is told as if these events had actually happened. However, it is written in symbolic language and all the realistic events described are symbols for the inner experiences of the hero. We find a sequence of symbols which follow one another: going into the ship, going into the ship's belly, falling asleep, being in the ocean, and being in the fish's belly. All these symbols stand for the same inner experience: for a condition of being protected and isolated, of safe withdrawal from communication with other human beings. They represent what could be represented in another symbol, the fetus in the mother's womb. Different as the ship's belly, deep sleep, the ocean, and a fish's belly are realistically, they are expressive of the same inner experience, of the blending between protection and isolation.

In the manifest story events happen in space and time: *first,* going into the ship's belly; *then,* falling asleep; *then,* being thrown into the ocean; *then,* being swallowed by the fish. One thing happens after the other, and although some events are obviously unrealistic, the story has its own logical consistency in terms of time and space. But if we understand that the writer did not intend to tell us the story of external events, but of the inner experience of a man torn between his conscience and his wish to escape from his inner voice, it becomes clear that his various actions following one after the other express the same mood in him; and that *sequence in time* is expressive of *growing intensity* of the same feeling. In his attempt to escape from his obligation to his fellow men Jonah isolates himself more and more until, in the belly of the fish, the protective[22] element has so given way to the imprisoning element that he can stand it no longer and is forced to pray to God to be released from where he had put himself. (This is a mechanism which we find so characteristic of neurosis. An attitude is assumed as a defense against a danger, but then it grows far beyond its original defense function and becomes a neurotic symptom from which the person tries to be relieved.) Thus Jonah's escape into protective isolation ends in the terror of being imprisoned, and he takes up his life at the point where he had tried to escape.

There is another difference between the logic of the manifest and the latent story. In the manifest story the logical connection is one of causality of external events. Jonah wants to go overseas *because* he wants to flee from God, he falls asleep *because* he is tired, he is thrown overboard *because* he is supposed to be the reason for the storm, and he is swallowed by the fish *because* there are man-eating fish in the ocean. One event occurs because of a previous event. (The last part of the story is unrealistic, but not illogical) But in the latent story the logic is different. The various events are related to each other by their association with the same inner experience. What appears to be a causal sequence of external events stands for a connection of experiences linked with each other by their association in terms of inner events. This is as logical as the manifest story—but it is a logic of a different kind.[23]

# 5. NATHANIEL HAWTHORNE—"Young Goodman Brown"

From *Mosses from an Old Manse* [1846]. Reprinted in *Nathaniel Hawthorne: Selected Tales and Sketches,* edited by Hyatt H. Waggoner. New York: Rinehart, 1950.

Young Goodman Brown came forth at sunset into the street at Salem village; but put his head back, after crossing the threshold, to exchange a parting kiss with his young wife. And Faith, as the wife was aptly named, thrust her own pretty head into the street, letting the wind play with the pink ribbons of her cap while she called to Goodman Brown.

"Dearest heart," whispered she, softly and rather sadly, when her lips were close to his ear, "prithee put off your journey until sunrise and sleep in your own bed to-night. A lone woman is troubled with such dreams and such thoughts that she's afeard of herself sometimes. Pray tarry with me this night, dear husband, of all nights in the year."

"My love and my Faith," replied young Goodman Brown, "of all nights in the year, this one night must I tarry away from thee. My journey, as thou callest it, forth and back again, must needs be done 'twixt now and sunrise. What, my sweet, pretty wife, dost thou doubt me already, and we but three months married?"

"Then God bless you!" said Faith, with the pink ribbons; "and may you find all well when you come back."

"Amen!" cried Goodman Brown. "Say thy prayers, dear Faith, and go to bed at dusk, and no harm will come to thee."

So they parted; and the young man pursued his way until, being about to turn the corner by the meeting-house, he looked back and saw the head of Faith still peeping after him with a melancholy air, in spite of her pink ribbons.

"Poor little Faith!" thought he, for his heart smote him. "What a wretch am I to leave her on such an errand! She talks of dreams,[108] too. Methought as she spoke there was trouble in her face, as if a dream had warned her what work is to be done to-night. But no, no;

'twould kill her to think it. Well, she's a blessed angel on earth; and after this one night I'll cling to her skirts and follow her to heaven."

With this excellent resolve for the future, Goodman Brown felt himself justified in making more haste on his present evil purpose. He had taken a dreary road, darkened by all the gloomiest trees of the forest, which barely stood aside to let the narrow path creep through, and closed immediately behind. It was all as lonely as could be; and there is this peculiarity in such a solitude, that the traveller knows not who may be concealed by the innumerable trunks and the thick boughs overhead; so that with lonely footsteps he may yet be passing through an unseen multitude.

"There may be a devilish Indian behind every tree," said Goodman Brown to himself; and he glanced fearfully behind him as he added, "What if the devil himself should be at my very elbow!"

His head being turned back, he passed a crook of the road, and, looking forward again, beheld the figure of a man, in grave and decent attire, seated at the foot of an old tree. He arose at Goodman Brown's approach and walked onward side by side with him.

"You are late, Goodman Brown," said he. "The clock of the Old South was striking as I came through Boston, and that is full fifteen minutes agone."

"Faith kept me back a while," replied the young man, with a tremor in his voice, caused by the sudden appearance of his companion, though not wholly unexpected.

It was now deep dusk in the forest, and deepest in that part of it where these two were journeying. As nearly as could be discerned, the second traveller was about fifty years old, apparently in the same rank of life as Goodman Brown, and bearing a considerable resemblance to him, though perhaps more in expression than features. Still they might have been taken for father and son. And yet, though the elder person was as simply clad as the[109] younger, and as simple in manner too, he had an indescribable air of one who knew the world, and who would not have felt abashed at the governor's dinner table or in King William's court, were it possible that his affairs should call him thither. But the only thing about him that could be fixed upon as remarkable was his staff, which bore the likeness of a great black snake, so curiously wrought that it might almost be seen to twist and wriggle itself like a living serpent. This, of course, must have been an ocular deception, assisted by the uncertain light.

"Come, Goodman Brown," cried his fellow-traveller, "this is a dull pace for the beginning of a journey. Take my staff, if you are so soon weary."

"Friend," said the other, exchanging his slow pace for a full stop, "having kept covenant by meeting thee here, it is my purpose now to return whence I came. I have scruples touching the matter thou wot'st of."

"Sayest thou so?" replied he of the serpent, smiling apart. "Let us walk on, nevertheless, reasoning as we go; and if I convince thee not thou shalt turn back. We are but a little way in the forest yet."

"Too far! too far!" exclaimed the goodman, unconsciously resuming his walk. "My father never went into the woods on such an errand, nor his father before him. We have been a race of honest men and good Christians since the days of the martyrs; and shall I be the first of the name of Brown that ever took this path and kept"—

"Such company, thou wouldst say," observed the elder person, interpreting his pause. "Well said, Goodman Brown! I have been as well acquainted with your family as with ever a one among the Puritans; and that's no trifle to say. I helped your grandfather, the constable, when he lashed the Quaker woman so smartly through the streets of Salem; and it was I that brought your father a pitch-pine knot, kindled at my own hearth, to set fire to an Indian village, in King Philip's war. They were my good friends, both; and many a pleasant walk have we had along this path, and returned[110] merrily after midnight. I would fain be friends with you for their sake."

"If it be as thou sayest," replied Goodman Brown, "I marvel they never spoke of these matters; or, verily, I marvel not, seeing that the least rumor of the sort would have driven them from New England. We are a people of prayer, and good works to boot, and abide no such wickedness."

"Wickedness or not," said the traveller with the twisted staff, "I have a very general acquaintance here in New England. The deacons of many a church have drunk the communion wine with me; the selectmen of divers towns make me their chairman; and a majority of the Great and General Court are firm supporters of my interest. The governor and I, too—But these are state secrets."

"Can this be so?" cried Goodman Brown, with a stare of amazement at his undisturbed companion. "Howbeit, I have nothing to do with the governor and council; they have their own ways, and are no rule for a simple husbandman like me. But, were I to go on with thee, how should I meet the eye of that good old man, our minister, at Salem village? Oh, his voice would make me tremble both Sabbath day and lecture day."

Thus far the elder traveller had listened with due gravity; but now burst into a fit of irrepressible mirth, shaking himself so violently that his snake-like staff actually seemed to wriggle in sympathy.

"Ha! ha! ha!" shouted he again and again; then composing himself, "Well, go on, Goodman Brown, go on; but, prithee, don't kill me with laughing."

"Well, then, to end the matter at once," said Goodman Brown, considerably nettled, "there is my wife, Faith. It would break her dear little heart; and I'd rather break my own."

"Nay, if that be the case," answered the other, "e'en go thy ways, Goodman Brown. I would not for twenty old women like the one hobbling before us that Faith should come to any harm."

As he spoke he pointed his staff at a female figure on the path, in whom Goodman Brown recognized a very pious and exemplary[111] dame, who had taught him his catechism in youth, and was still his moral and spiritual adviser, jointly with the minister and Deacon Gookin.

"A marvel, truly, that Goody Cloyse should be so far in the wilderness at nightfall," said he. "But with your leave, friend, I shall take a cut through the woods until we have left this Christian woman behind. Being a stranger to you, she might ask whom I was consorting with and whither I was going."

"Be it so," said his fellow-traveller. "Betake you to the woods, and let me keep the path."

Accordingly the young man turned aside, but took care to watch his companion, who advanced softly along the road until he had come within a staff's length of the old dame. She, meanwhile, was making the best of her way, with singular speed for so aged a woman, and mumbling some indistinct words—a prayer, doubtless—as she went. The traveller put forth his staff and touched her withered neck with what seemed the serpent's tail.

"The devil!" screamed the pious old lady.

"Then Goody Cloyse knows her old friend?" observed the traveller, confronting her and leaning on his writhing stick.

"Ah, forsooth, and is it your worship indeed?" cried the good dame. "Yea, truly is it, and in the very image of my old gossip, Goodman Brown, the grandfather of the silly fellow that now is. But—would your worship believe it?—my broomstick hath strangely disappeared, stolen, as I suspect, by that unhanged witch, Goody Cory, and that, too, when I was all anointed with the juice of smallage, and cinquefoil, and wolf's bane"—

"Mingled with fine wheat and the fat of a new-born babe," said the shape of old Goodman Brown.

"Ah, your worship knows the recipe," cried the old lady, cackling aloud. "So, as I was saying, being all ready for the meeting, and no horse to ride on, I made up my mind to foot it; for they tell me there is a nice young man to be taken into communion tonight. But now your good worship will lend me your arm, and we shall be there in a twinkling."[112]

"That can hardly be," answered her friend. "I may not spare you my arm, Goody Cloyse; but here is my staff, if you will."

So saying, he threw it down at her feet, where, perhaps, it assumed life, being one of the rods which its owner had formerly lent to the Egyptian magi. Of this fact, however, Goodman Brown could not take cognizance. He had cast up his eyes in astonishment, and, looking down again, beheld neither Goody Cloyse nor the serpentine staff, but his fellow-traveller alone, who waited for him as calmly as if nothing had happened.

"That old woman taught me my catechism," said the young man; and there was a world of meaning in this simple comment.

They continued to walk onward, while the elder traveller exhorted his companion to make good speed and persevere in the path, discoursing so aptly that his arguments seemed rather to spring up in the bosom of his auditor than to be suggested by himself. As they went, he plucked a branch of maple to serve for a walking stick, and began to strip it of the twigs and little boughs, which were wet with evening dew. The moment his fingers touched them they became strangely withered and dried up as with a week's sunshine. Thus the pair proceeded, at a good free pace, until suddenly, in a gloomy hollow of the road, Goodman Brown sat himself down on the stump of a tree and refused to go any farther.

"Friend," said he, stubbornly, "my mind is made up. Not another step will I budge on this errand. What if a wretched old woman do choose to go to the devil when I thought she was going to heaven: is that any reason why I should quit my dear Faith and go after her?"

"You will think better of this by and by," said his acquaintance, composedly. "Sit here and rest yourself a while; and when you feel like moving again, there is my staff to help you along."

Without more words, he threw his companion the maple stick, and was as speedily out of sight as if he had vanished into the deepening gloom. The young man sat a few moments by the roadside, applauding himself greatly, and thinking with how[113] clear a conscience he should meet the minister in his morning walk, nor shrink from the eye of good old Deacon Gookin. And what calm sleep would be his that very night, which was to have been spent so wickedly, but so purely and sweetly now, in the arms of Faith! Amidst these pleasant and praiseworthy meditations, Goodman Brown heard the tramp of horses along the road, and deemed it advisable to conceal himself within the verge of the forest, conscious of the guilty purpose that had brought him thither, though now so happily turned from it.

On came the hoof tramps and the voices of the riders, two grave old voices, conversing soberly as they drew near. These mingled sounds appeared to pass along the road, within a few yards of the young man's hiding-place; but, owing doubtless to the depth of the gloom at that particular spot, neither the travellers nor their steeds were visible. Though their figures brushed the small boughs by the wayside, it could not be seen that they intercepted, even for a moment, the faint gleam from the strip of bright sky athwart which they must have passed. Goodman Brown alternately crouched and stood on tiptoe, pulling aside the branches and thrusting forth his head as far as he durst without discerning so much as a shadow. It vexed him the more, because he could have sworn, were such a thing possible, that he recognized the voices of the minister and Deacon Gookin, jogging along quietly, as they were wont to do, when bound to some ordination or ecclesiastical council. While yet within hearing, one of the riders stopped to pluck a switch.

"Of the two, reverend sir," said the voice like the deacon's, "I had rather miss an ordination dinner than to-night's meeting. They tell me that some of our community are to be here from Falmouth and beyond, and others from Connecticut and Rhode Island, besides several of the Indian powwows, who, after their fashion, know almost as much deviltry as the best of us. Moreover, there is a goodly young woman to be taken into communion."

"Mighty well, Deacon Gookin!" replied the solemn old tones of[114] the minister. "Spur up, or we shall be late. Nothing can be done you know until I get on the ground."

The hoofs clattered again; and the voices, talking so strangely in the empty air, passed on through the forest, where no church had ever been gathered or solitary Christian prayed. Whither, then, could these holy men be journeying so deep into the heathen wilderness? Young Goodman Brown caught hold of a tree for support, being ready to sink down on the ground, faint and overburdened with the heavy sickness of his heart. He looked up to the sky, doubting whether there really was a heaven above him. Yet there was the blue arch, and the stars brightening in it.

"With heaven above and Faith below, I will yet stand firm against the devil!" cried Goodman Brown.

While he still gazed upward into the deep arch of the firmament and had lifted his hands to pray, a cloud, though no wind was stirring, hurried across the zenith and hid the brightening stars. The blue sky was still visible, except directly overhead, where this black mass of cloud was sweeping swiftly northward. Aloft in the air, as if from the depths of the cloud, came a confused and doubtful sound of voices. Once the listener fancied that he could distinguish the accents of towns-people of his own, men, and women, both pious and ungodly, many of whom he had met at the communion table, and had seen others rioting at the tavern. The next moment, so indistinct were the sounds, he doubted whether he had heard aught but the murmur of the old forest, whispering without a wind. Then came a stronger swell of those familiar tones, heard daily in the sunshine at Salem village, but never until now from a cloud of night. There was one voice of a young woman, uttering lamentations, yet with an uncertain sorrow, and entreating for some favor, which, perhaps, it would grieve her to obtain; and all the unseen multitude, both saints and sinners, seemed to encourage her onward.

:"Faith!" shouted Goodman Brown, in a voice of agony and desperation; and the echoes of the forest mocked him, crying, "Faith![115]

Faith!" as if bewildered wretches were seeking her all through the wilderness.

The cry of grief, rage, and terror was yet piercing the night, when the unhappy husband held his breath for a response. There was a scream, drowned immediately in a louder murmur of voices, fading into far-off laughter, as the dark cloud swept away, leaving the clear and silent sky above Goodman Brown. But something fluttered lightly down through the air and caught on the branch of a tree. The young man seized it, and beheld a pink ribbon.

"My Faith is gone!" cried he, after one stupefied moment. "There is no good on earth; and sin is but a name. Come, devil; for to thee is this world given."

And, maddened with despair, so that he laughed loud and long, did Goodman Brown grasp his staff and set forth again, at such a rate that he seemed to fly along the forest path rather than to walk or run. The road grew wilder and drearier and more faintly traced, and vanished at length, leaving him in the heart of the dark wilderness, still rushing onward with the instinct that guides mortal man to evil. The whole forest was peopled with frightful sounds—the creaking of the trees, the howling of wild beasts, and the yell of Indians; while sometimes the wind tolled like a distant church bell, and sometimes gave a broad roar around the traveller, as if all Nature were laughing him to scorn. But he was himself the chief horror of the scene, and shrank not from its other horrors.

"Ha! ha! ha!" roared Goodman Brown when the wind laughed at him. "Let us hear which will laugh loudest. Think not to frighten me with your deviltry. Come witch, come wizard, come Indian pow-wow, come devil himself, and here comes Goodman Brown. You may as well fear him as he fear you."

In truth, all through the haunted forest there could be nothing more frightful than the figure of Goodman Brown. On he flew among the black pines, brandishing his staff with frenzied gestures, now giving vent to an inspiration of horrid blasphemy, and now shouting forth such laughter as set all the echoes of the forest[116] laughing like demons around him. The fiend in his own shape is less hideous than when he rages in the breast of man. Thus sped the demoniac on his course, until, quivering among the trees, he saw a red light before him, as when the felled trunks and branches of a clearing have been set on fire, and throw up their lurid blaze against the sky, at the hour of midnight. He paused, in a lull of the tempest that had driven him onward, and heard the swell of what seemed a hymn, rolling solemnly from a distance with the weight of many voices. He knew the tune; it was a familiar one in the choir of the village meeting-house. The verse died heavily away, and was lengthened by a chorus, not of human voices, but of all the sounds of the benighted wilderness pealing in awful harmony together. Goodman Brown cried out, and his cry was lost to his own ear by its unison with the cry of the desert.

In the interval of silence he stole forward until the light glared full upon his eyes. At one extremity of an open space, hemmed in by the dark wall of the forest, arose a rock, bearing some rude, natural resemblance either to an altar or a pulpit, and surrounded by four blazing pines, their tops aflame, their stems untouched, like candles at an evening meeting. The mass of foliage that had overgrown the summit of the rock was all on fire, blazing high into the night and fitfully illuminating the whole field. Each pendent twig and leafy festoon was in a blaze. As the red light arose and fell, a numerous congregation alternately shone forth, then disappeared in shadow, and again grew, as it were, out of the darkness, peopling the heart of the solitary woods at once.

"A grave and dark-clad company," quoth Goodman Brown.

In truth they were such. Among them, quivering to and fro between gloom and splendor, appeared faces that would be seen next day at the council board of the province, and others which, Sabbath after Sabbath, looked devoutly heavenward, and benignantly over the crowded pews, from the holiest pulpits in the land. Some affirm that the lady of the governor was there. At least there were high dames well known to her, and wives of honored husbands, and widows, a great multitude, and ancient maidens, all of excellent[117] repute, and fair young girls, who trembled lest their mothers should espy them. Either the sudden gleams of light flashing over the obscure field bedazzled Goodman Brown, or he recognized a score of the church members of Salem village famous for their especial sanctity. Good old Deacon Gookin had arrived, and waited at the skirts of that venerable saint, his revered pastor. But, irreverently consorting with these grave, reputable, and pious people, these elders of the church, these chaste dames and dewy virgins, there were men of dissolute lives and women of spotted fame, wretches given over to all mean and filthy vice, and suspected even of horrid crimes. It was strange to see that the good shrank not from the wicked, nor were the sinners abashed by the saints. Scattered also among their pale-faced enemies were the Indian priests, or powwows, who had often scared their native forest with more hideous incantations than any known to English witchcraft.

"But where is Faith?" thought Goodman Brown; and, as hope came into his heart, he trembled.

Another verse of the hymn arose, a slow and mournful strain, such as the pious love, but joined to words which expressed all that our nature can conceive of sin, and darkly hinted at far more. Unfathomable to mere mortals is the lore of fiends. Verse after verse was sung; and still the chorus of the desert swelled between like the deepest tone of a mighty organ; and with the final peal of that dreadful anthem there came a sound, as if the roaring wind, the rushing streams, the howling beasts, and every other voice of the unconcerted wilderness were mingling and according with the voice of guilty man in homage to the prince of all. The four blazing pines threw up a loftier flame, and obscurely discovered shapes and visages of horror on the smoke wreaths above the impious assembly. At the same moment the fire on the rock shot redly forth and formed a glowing arch above its base, where now appeared a figure. With reverence be it spoken, the figure bore no slight similitude, both in garb and manner, to some grave divine of the New England churches.[118]

"Bring forth the converts!" cried a voice that echoed through the field and rolled into the forest.

At the word, Goodman Brown stepped forth from the shadow of the trees and approached the congregation, with whom he felt a loathful brotherhood by the sympathy of all that was wicked in his heart. He could have well-nigh sworn that the shape of his own dead father beckoned him to advance, looking downward from a smoke wreath, while a woman, with dim features of despair, threw out her hand to warn him back. Was it his mother? But he had no power to retreat one step, nor to resist, even in thought, when the minister and good old Deacon Gookin seized his arms and led him to the blazing rock. Thither came also the slender form of a veiled female, led between Goody Cloyse, that pious teacher of the catechism, and Martha Carrier, who had received the devil's promise to be queen of hell. A rampant hag was she. And there stood the proselytes beneath the canopy of fire.

"Welcome, my children," said the dark figure, "to the communion of your race. Ye have found thus young your nature and your destiny. My children, look behind you!"

They turned; and flashing forth, as it were, in a sheet of flame, the fiend worshippers were seen; the smile of welcome gleamed darkly on every visage.

"There," resumed the sable form, "are all whom ye have reverenced from youth. Ye deemed them holier than yourselves, and shrank from your own sin, contrasting it with their lives of righteousness and prayerful aspirations heavenward. Yet here are they all in my worshipping assembly. This night it shall be granted you to know their secret deeds: how hoary-bearded elders of the church have whispered wanton words to the young maids of their households; how many a woman, eager for widows' weeds, has given her husband a drink at bedtime and let him sleep his last sleep in her bosom; how beardless youths have made haste to inherit their fathers' wealth; and how fair damsels—blush not, sweet ones—have dug little graves in the garden, and bidden me, the sole[119] guest, to an infant's funeral. By the sympathy of your human hearts for sin ye shall scent out all the places—whether in church, bedchamber, street, field, or forest—where crime has been committed, and shall exult to behold the whole earth one stain of guilt, one mighty blood spot. Far more than this. It shall be yours to penetrate, in every bosom, the deep mystery of sin, the fountain of all wicked arts, and which inexhaustibly supplies more evil impulses than human power—than my power at its utmost—can make manifest in deeds. And now, my children, look upon each other."

They did so; and, by the blaze of the hell-kindled torches, the wretched man beheld his Faith, and the wife her husband, trembling before that unhallowed altar.

"Lo, there ye stand, my children," said the figure, in a deep and solemn tone, almost sad with its despairing awfulness, as if his once angelic nature could yet mourn for our miserable race. "Depending upon one another's hearts, ye had still hoped that virtue were not all a dream. Now are ye undeceived. Evil is the nature of mankind. Evil must be your only happiness. Welcome again, my children, to the communion of your race."

"Welcome," repeated the fiend worshippers, in one cry of despair and triumph.

And there they stood, the only pair, as it seemed, who were yet hesitating on the verge of wickedness in this dark world. A basin was hollowed, naturally, in the rock. Did it contain water, reddened by the lurid light? or was it blood? or, perchance, a liquid flame? Herein did the shape of evil dip his hand and prepare to lay the mark of baptism upon their foreheads, that they might be partakers of the mystery of sin, more conscious of the secret guilt of others, both in deed and thought, than they could now be of their own. The husband cast one look at his pale wife, and Faith at him. What polluted wretches would the next glance show them to each other, shuddering alike at what they disclosed and what they saw!

"Faith! Faith!" cried the husband, "look up to heaven, and resist the wicked one." [120]

Whether Faith obeyed he knew not. Hardly had he spoken when he found himself amid calm night and solitude, listening to a roar of the wind which died heavily away through the forest. He staggered against the rock, and felt it chill and damp; while a hanging twig, that had been all on fire, besprinkled his cheek with the coldest dew.

The next morning young Goodman Brown came slowly into the street of Salem village, staring around him like a bewildered man. The good old minister was taking a walk along the graveyard to get an appetite for breakfast and meditate his sermon, and bestowed a blessing, as he passed, on Goodman Brown. He shrank from the venerable saint as if to avoid an anathema. Old Deacon Gookin was at domestic worship, and the holy words of his prayer were heard through the open window. "What God doth the wizard pray to?" quoth Goodman Brown. Goody Cloyse, that excellent old Christian, stood in the early sunshine at her own lattice, catechizing a little girl who had brought her a pint of morning's milk. Goodman Brown snatched away the child as from the grasp of the fiend himself. Turning the corner by the meeting-house, he spied the head of Faith, with the pink ribbons, gazing anxiously forth, and bursting into such joy at sight of him that she skipped along the street and almost kissed her husband before the whole village. But Goodman Brown looked sternly and sadly into her face, and passed on without a greeting.

Had Goodman Brown fallen asleep in the forest and only dreamed a wild dream of a witch-meeting?

Be it so if you will; but, alas! it was a dream of evil omen for young Goodman Brown. A stern, a sad, a darkly meditative, a distrustful, if not a desperate man did he become from the night of that fearful dream. On the Sabbath day, when the congregation were singing a holy psalm, he could not listen because an anthem of sin rushed loudly upon his ear and drowned all the blessed strain. When the minister spoke from the pulpit with power and fervid eloquence, and, with his hand on the open Bible, of the sacred truths of our religion, and of saint-like lives and triumphant[121] deaths, and of future bliss or misery unutterable, then did Goodman Brown turn pale, dreading lest the roof should thunder down upon the gray blasphemer and his hearers. Often, waking suddenly at midnight, he shrank from the bosom of Faith; and at morning or eventide, when the family knelt down at prayer, he scowled and muttered to himself, and gazed sternly at his wife, and turned away. And when he had lived long, and was borne to his grave a hoary corpse, followed by Faith, an aged woman, and children and grandchildren, a goodly procession, besides neighbors not a few, they carved no hopeful verse upon his tombstone, for his dying hour was gloom.

## AUSTIN WARREN

From *Nathaniel Hawthorne: Representative Selections, with Introduction, Bibliography, and Notes.* New York: American Book Company, 1934. Reprinted by permission of the publishers.

The materials for this tale Hawthorne gathered, without doubt, from Cotton Mather's *Wonders of the Invisible World.* The following are the relevant passages: "The *Devil,* exhibiting himself ordinarily as a small *Black Man,* has decoy'd a fearful knot of proud, froward, ignorant, envious and malicious Creatures, to list themselves in his horrid Service, by entring their Names in a Book by him tendred unto them. These Witches...have met in Hellish *Randezvouzes* [*sic*],[361] wherein the Confessors do say, they have had their Diabolical Sacraments, imitating the *Baptism* and the *Supper* [the communion or mass] of our Lord" (1693 edition, 17). "But that which makes this Descent [of the Devil] the more formidable, is the *multitude* and *quality* [i.e., social rank] of Persons accused of an Interest in this *Witchcraft,* by the Efficacy of the *Spectres* which take their Name and Shape upon them....That the Devils have obtain'd the power, to take on them the likeness of harmless people...." (*ibid.,* 19).

"Had Goodman Brown fallen asleep in the forest and only dreamed a wild dream of a witch meeting? Be it so if you will." Hawthorne has no desire to insist on a literal interpretation of his narrative, and would indeed have rejected it, had he been faced with a bare alternative. His point is the devastating effect of moral scepticism. All men are hero-worshippers; and the consequence of discovering, or fancying one has discovered, obliquity in those whom one has deemed sages and saints is the destruction of one's courage to struggle for the mastery of his own passions. If the elect have fallen, what hope for ordinary men? Hawthorne educes no positive counsel from his tale; he does not bid us put our trust in God instead of in men, or in virtue rather than the virtuous. He merely depicts a state of mind: a perilous sort of disillusionment. The historical setting adds color and eases the strain of the supernatural penumbra; but the tale is universal in its implications, and transcends its setting.[362]

RICHARD HARTER FOGLE

> From "Young Goodman Brown." In his *Hawthorne's Fiction: The Light and the Dark.* Norman: University of Oklahoma Press, 1952. Pp. 15-32. Reprinted by permission of the publisher and the author.

. . . . The broad antitheses of day and night, town and forest, both of which signify in general a sharp dualism of Good and Evil, are supplemented by a color contrast of red and black at the witch meeting, by the swift transition of the forest scene from leaping flame to damp and chill, and by the consistent cleavage between outward decorum and inner corruption in the characters.

The symbols of Day and Night, of Town and Forest, are almost indistinguishable in meaning. Goodman Brown leaves the limits of Salem at dusk and re-enters them at[25] sunrise; he spends the intervening night in the forest. Day and the Town are clearly emblematic of Good, of the seemly outward appearance of human convention and society. They stand for the safety of an unquestioning and unspeculative faith. Oddly enough, in the daylight of the Salem streets Goodman Brown is too simple and straightforward to be interesting and is somewhat distasteful in his boundless reverence for such unspectacular worthies as the minister, the deacon, and Goody Cloyse. Night and the Forest, symbols of doubt and wandering, are the domains of the Evil One, where the dark subterranean forces of the human spirit riot unchecked. By the dramatic necessities of the plot Brown is a larger figure in the Forest of Evil and at the witch-meeting than he is within the safe bounds of the town.

The contrast of the red of fire and blood and the black of night and forest at the witch-meeting has a different import. As the flames rise and fall, the faces of the worshipers of Evil are alternately seen in clear outline and in deep shadow, and all the details of the scene are at one moment revealed, the next obscured. It seems, then, that red represents Sin or Evil, plain and unequivocal; black represents that doubt of the reality of either Evil or Good which tortures Goodman Brown. A further contrast follows in the swift transformation of scene, when young Goodman Brown finds himself "amid calm night and solitude....He staggered against the rock, and felt it chill and damp; while a hanging twig, that had been all on fire, besprinkled his cheek with the coldest dew." . . .[26]

In "Young Goodman Brown," then, Hawthorne has achieved that reconciliation of opposites which Coleridge considered the highest art. The combination of clarity of technique—embodies in simplicity and balance of structure, in firm pictorial composition, in contrast and climactic arrangement, in irony and detachment—with ambiguity of meaning, as signalized by the "device of multiple choice," in its interrelationships produces the story's characteristic effect. By means of these two elements Hawthorne reconciles oneness of action with multiplicity of suggestion and enriches the bareness of systematic allegory. Contrarily, by them he avoids lapsing into mere speculation without substance or form. The phantasmagoric light and shadow of the rising and falling fire, which obscures and softens the clear, hard outline of the witch-meeting, is an image which will stand for the essential effect of the story itself, an effect compacted of ambiguity and clarity harmoniously interfused.[32]

D. M. McKEITHAN

From "Hawthorne's 'Young Goodman Brown':
An Interpretation." *Modern Language Notes,*
LXVII (February, 1952), 93-96. Reprinted
by permission of The Johns Hopkins Press.

. . . . This is not a story of the disillusionment that comes to
a person when he discovers that many supposedly religious and virtuous people are really sinful; it is,[95] rather, a story of a man whose
sin led him to consider all other people sinful. Brown came eventually
to judge others by himself: he thought them sinful and hypocritical
because he was sinful and hypocritical himself. He did not judge them
accurately: he misjudged them. The minister of Salem village, Deacon
Gookin, Goody Cloyse, and Faith were all good in spite of what Goodman Brown eventually came to think of them.

Moreover, it is not necessary to choose between interpreting the
story literally and taking it as a dream. "Young Goodman Brown" is
an allegory—which is what Hawthorne meant when he suggested that
it might have been a dream—and an allegory is a fictitious story designed to teach an abstract truth. In reality, Brown did not go into a
forest at night nor did he dream that he did. What Brown did was to
indulge in sin (represented by the journey into the forest at night—
and of course the indulgence might have lasted much longer than a
night. weeks, months, even years) under the mistaken notion that he
could break off whenever he wanted to. Instead of breaking off
promptly, he continued to indulge in sin longer than he had expected
and suffered the consequences, which were the loss of religious faith
and faith in all other human beings.

What Brown's sin was at the beginning of the story Hawthorne
does not say, but it was not cynicism: at that time he was not cynical,
although he was already engaged in evil dealings with Satan. Cynicism
was merely the result of the sin and came later and gradually. By not
identifying the sin Hawthorne gives the story wider application.
Which sin it was does not greatly matter: what Hawthorne puts the
stress on is the idea that this sin had evil consequences.

ROY R. MALE

From *Hawthorne's Tragic Vision*. Austin: University of Texas Press, 1957. Reprinted by permission of the author and the publisher.

. . . we are now ready to confront the devil's staff and the pink ribbon of "Young Goodman Brown." One of the world's great short stories, it has prompted considerable critical comment. Fogle has very effectively shown how ambiguity of meaning and clarity of technique combine in the art of the[76] story, and F. O. Matthiessen praised it highly, though he was troubled by the pink ribbons. As I shall try to demonstrate, the ribbons lead to that aspect of the story which is usually missed—the fact that Faith's ambiguity is the ambiguity of womanhood and that the dark night in the forest is essentially a sexual experience, though it is also much more.

Young Goodman Brown, whose name indicates his kinship with Goody Cloyse and Deacon Gookin—that is, his role as Everyman —seems destined to spend a night in the forest, just as his wife's pink ribbons seem to be part of her. In the town daylight his Faith is simple and innocuous. "She's a blessed angel on earth; and after this one night I'll cling to her skirts and follow her to heaven," he says. But this one night, this one involvement with the ambiguity of good and evil, will so shatter him that his dying hour will be gloom. For Faith and her pink ribbon, so pure in the sunlight, are fiendish at night. There is just a faint suggestion of the transition at sunset, when Faith whispers softly to Brown, "tarry with me."

Faith, like Beatrice Rappaccini, is both pure and poisonous, saint and sinner. She *is* in the forest that night, and the pink ribbons blend with the serpentine staff in what becomes a fiery orgy of lust. In marrying her, Brown has been introduced to a devilish traveler who strongly resembles his father. The most conspicuous thing about this stranger is his wriggling staff, which suggests the knowledge of the serpent—and also serves as a means of penetrating into space.

One of the guests who will attend the midnight ceremonies is Goody Cloyse. She has lost her broomstick—"and that, too, when I was all anointed with the juice of smallage, and cinquefoil, and wolf's bane"—but she borrows the devil's[77] staff to help her speed onward.

"They tell me there is a nice young man to be taken into communion tonight," she cackles. Brown balks at going further; the devil lends him a staff and disappears into the gloom. Next the voices of two riders are heard. As one stops to pluck a switch, the voices become more distinct and seem to belong to Deacon Gookin and the minister. "There is a goodly young woman to be taken into communion," announces the deacon. And his lecherous old companion makes this double-edged rejoinder: "Spur up, or we shall be late. Nothing can be done, you know, until I get on the ground."

Almost everything in the forest scene suggests that the communion of sinners is essentially sexual and that Brown qualifies for it by his marriage. Having witnessed the pink ribbon impaled upon the branch of a tree, Brown seizes the devil's staff and speeds towards the sounds of the gathering multitude. The details of the setting subtly reveal further images of penetration and investment:

At one extremity of an open space, hemmed in by the dark wall of the forest, arose a rock, bearing some rude, natural resemblance either to an altar or a pulpit, and surrounded by four blazing pines, their tops aflame, their stems untouched, like candles at an evening meeting. The mass of foliage that had overgrown the summit of the rock was all on fire, blazing high into the night and fitfully illuminating the whole field. Each pendant twig and leafy festoon was in a blaze.

The ceremony is a magnificent blending of folklore and superstition, containing elements of the Black Mass and the witch sabbath. It is also a dark marriage, in which Brown and Faith are taken into communion with their race. The "one stain of guilt," the "deep mystery of sin," is set forth[78] in the crimes of sexual passion described by the devil. He tells how

hoary-bearded elders of the church have whispered wanton words to the young maids of their household; how many a woman, eager for widow's weeds, has given her husband a drink at bedtime and let him sleep his last sleep in her bosom; how beardless youths have made haste to inherit their fathers' wealth; and how fair damsels—blush not, sweet ones—have dug little graves in the garden, and bidden me, the sole guest, to an infant's funeral.

The whole affair, of course, may well have been a dream, but, whether dream or no, the ultimate effect on Brown is the same. "Truth," as Hawthorne wrote in "The Birthmark," "often finds its way to the mind close muffled in robes of sleep."

One effect of "marriage"—whether the wedding is of man and woman or a complete involvement with an art or a religion—is the shock of recognizing the reality of the past. The tapestry conserving the vital patterns of man's limitations and potentialities as expressed in myth, legend, and superstition gradually unfolds, and the young man becomes painfully aware of his cultural and familial parentage.

For Brown the shocks are too much to bear. He sees the devil in his father's shape; he hears him say, "I helped your grandfather, the constable, when he lashed the Quaker woman so smartly through the streets of Salem; and it was I that brought your father a pitch-pine knot, kindled at my own hearth, to set fire to an Indian village." Brown is also stupefied by the vision of evil that seems to infest all the foundations of church and state.

Brown's dying hour is gloom, then, because he fails to attain a tragic vision, a perspective broad enough and deep[79] enough to see the dark night as an essential part of human experience, but a part that may prelude a new and richer dawn. Returning from the forest, he sees "Faith, with the pink ribbons, gazing anxiously forth, and bursting into such joy at the sight of him that she skipped along the street and almost kissed her husband before the whole village." But Brown . . . is unable to grasp this higher faith.[80]

## THOMAS E. CONNOLLY

> "Hawthorne's 'Young Goodman Brown': An Attack on Puritanic Calvinism." *American Literature,* XXVIII (November, 1956), 370-375. Reprinted by permission of the publisher and the author.

It is surprising, in a way, to discover how few of the many critics who have discussed "Young Goodman Brown" agree on any aspect of the work except that it is an excellent short story. D. M.[370] McKeithan says that its theme is "sin and its blighting effects."[1] Richard H. Fogle observes, "Hawthorne the artist refuses to limit himself to a single and doctrinaire conclusion, proceeding instead by indirection,"[2] implying, presumably, that it is inartistic to say something which can be clearly understood by the readers. Gordon and Tate assert, "Hawthorne is dealing with his favorite theme: the unhappiness which the human heart suffers as a result of its innate depravity."[3] Austin War-

---

[1] D M McKeithan, "Hawthorne's 'Young Goodman Brown' An Interpretation," *Modern Language Notes,* LXVII (Feb , 1952), 94

[2] Richard H Fogle, "Ambiguity and Clarity in Hawthorne's 'Young Goodman Brown,'" *New England Quarterly,* XVIII (Dec , 1945), 453

[3] Caroline Gordon and Allen Tate (eds ), *The House of Fiction* (New York, 1950), p 38.

ren says, "His point is the devastating effect of moral scepticism."[4] Almost all critics agree, however, that Young Goodman Brown lost his faith. Their conclusions are based, perhaps, upon the statement, "My Faith is gone!" made by Brown when he recognizes his wife's voice and ribbon. I should like to examine the story once more to show that Young Goodman Brown did not lose his faith at all. In fact, not only did he retain his faith, but during his horrible experience he actually discovered the full and frightening significance of his faith.

Mrs. Leavis comes closest to the truth in her discussion of the story in the *Sewanee Review* in which she says, "Hawthorne has imaginatively recreated for the reader that Calvinist sense of sin, that theory which did in actuality shape the early social and spiritual history of New England."[5] But Mrs. Leavis seems to miss the critical implications of the story, for she goes on to say: "But in Hawthorne, by a wonderful feat of transmutation, it has no religious significance, it is a psychological state that is explored. Young Goodman Brown's Faith is not faith in Christ but faith in human beings, and losing it he is doomed to isolation forever."[6] Those who persist in reading this story as a study of the effects of sin on Brown come roughly to this conclusion: "Goodman Brown became evil as a result of sin and thought he saw evil *where none existed.*"[7] Hawthorne's message is far more depressing and horrifying than this The story is obviously an individual tragedy, and those who treat it as such are[371] right, of course: but, far beyond the personal plane, it has universal implications.

Young Goodman Brown, as a staunch Calvinist, is seen at the beginning of this allegory to be quite confident that he is going to heaven. The errand on which he is going is presented mysteriously and is usually interpreted to be a deliberate quest of sin. This may or may not be true; what is important is that he is going out to meet the devil by prearrangement. We are told by the narrator that his purpose in going is evil. When the devil meets him, he refers to the "beginning of a journey." Brown admits that he "kept covenant" by meeting the devil and hints at the evil purpose of the meeting.

Though his family has been Christian for generations, the point is made early in the story that Young Goodman Brown has been married to his Faith for only three months. Either the allegory breaks down at this point or the marriage to Faith must be looked upon as the moment of conversion to grace in which he became fairly sure of his election to heaven. That Goodman Brown is convinced he is of the elect is made clear at the beginning: ".. and after this one night I'll

---

4 Austin Warren, *Nathaniel Hawthorne* (New York, 1934), p 362.

5 Q D Leavis, "Hawthorne as Poet," *Sewanee Review,* LIX (Spring, 1951), 197-198.

6 *Ibid.*

7 McKeithan, *op cit ,* p. 95 Italics mine.

cling to her skirts and follow her to heaven." In other words, at the start of his adventure, Young Goodman Brown is certain that his faith will help man get to heaven. It is in this concept that his disillusionment will come. The irony of this illusion is brought out when he explains to the devil the reason for his tardiness: "Faith kept me back awhile." That is what he thinks! By the time he gets to the meeting place he finds that his Faith is already there. Goodman Brown's disillusionment in his belief begins quickly after meeting the devil. He has asserted proudly that his ancestors "have been a race of honest men and good Christians since the days of the martyrs," and the devil turns his own words on him smartly.

Well said, Goodman Brown! I have been as well acquainted with your family as with ever a one among the Puritans; and that's no trifle to say. I helped your grandfather, the constable, when he lashed the Quaker woman so smartly through the streets of Salem; and it was I that brought your father a pitch-pine knot, kindled at my own hearth, to set fire to an Indian village, in King Philip's war. They were my good friends, both; and many a pleasant walk have we had along this path, and[372] returned merrily after midnight. I would fain be friends with you for their sake.

Goodman Brown manages to shrug off this identification of his parental and grandparental Puritanism with the devil, but the reader should not overlook the sharp tone of criticism in Hawthorne's presentation of this speech.

When the devil presents his next argument, Brown is a little more shaken. The devil has shown him that Goody Cloyse is of his company and Brown responds: "What if a wretched old woman do choose to go to the devil when I thought she was going to heaven: is that any reason why I should quit my dear Faith and go after her?" He still believes at this point that his faith will lead him to heaven. The devil's reply, "You will think better of this by and by," is enigmatic when taken by itself, but a little earlier the narrator had made a comment which throws a great deal of light on this remark by the devil. When he recognized Goody Cloyse, Brown said, "That old woman taught me my catechism," and the narrator added, "and there was a world of meaning in this simple comment." The reader at this point should be fairly well aware of Hawthorne's criticism of Calvinism. The only way there can be a "world of meaning" in Brown's statement is that her catechism teaches the way to the devil and not the way to heaven.

From this point on Brown is rapidly convinced that his original conception about his faith is wrong. Deacon Gookin and the "good old minister," in league with Satan, finally lead the way to his recognition that this faith is diabolic rather than divine. Hawthorne points up this fact by a bit of allegorical symbolism. Immediately after he recognizes the voices of the deacon and the minister, we are told by the narrator that "Young Goodman Brown caught hold of a tree for support, being ready to sink down on the ground, faint and overburdened with the heavy sickness of his heart. He looked up to the sky, doubting whether there really was a heaven above him. Yet there was a blue arch, and the stars brightened in it." Here the doubt has begun to gnaw, but the stars are symbols of the faint hope which he is still able to cherish, and he is able to say: "With heaven above and Faith below, I will yet stand firm against the devil." But immediately a symbolic cloud hides the symbolic stars: "While he still gazed upward into the deep arch of the firmament[373] and had lifted his hands to pray, a cloud, though no wind was stirring, hurried across the zenith and hid the brightening stars." And it is out of this black cloud of doubt that the voice of his faith reaches him and the pink ribbon of his Faith falls.[8] It might be worthwhile to discuss Faith's pink ribbons here, for Hawthorne certainly took great pains to call them to our attention. The ribbons seem to be symbolic of his initial illusion about the true significance of this faith, his belief that his faith will lead him to heaven. The pink ribbons on a Puritan lady's cap, signs of youth, joy, and happiness, are actually entirely out of keeping with the severity of the rest of her dress which, if not somber black, is at least gray. When the ribbon falls from his cloud of doubt, Goodman Brown cries in agony, "My Faith is gone!" and it is gone in the sense that it now means not what it once meant. He is quick to apply the logical, ultimate conclusion of Goody Cloyse's catechizing: "Come, devil; for to thee is this world given."

Lest the reader miss the ultimate implication of the doctrine of predestination, Hawthorne has the devil preach a sermon at his communion service: "Welcome, my children...to the communion of your race. Ye have found thus young your nature and your destiny." Calvinism teaches that man is innately depraved and that he can do nothing to merit salvation. He is saved only by the whim of God who selects some, through no deserts of their own, for heaven while the great mass of mankind is destined for hell. The devil concludes his sermon: "Evil is the nature of mankind. Evil must be your only happiness. Welcome again, my children, to the communion of your race." It is not at all insignificant that the word *race* is used several times in this passage, for it was used earlier by Goodman Brown when he said, "We have been a race of honest men and Christians...." After this sermon by the devil, Young Goodman Brown makes one last effort to retain the illusion that faith will lead him to heaven; he calls out, "Faith! Faith!...look up to heaven, and resist the wicked one."

---

8 F. O. Matthiessen made entirely too much of the wrong thing of this ribbon. Had Young Goodman Brown returned to Salem Village clutching the ribbon, there might be some point in what Matthiessen says (*American Renaissance*, New York, 1941, pp. 282-284). As it is, the ribbon presents no more of a problem than do the burning trees turned suddenly cold again.

But we are fairly sure that he is unsuccessful, for we are immediately told: "Whether Faith obeyed he knew not."[374]

Young Goodman Brown did not lose his faith (we are even told that his Faith survived him); he learned its full and terrible significance. This story is Hawthorne's criticism of the teachings of Puritanic-Calvinism. His implication is that the doctrine of the elect and damned is not a faith which carries man heavenward on its skirts, as Brown once believed, but, instead, condemns him to hell—bad and good alike indiscriminately—and for all intents and purposes so few escape as to make one man's chance of salvation almost disappear. It is this awakening to the full meaning of his faith which causes Young Goodman Brown to look upon his minister as a blasphemer when he teaches "the sacred truths of our religion, and of saint-like lives and triumphant deaths, and of future bliss or misery unutterable," for he has learned that according to the truths of his faith there is probably nothing but "misery unutterable" in store for him and all his congregation; it is this awakening which causes him to turn away from prayer; it is this awakening which makes appropriate the fact that "they carved no hopeful verse upon his tombstone."

Though much is made of the influence of Puritanism on the writings of Hawthorne, he must also be seen as a critic of the teachings of Puritanism. Between the position of Vernon L. Parrington,[9] who saw Hawthorne as retaining "much of the older Calvinistic view of life and human destiny," and that of Régis Michaud,[10] who saw him as "an anti-puritan and prophet heralding the Freudian gospel," lies the truth about Hawthorne.[375]

---

9 *Main Currents in American Thought* (New York, 1927), II, 443

10 "How Nathaniel Hawthorne Exorcised Hester Prynne." *The American Novel Today* (Boston, 1928), pp 25-46.

# 6. JAMES JOYCE—"Clay"

From *Dubliners* [1914]. New York: Compass Books, 1958. Reprinted by permission of the publisher, The Viking Press, Inc.

The matron had given her leave to go out as soon as the women's tea was over and Maria looked forward to her evening out. The kitchen was spick and span: the cook said you could see yourself in the big copper boilers. The fire was nice and bright and on one of the side-tables were four very big barmbracks. These barmbracks seemed uncut; but if you went closer you would see that they had been cut into long thick even slices and were ready to be handed round at tea. Maria had cut them herself.

Maria was a very, very small person indeed but she had a very long nose and a very long chin. She talked a little through her nose, always soothingly: *"Yes, my dear,"* and *"No, my dear."* She was always sent for when the women quarrelled over their tubs and always succeeded in making peace. One day the matron had said to her:

"Maria, you are a veritable peace-maker!"

And the sub-matron and two of the Board ladies had heard the compliment. And Ginger Mooney was always saying[99] what she wouldn't do to the dummy who had charge of the irons if it wasn't for Maria. Everyone was so fond of Maria.

The women would have their tea at six o'clock and she would be able to get away before seven. From Ballsbridge to the Pillar, twenty minutes; from the Pillar to Drumcondra, twenty minutes; and twenty minutes to buy the things. She would be there before eight. She took out her purse with the silver clasps and read again the words *A Present from Belfast*. She was very fond of that purse because Joe had brought it to her five years before when he and Alphy had gone to Belfast on a Whit-Monday trip. In the purse were two half-crowns and some coppers. She would have five shillings clear after paying tram fare. What a nice evening they would have, all the children singing! Only she hoped that Joe wouldn't come in drunk. He was so different when he took any drink.

Often he had wanted her to go and live with them; but she

would have felt herself in the way (though Joe's wife was ever so nice with her) and she had become accustomed to the life of the laundry. Joe was a good fellow. She had nursed him and Alphy too; and Joe used often say:

"Mamma is mamma but Maria is my proper mother."

After the break-up at home the boys had got her that position in the *Dublin by Lamplight* laundry, and she liked it. She used to have such a bad opinion of Protestants but now she thought they were very nice people, a little quiet and serious, but still very nice people to live with. Then she had her plants in the conservatory and she liked looking after them. She had lovely ferns and wax-plants and, whenever anyone came to visit her, she always gave the visitor one or two slips from her conservatory. There was one thing she didn't like and that was the tracts on the walks; but the matron was such a nice person to deal with, so genteel.

When the cook told her everything was ready she went into the women's room and began to pull the big bell. In a few minutes[100] the women began to come in by twos and threes, wiping their steaming hands in their petticoats and pulling down the sleeves of their blouses over their red steaming arms. They settled down before their huge mugs which the cook and the dummy filled up with hot tea, already mixed with milk and sugar in huge tin cans. Maria superintended the distribution of the barmbrack and saw that every woman got her four slices. There was a great deal of laughing and joking during the meal. Lizzie Fleming said Maria was sure to get the ring and, though Fleming had said that for so many Hallow Eves, Maria had to laugh and say she didn't want any ring or man either; and when she laughed her grey-green eyes sparkled with disappointed shyness and the tip of her nose nearly met the tip of her chin. Then Ginger Mooney lifted up her mug of tea and proposed Maria's health while all the other women clattered with their mugs on the table, and said she was sorry she hadn't a sup of porter to drink it in. And Maria laughed again till the tip of her nose nearly met the tip of her chin and till her minute body nearly shook itself asunder because she knew that Mooney meant well though, of course, she had the notions of a common woman.

But wasn't Maria glad when the women had finished their tea and the cook and the dummy had begun to clear away the tea-things! She went into her little bedroom and, remembering that the next morning was a mass morning, changed the hand of the alarm from seven to six. Then she took off her working skirt and her house-boots and laid her best skirt out on the bed and her tiny dress-boots beside the foot of the bed. She changed her blouse too and, as she stood before the mirror, she thought of how she used to dress for mass on Sunday morning when she was a young girl, and she looked with quaint affection at the diminutive body which she had so often adorned. In spite of its years she found it a nice tidy little body.

When she got outside the streets were shining with rain and[101] she was glad of her old brown waterproof. The tram was full and she had to sit on the little stool at the end of the car, facing all the people, with her toes barely touching the floor. She arranged in her mind all she was going to do and thought how much better it was to be independent and to have your own money in your pocket. She hoped they would have a nice evening. She was sure they would but she could not help thinking what a pity it was Alphy and Joe were not speaking. They were always falling out now but when they were boys together they used to be the best of friends: but such was life.

She got out of her tram at the Pillar and ferreted her way quickly among the crowds. She went into Downes's cake-shop but the shop was so full of people that it was a long time before she could get herself attended to. She bought a dozen of mixed penny cakes, and at last came out of the shop laden with a big bag. Then she thought what else would she buy: she wanted to buy something really nice. They would be sure to have plenty of apples and nuts. It was hard to know what to buy and all she could think of was cake. She decided to buy some plumcake but Downes's plumcake had not enough almond icing on top of it so she went over to a shop in Henry Street. Here she was a long time in suiting herself and the stylish young lady behind the counter, who was evidently a little annoyed by her, asked her was it wedding-cake she wanted to buy. That made Maria blush and smile at the young lady; but the young lady took it all very seriously and finally cut a thick slice of plumcake, parcelled it up and said:

"Two-and-four, please."

She thought she would have to stand in the Drumcondra tram because none of the young men seemed to notice her but an elderly gentleman made room for her. He was a stout gentleman and he wore a brown hard hat; he had a square red face and a greyish moustache. Maria thought he was a colonel-looking[102] gentleman and she reflected how much more polite he was than the young men who simply stared straight before them. The gentleman began to chat with her about Hallow Eve and the rainy weather. He supposed the bag was full of good things for the little ones and said it was only right that the youngsters should enjoy themselves while they were young. Maria agreed with him and favoured him with demure nods and hems. He was very nice with her, and when she was getting out at the Canal Bridge she thanked him and bowed, and he bowed to her and raised his hat and smiled agreeably; and while she was going up along the terrace, bending her tiny head under the rain, she thought how easy it was to know a gentleman even when he has a drop taken.

Everybody said: *"O, here's Maria!"* when she came to Joe's house. Joe was there, having come home from business, and all the children had their Sunday dresses on. There were two big girls in from next door and games were going on. Maria gave the bag of cakes to the eldest boy, Alphy, to divide and Mrs. Donnelly said it was too good of her to bring such a big bag of cakes and made all the children say:

"Thanks, Maria."

But Maria said she had brought something special for papa and mamma, something they would be sure to like, and she began to look for her plumcake. She tried in Downes's bag and then in the pockets of her waterproof and then on the hallstand but nowhere could she find it. Then she asked all the children had any of them eaten it—by mistake, of course—but the children all said no and looked as if they did not like to eat cakes if they were to be accused of stealing. Everybody had a solution for the mystery and Mrs. Donnelly said it was plain that Maria had left it behind her in the tram. Maria, remembering how confused the gentleman with the greyish moustache had made her, coloured with shame and vexation and[103] disappointment. At the thought of the failure of her little surprise and of the two and fourpence she had thrown away for nothing she nearly cried outright.

But Joe said it didn't matter and made her sit down by the fire. He was very nice with her. He told her all that went on in his office, repeating for her a smart answer which he had made to the manager. Maria did not understand why Joe laughed so much over the answer he had made but she said that the manager must have been a very overbearing person to deal with. Joe said he wasn't so bad when you knew how to take him, that he was a decent sort so long as you didn't rub him the wrong way. Mrs. Donnelly played the piano for the children and they danced and sang. Then the two next-door girls handed round the nuts. Nobody could find the nutcrackers and Joe was nearly getting cross over it and asked how did they expect Maria to crack nuts without a nutcracker. But Maria said she didn't like nuts and that they weren't to bother about her. Then Joe asked would she take a bottle of stout and Mrs. Donnelly said there was port wine too in the house if she would prefer that. Maria said she would rather they didn't ask her to take anything: but Joe insisted.

So Maria let him have his way and they sat by the fire talking over old times and Maria thought she would put in a good word for Alphy. But Joe cried that God might strike him stone dead if ever he spoke a word to his brother again and Maria said she was sorry she had mentioned the matter. Mrs. Donnelly told her husband it was a great shame for him to speak that way of his own flesh and blood but Joe said that Alphy was no brother of his and there was nearly being a row on the head of it. But Joe said he would not lose his temper on account of the night it was and asked his wife to open some more stout.

The two next-door girls had arranged some Hallow Eve games and soon everything was merry again. Maria was delighted to see the children so merry and Joe and his wife in such good spirits. The[104] next-door girls put some saucers on the table and then led the children up to the table, blindfold. One got the prayer-book and the other three got the water; and when one of the next-door girls got the ring Mrs. Donnelly shook her finger at the blushing girl as much as to say: *O, I know all about it!* They insisted then on blindfolding Maria and leading her up to the table to see what she would get; and, while they were putting on the bandage, Maria laughed and laughed again till the tip of her nose nearly met the tip of her chin.

They led her up to the table amid laughing and joking and she put her hand out in the air as she was told to do. She moved her hand about here and there in the air and descended on one of the saucers. She felt a soft wet substance with her fingers and was surprised that nobody spoke or took off her bandage There was a pause for a few seconds; and then a great deal of scuffling and whispering. Somebody said something about the garden, and at last Mrs. Donnelly said something very cross to one of the next-door girls and told her to throw it out at once: that was no play. Maria understood that it was wrong that time and so she had to do it over again: and this time she got the prayer-book.

After that Mrs. Donnelly played Miss McCloud's Reel for the children and Joe made Maria take a glass of wine. Soon they were all quite merry again and Mrs. Donnelly said Maria would enter a convent before the year was out because she had got the prayer-book. Maria had never seen Joe so nice to her as he was that night, so full of pleasant talk and reminiscences. She said they were all very good to her.

At last the children grew tired and sleepy and Joe asked Maria would she not sing some little song before she went, one of the old songs Mrs. Donnelly said *"Do, please, Maria!"* and so Maria had to get up and stand beside the piano. Mrs. Donnelly bade the children be quiet and listen to Maria's song. Then she played the prelude and said *"Now, Maria!"* and Maria,[105] blushing very much, began to sing in a tiny quavering voice. She sang *I Dreamt that I Dwelt,* and when she came to the second verse she sang again:

> I dreamt that I dwelt in marble halls
>   With vassals and serfs at my side,
> And of all who assembled within those walls
>   That I was the hope and the pride.
>
> I had riches too great to count, could boast
>   Of a high ancestral name,
> But I also dreamt, which pleased me most,
>   That you loved me still the same.

But no one tried to show her her mistake; and when she had ended her song Joe was very much moved. He said that there was no time like the long ago and no music for him like poor old Balfe, whatever other people might say, and his eyes filled up so much with tears that he could not find what he was looking for and in the end he had to ask his wife to tell him where the corkscrew was.

RICHARD B. HUDSON

> "Joyce's 'Clay.'" *The Explicator*, VI (March, 1948), item 30 [no pagination]. Reprinted by permission of the publisher.

The key to the meaning of James Joyce's "Clay" (*Dubliners*) is, I think, to be found in the title. There are three associations common to clay itself, and Joyce makes use of all three of them.

First, there is clay as the common substance out of which we are all compounded. Maria's is just another life, living out its days in deadening routine livened now and then by rather pathetic holidays such as this one. The basic irony is that this worn and unloved laundry worker sings—and no doubt dreams—of servants, vassals, marble halls, and "riches too great to count." Her drunken brother weeps, but he weeps sentimentally for the old days, not for Maria or for himself.

Then there is clay as a substance susceptible of molding. Maria is a weak character; everyone in the story senses this in one way or another, and takes advantage of the fact. She is imposed upon at the laundry, where she has a reputation as a peacemaker. Where the issue is important, where she really wants to make peace, as she does between her brothers, she cannot do so; Joe simply will not listen to her. The Protestants at the laundry, the clerk in the cake shop, the gentleman in the tram, Joe and his family, all perceive her weakness and imprint their personalities on her. She resists no more than clay resists the hand of the potter.

The third common association of clay is with death. Joyce's application of this concept to the story is, I think, the most subtle, but at the same time most meaningful, of all. The association of clay with death is first evident in the last part of the story when Maria takes part in the divination game, but its relation to earlier events in the story is clear. Maria is led blindfolded to the table to choose one of four saucers—one containing clay, another water, the third a prayer book, and the last a ring. According to the tradition of All Hallow's Eve, her choice will determine her fate for the year, and many such games for this holiday are listed in Fraser's *Golden Bough,* although I did not find this specific one. She chooses the clay, which the neighbor girls have apparently included without the knowledge of Mrs. Donnelly, Maria's sister-in-law. Mrs. Donnelly reproves them and has the clay thrown back in the garden. Maria chooses again and gets the prayer book. Mrs. Donnelly is not disturbed at the clay because she believes in the portent and does not want Maria to know that she is to die within the year; Mrs. Donnelly simply thinks that the idea of death, introduced by thoughtless children who do not worry about such things, is a needless intrusion into a happy family party.

Mrs. Donnelly and the others, however, are not aware of how appropriate to Maria the symbol of death is. Maria is death-in-life. No portent is needed because for all practical purposes Maria is already dead. Her spinsterhood and her subconscious longing for marriage and children mark her life as unfulfilled, a kind of walking death. This is especially true now that her brothers have grown up and no longer need her. This subconscious longing of hers is apparent in many incidents: her attitude towards the ring in the barmbrack (another divination game), her thoughts about her "tidy" body when she is dressing, her insistence that independence is best, and her confusion as a result of the old gentleman's error in the train (which she does not correct).

Most important in this connection, however, is the error that she makes in Balfe's song. She sings the first verse and then repeats it (as printed in the story) because, consciously or unconsciously, she rejects such a direct statement of her own situation. What she should have sung but did not is as follows:

> I dreamt that suitors sought my hand
> That knights on bended knee,
> And with vows no maiden heart could withstand,
> They pledged their faith to me.
>
> And I dreamt that one of that noble band
> Came forth my heart to claim,
> But I also dreamt, which charmed me most,
> That you loved me still the same.

The attention Joyce calls to his error makes it all too clear how the reader is to regard Maria.

One other point, does, I think, support the death-in-life theme suggested by clay. The action takes place on All Hallow's Eve, and Maria's holiday that night at the fireside of her brother Joe is like that of the ghost allowed to return to life on this night until the crowing of the cock. At least at Joe's there is a kind of life, of fulfillment—love, children, anger, sentiment, drink.

## MARVIN MAGALANER

From "The Other Side of James Joyce." *Arizona Quarterly*, IX (Spring, 1953), 5-16. Reprinted by permission of the publisher and the author.

A quick reading of "Clay" deceives the reader into thinking that the sketch concerns nothing more than the frustrated longings of a timid old maid for the joys of life which have been denied to her—a husband, children, romantic adventures. There is much more in the fewer than nine pages which the author takes to tell the story. The first point to be noted is the number of social relationships which are awry. For centuries, the civilized world has considered marriage the wholesome, normal state for mature people. Yet Maria has wasted her sterile, barren life as an unmarried woman. Since Cain slew Abel, it has been considered sinful for brothers to fight; yet the brothers, Alphy and Joe, are constantly at each other's throats. Nor are relationships amicable among the other minor characters. When her husband, Joe, is drunk, a frequent state for him, Mrs. Donnelly has difficulty in maintaining the peace and decorum of her household. In the laundry where Maria is employed, the women quarrel often and make threats against their subordinates. "Ginger Mooney was always saying what she wouldn't do to the dummy who had charge of the irons..." The saleslady in the cake shop is deliberately impudent to the most inoffensive of customers. The young men on the tram ignore her and allow her to stand—an ordinary occurrence today but noteworthy in 1900. And even the innocent children are half accused of stealing the missing cakes. Through this maze of human unpleasantness moves the old maid, Maria, a steadying and moderating influence on all those who have dealings with her.

Her role as peacemaker is stressed by Joyce. In the Protestant laundry in which she worked, she "was always sent for when the women quarreled over their tubs and always succeeded in making peace." Her employer compliments her on her ability as mediator: "Maria, you are a veritable peacemaker." Her calm moderation alone keeps Ginger Mooney from using violence against another worker. "Everyone," says Joyce, concluding the paragraph, "was so[7] fond of Maria." And for good reason. She worries about Joe's drunkenness; she refuses to live with Joe and his family, though she loves them, for fear of putting them out. She is grieved terribly over the unnecessary estrangement of Joe and Alphy. Very tactful, Maria prevents a family quarrel over the loss of a nutcracker, by saying that "she didn't like nuts and that they weren't to bother about her." Though she does not wish a drink of wine offered by Joe, she "let him have his way." Maria cannot resist, however, attempting to make peace between the brothers, but on this point Joe is violently adamant.

The old maid's success at peacemaking in the laundry is remarkable inasmuch as she must deal with women whose morality is questionable. For the Dublin by Lamplight laundry was part of a larger institution called Dublin by Lamplight, an asylum for delinquent women. Located in the Ballsbridge section of Dublin, it existed through charitable donations. It was kept up also "by the inmates' own exertions. It has an excellent laundry attached, furnished with all modern appliances...Terms moderate." The motto of the organization is indicative of the task which faced Maria: "That they may recover themselves out of the snare of the devil, who are taken captive by him at his will." (2 Tim. ii:26). Maria's position in the laundry is unclear. She certainly does not appear to be in the snare of the devil or to require reformation. Since she apparently works in the kitchen, not in the laundry with the vulgar inmates, she may be one of the hired staff. Even so, all twenty-four hours of her day are regulated by the matron, for she needs permission to leave the building, even after working hours.

Maria's role as peacemaker, dovetailing as it does with a great many other details of the story, suggests the hypothesis that Joyce intended to build up a rough analogy between the laundry worker Maria and the Virgin Mary. Had not Christ said, in the Sermon on the Mount, "Blessed are the peacemakers. For they shall be called the children of God." Along certain lines, the relationship seems fairly obvious.[8]

Maria, of course, is a variant of the name Mary. Certainly there is nothing subtle about the associations which the name of the main character evokes. The Virgin is well-known for her role as peacemaker, for the invocations to her especially by women to prevent conflict. Accordingly, she is invoked ("sent for") whenever the laundresses argue and she "always succeeded in making peace." Without her restraining and comforting influence, much more violence would occur. There is surely a suggestion of the church in Maria, for, like Mrs.

Kearney (in "A Mother") and the two old women (in "The Sisters"), she offers communion to the women by distributing the barmbrack cakes.

Carrying the argument further, Joyce makes much of the fact that Maria is a virgin. At the same time, and this seems very significant, she has children, though they are not born from her womb. "She had nursed...[Joe] and Alphy too; and Joe used often to say: 'Mamma is mamma but Maria is my proper mother.' " There would seem to be no reason, in a very short story, to quote Joe directly here unless more was intended by the author than the bare statement that Maria had aided his mother in bringing up her sons. It appears to be an attempt to hint that Maria's offspring are conceived without sin or that she is the Mother Church. But there are further biblical parallels. It will be recalled that in the Gospel according to Luke, it is Elizabeth who announces to Mary that she is blessed and will have blessed offspring. Interestingly enough, in "Clay" it is Lizzie (Elizabeth) Fleming, Maria's co-worker in the laundry, who "said Maria was sure to get the ring and, though Fleming had said that for so many Hallow Eves, Maria had to laugh and say she didn't want any ring or man either..."

Other facts crowd in to lend support to the idea. Maria works in a laundry, where things are made clean; Mary is the instrument of cleansing on the spiritual plane. All the children sing for Maria, and two bear gifts to her on a Whit-Monday trip. That one gift is a purse has ironic implications in Joyce's modern Dublin. The laundress finds her appearance "nice" and "tidy" "in spite of its[9] years." This may be a circumspect way of saying that, after centuries, the freshness of Mary as a symbol is still untarnished. On the other hand, Maria finds on the tram that she is ignored by the young men, and in the bake shop treated insolently by the young clerk. Only the elderly and the slightly drunk treat her with the respect which she merits but which she is too timid to demand. Only the old and muddled in Dublin any longer pay homage to the Virgin. The fact that Maria finally gets the prayer book, in the ceremony of the three dishes, and is therefore slated to enter a convent and retire from the world, is additional grist for this mill.

Why Joyce would want to work on these two levels simultaneously and what artistic purpose he might have in so doing are fair questions. Knowing his love of multi-leveled symbolism in *Ulysses* and *Finnegans Wake*, one might well expect to find similar levels in his earlier books. To take his stories merely at their surface meaning would hardly do justice to the painstaking care with which he worked out their over-all structure and the minutest details of their execution. An answer which is perhaps close to the truth may be that, just as in *Ulysses* the juxtaposition of the heroic age and the human—of wily Odysseus and sly Leopold Bloom—serves to point up the glory that was Greece and the hell that was Dublin for the artist of 1900, so the superimposition of modern Maria upon the ancient and venerable symbol of Mary is aesthetically effective.

There is still a third level in "Clay" which demands mention. The story, originally entitled "Hallow Eve," takes place on the spooky night of October thirty-first.

the night set apart for a universal walking abroad of spirits, both of the visible and invisible world; for..one of the special characteristics attributed to this mystic evening, is the faculty conferred on the immaterial principle in humanity to detach itself from its corporeal tenement and wander abroad through the realms of space (Robert Chambers: *The Book of Days*)

Putting this more bluntly than Joyce would have wished, Maria on the spirit level is a witch on this Hallowe'en night—and as a traditional witch Joyce describes her. "Maria was a very, very small[10] person indeed but she had a very long nose and a very long chin." To fix this almost caricature description in the minds of his readers, the author repeats that "when she laughed...the tip of her nose nearly met the tip of her chin." And two sentences further down in the same paragraph, he reiterates the sentence for the third time, and for a fourth before the story is through. The intention . . . is very plain. In addition to these frequent iterations, Joyce's first sentence in "Clay"— and his story openings are almost always fraught with special significance—discloses that this was "her evening out." By right it should be, for witches walk abroad on Hallow Eve. In itself, however, implying that the old woman is a witch is of minor importance. It derives fuller meaning from the illusion-reality motif of which it is a small part.

This motif is central to the story, gives it, in fact, its point. Joyce selected titles for his works with great care and deliberation. That he first called this one "Hallow Eve" means that to him the day on which the action occurs is significant. Hallowe'en is famous in modern times for its masquerades, its hiding of identity of celebrants, conjuring tricks, illusions of goblins and ghosts—in other words, famed for the illusions which are created in the name of celebrating the holiday. It is a night too on which it is hard to tell the material from the supernatural, witch from woman, ghost from sheeted youngster. On this night things are not what they seem.

In the first paragraph, Joyce touches gently upon the motif more than once. Maria's work in the kitchen is done. Barmbracks (raisin bread baked as part of the holiday celebration) have been prepared and stand ready to be eaten. The author does not reveal the details of the baking process, but it is legitimate to wonder whether he had this Irish custom in mind: unmarried girls would knead a cake with their left thumbs Not a sound escaped from their clenched lips; the work proceeded in mute solemnity, a single word would have broken the charm and destroyed their ardent hopes of beholding their future husbands in their dreams after having partaken of the mystic 'dumb-cake.' (E H. Sechrist, *Red Letter Days*)[11]

The finished barmbracks "seemed uncut, but if you went closer you would see that they had been cut into long thick even slices and were ready...Maria had cut them herself " The contrast between the illusion of wholeness and the reality of the actual slices is given prominent mention only because it belongs within the larger framework of the motif. Also, in the same paragraph, the cook delights in the cleanliness of the big copper boilers in which "you could see yourself," another reference to illusion, possibly connected in Joyce's mind with the Hallow Eve custom of looking into a mirror to see one's future husband.

In other respects, also, the spirits are at work in this story. Things, as things, lose their materiality and become invisible. At least they are missing and cannot be located. The *pièce de resistance* of the evening, the plumcake, is missing and "nowhere could she find it." On the heels of this annoying mystery comes the disclosure that "Nobody could find the nutcrackers." Finally, Joe, trying to locate the corkscrew, "could not find what he was looking for" and is forced to seek assistance. Whether this repetitious inability to find small implements and objects is symbolic, on a broader level, of the inability of Dubliners to get anything but frustrated failure from their search for the world's goods is a valid question but must wait for an answer.

Maria herself is ambiguous, sometimes more a disembodied spirit than a person. Her body, though it exists, is "very, very small," and a hearty burst of laughter grips her "till her minute body nearly shook itself asunder." On this night she is able almost to get outside of her body and look at it objectively: "she looked with quaint affection at the diminutive body which she had so often adorned...she found it a nice tidy little body."

It is in dreams, however, that Maria is able to put the greatest distance between illusion, namely the love and adventure which have never entered her life, and reality, the drab, methodical existence of a servant in a laundry. Or if not in dreams, in the reverie induced by a dream song, "I dreamt that I dwelt in marble halls."[12] The whole story builds up to this central split, at which point all the minor examples of the thin line between fantasy and actuality attain their *raison d'être*. In these rich and sensuous lines, sung in a "tiny quavering voice" by a "blushing" Maria, are packed the antitheses to the frustrating life of the average Dubliner, made to seem even more pallid and unlovely by close contact with richness. Mary in contemporary life has decayed in scope to Maria. The "marble halls" have been converted into laundry kitchens. Far from having "riches too great to count," Maria wants to cry because she has wasted a few shillings. Most tragic of all, there is no one in the world to whom the old maid can, with truth, sing "that you loved me just the same." In this song, and in dream, her spirit can "detach itself from its corporeal tenement and wander abroad through the realms of space," and appropriately on Hallow Eve it does just that.

In Maria's rendition of the song, she inadvertently omits the second and third stanzas. By mistake she sings the first verse twice. Joyce emphasizes that "no one tried to show her her mistake." Little wonder that her audience remains tactfully silent, since the missing verses are these:

> I dreamt that suitors sought my hand
> That knights on bended knee,
> And with vows no maiden heart could withstand,
> They pledged their faith to me.
>
> And I dreamt that one of that noble band
> Came forth my heart to claim,
> But I also dreamt, which charmed me most,
> That you loved me still the same .

Maria's error is probably attributable to an emotional block which prevents her from giving voice to remarks so obviously at variance with the reality of her dull life. The psychoanalysts would have a name for this unconscious repression of a painful remark, similar to the Freudian stutter. Leopold Bloom suffers such a lapse when thinking of Boylan's affair with Molly. He speaks of "the wife's[13] admirers" and then in confusion adds, "The wife's advisers, I mean."

Joyce's decision to change the title of the story from "Hallow Eve" to "Clay" needs explanation. The result of the change is a slight shift of emphasis from the singing of the stanzas to the ceremony of the three dishes. There are many variations of this holiday game, one of which requires this set-up:

> Two of these [dishes] are respectively filled with clean and foul water, and one is empty...the parties, blindfolded, advance in succession, and dip their fingers into one  If they dip into the clean water, they are to marry a maiden; if into the foul water, a widow, if into the empty dish, the party so dipping is destined to be either a bachelor or an old maid...(Chambers: *The Book of Days*)

The game played in "Clay" is slightly different, but the principle is the same. Poor Maria puts her fingers into a dish which the thoughtless children have jokingly filled with clay. She is to get neither the prayer book (life in a convent) or the ring (marriage). Death is her fate. There is a subdued shock when even the insensitive people present at the Hallowe'en party realize the symbolic significance of selecting clay as an omen of things to come. Joyce, leaving nothing to chance, has earlier prepared the reader for the symbolic action by showing that Maria is half in love with easeful death: "She had her plants...and she liked looking after them. She had lovely ferns and wax-plants..." It is interesting to remember at this point that in *A Portrait of the Artist* Joyce tells the reader that the emblems of the Virgin Mary, too, are late-flowering plants and late-blossoming trees. It is very probable that the young writer was not sure where to place the emphasis in this short story—or, at least, which hint to offer his readers. Certainly the final version of the title accentuates the motif of decay though it robs the story of an element of surprise which it might otherwise have.[14]

## WILLIAM T. NOON, S. J.

"Joyce's 'Clay': An Interpretation." *College English*, XVII (November, 1955). Reprinted by permission of the author and the publisher.

> Blessed are the peace-makers; they shall
> be counted the children of God.

In the James Joyce Collection at the University of Buffalo Library there is a large notebook containing in Joyce's own hand further notes to his already published works. The new notes to "Clay," one of the shortest of the *Dubliners* stories, are cryptic:

> Gentleman horse (stallion):
> sie studiert immer etwas:
> murders child.

Such jottings are mysterious enough to afford several slants of the critical glass in an effort to catch the meaning of "Clay." Since these late marginal comments are outside of the story's own texture, the interpreter can hope at best to accommodate them to the meaning which emerges, which "epiphanizes," in the story itself. I should like to accommodate them to my own view of "Clay" as a spiritually re-vitalized version of a Hallowe'en tale. (I am grateful to the University Librarian for permission to quote the phrases.)

All Hallows Eve, or Hallowe'en, has a spiritual core of meaning in Catholic countries like Ireland which has been almost altogether forgotten in our own secular observance of the holiday. Hallow Eve, or "Holy Eve," began not just as a holiday of false faces and funny pranks, but as the vigil of holy day, the feast of All the Saints. Once a year at the end of the Church's liturgical cycle in the autumn, this holy day is observed in honor of all the little men and women, the G.I. Joes and Janes of the spiritual warfare, the unsung heroes, the "saints" (with a small *s*) who may not have done anything particularly memorable or striking by way of exploit, but who in the ordinary, everyday routine business of living showed holiness, saved their souls. This "feast" has always been a favorite with the vast rank and file of the faithful. It has been regarded in a very special way as their particular holy day. In a Catholic country like Ireland the evening before the holy day came to be celebrated with games and harmless pranks from which our Hallowe'en customs are derived.

Joyce's story "Clay" unfolds against this All Hallows background. Joyce takes advantage of the original meaning of All Hallows Eve to introduce us to a modern work-a-day saint, a saint with the small *s* indeed, somewhat vain and somewhat foolish, whose proudest moment of grace "epiphanizes" in the wordless, brave acceptance of herself as others see her—so much shapeless, loveless clay.

The plot-line of Joyce's story is simple. Maria, employee of a laundry (at Ballsbridge, the site of the annual Horse Show in Dublin), goes on Hallow Eve to the family of one of the Donnelly boys for whom she had been a childhood nurse. En route, she purchases some cookies and a plumcake for the Hallowe'en party which Joe Donnelly and his wife have arranged for their own and a neighbor's children. On the tram a stout, elderly "gentleman," somewhat intoxicated, makes room for Maria, and they chat together. Arriving at the Donnelly home Maria is disconcerted when she cannot find her plumcake surprise. In the course of the evening's games the children trick Maria, who is blindfolded, into choosing, instead of a ring (prophetic of marriage) which she had hoped for, a wet lump of clay (prophetic of death). Joe scolds the children and he and his wife arrange that on the next try Maria will choose the prayer-book (prophetic, so they say, of Maria's entering a convent). The party closes with Maria's singing, at Joe's and his wife's insistence, two stanzas from one of "the old songs" of Balfe. Only, Maria omits the second stanza and sings the first stanza twice.

The plot-line of the story gives little idea, however, of how Joyce manages his "epiphany" of Maria as a kind of average saint, aware and unaware of the humility in self-knowledge which existence and sanctity require. Quietly, in a seemingly casual, unpremeditated way, Joyce prepares us for this understanding of Maria in the very opening of the story. The incident of Maria's settling the quarrels of the work-house laundry women has its point in the matron's words: "Maria, you are a veritable peace-maker." Though Joyce's overt allusion is to but one of the Beatitudes, covertly he manages to suggest, after a fashion, all the Beatitudes. "Blessed are you who are poor; the Kingdom of God is yours": in Maria's purse, we are told, there "were but two half-crowns and some coppers." Also, Maria is patient ("Blessed are the sad of heart") when she suspects that her cakes have been stolen by the children (as possibly they were), when the nutcracker is misplaced by the children (most likely, deliberately) so that she cannot eat any of the nuts. In a subtle way Maria "suffers persecutions" and yet tries to appear "glad and light-hearted."

The lyric-like ambiguity of the story, however, comes from Joyce's focus on Maria as a woman as well as a saint. For all her beautiful moral traits, on which she somewhat prided herself, Maria was not physically attractive. When she laughed, for instance, the tip of her very long nose nearly met the tip of her very long chin. The poor drudges of the laundry loved Maria anyway for her gentle character. Joe Donnelly and his wife were old enough, had lived long enough to take Maria for granted. But children were instinctively "put off" by her physical ugliness. And there had never been any "beaux" for Maria; no "suitors sought her hand, no knights upon bended knee."

This, Joyce implies, was a great sorrow. For Maria at heart thought of herself as a great lady. *Sie studiert immer etwas;* Maria was always "studying something." She had a knack of fitting whatever harsh thing might happen into her dream. "All that is lovely, all that is gracious in the telling"—all this truly was the argument of Maria's thought. Maria knew that she was a lady, not like Ginger Mooney, "a common woman." Since she was a lady Maria thought she could tell a gentleman when she saw one. After talking with the "colonel-looking gentleman" on the tram she thought: "How easy it was to know a gentleman even when he has a drop taken." Maria was ever ready to make excuses. Maria was sometimes wrong. The gentleman of whom she had such a high opinion was in some respects, had she known them, hardly more than a stallion, a gentleman horse.

A lovely person like Maria should have been married, should have had a chance to know the love of a husband and children of her own, children who would have cared for her too much to have wanted to play tricks on her. It is only when we come to reflect on Maria's "mistake" at the end of the story that we realize how much the lack of love in her life had hurt Maria, how much it had cost her.

Joyce manages numerous details of the story in illumination

of Maria's mistake at its close. The laundry-women laugh and jest about the ring in the barmbrack which they truly wish Maria to have. Maria seemingly regards the jest as lightheartedly as they do. Actually she has to try to convince herself "how much better it was to be independent and have your own money in your pocket." The stylish clerk's ironical question at the cake-shop, "was it wedding-cake she wanted to buy," made Maria blush. The cruelty of the children's jest in offering her a saucer filled with moist clay from the garden is seemingly not registered by Maria, only because the illumination is all within. The child who is "murdered" in the story is not any one of the children at the party. The child is inside Maria. In a flash the lady Maria sees herself as ridiculous and rather ugly. In that flash she loses hold on her dream.

The crucial test of Maria's gentle character comes to focus a little while later in her singing of Balfe's romantic lovesong from *The Bohemian Girl*, "I Dreamt I Dwelt in Marble Halls." What an ironic contrast there is between Maria's actual situation and the words of the lyric as she sings them in her "tiny, quavering voice." There had been a time when Maria might have imagined that these words of the first stanza could conceivably come true in some sense for her. She was the hope and the pride of the laundry-folk, was she not? It was not altogether incongruous to dream that she could be rich, could have a high name. In spite of everything, she had once believed, or at least wanted to believe that people were good like herself—so that they would continue to love her *for what she was*, even if she were "to dwell in marble halls."

But Maria herself saw the incongruity of singing the second stanza of the lyric, hard as she had once tried to believe that people loved her just for what she was, and so she omitted:

> I dreamt that suitors sought my hand
>    That knights upon bended knee,
> And with vows no maiden heart could withstand
>    They pledged their faith to me.

> And I dreamt that one of that noble band
>    Came forth my hand to claim.
> But I also dreamt, which pleased me most,
>    That you loved me still the same.

Life had finally taught Maria the sheer impossibility of a dream like that ever coming true for her. Now after the games of the evening it would not be wise to expose herself to ridicule by singing this second verse. So, Joyce tells us, she sang the first verse twice. Joyce adds, "No one tried to show her her mistake!" Maria's goodness was not always able to restore peace: she had not succeeded that evening in making Joe any better disposed toward his estranged brother Alphy. But on this All Hallows Eve, she had succeeded in something. Her goodness was stronger than the children's hardness, their lack of understanding: "No one tried to show her her mistake." Her goodness was strong enough to trouble their parents' casual acceptance: Joe had to ask for the corkscrew. Life had been hard to Maria, but Maria had not become hard. Was Maria's singing the same stanza twice a mistake? Is living the life of the Beatitudes a mistake? Is it a mistake to be hallow on All Hallows Eve?

## 7. FRANZ KAFKA—"A Country Doctor"

In *Selected Short Stories of Franz Kafka,* translated by Willa and Edwin Muir. New York: Modern Library, 1952. Originally published in *The Penal Colony* (New York: Schocken Books, 1948). Reprinted by permission of Schocken Books.

I was in great perplexity; I had to start on an urgent journey; a seriously ill patient was waiting for me in a village ten miles off, a thick blizzard of snow filled all the wide spaces between him and me; I had a gig, a light gig with big wheels, exactly right for our country roads, muffled in furs, my bag of instruments in my hand, I was in the courtyard all ready for the journey; but there was no horse to be had, no horse. My own horse had died in the night, worn out by the fatigues of this icy winter; my servant girl was now running round the village trying to borrow a horse; but it was hopeless, I knew it, and I stood there forlornly, with the snow gathering more and more thickly upon me, more and more unable to move. In the gateway the girl appeared, alone, and waved the lantern; of course, who would lend a horse at this time for such a journey? I strode through the courtway once more; I could see no way out; in my confused distress I kicked at the dilapidated door of the yearlong uninhabited pigsty. It flew open and flapped to and fro on its hinges. A steam and smell as of horses came out of it. A dim stable lantern was swinging inside from a rope. A man, crouching on his[148] hams in that low space, showed an open blue-eyed face. "Shall I yoke up?" he asked, crawling out on all fours. I did not know what to say and merely stooped down to see what else was in the sty. The servant girl was standing beside me. "You never know what you're going to find in your own house," she said, and we both laughed. "Hey there, Brother, hey there, Sister!" called the groom, and two horses, enormous creatures with powerful flanks, one after the other, their legs tucked close to their bodies, each well-shaped head lowered like a camel's, by sheer strength of buttocking squeezed out through the door hole which they filled entirely. But at once they were standing up, with their long legs and their bodies steaming thickly. "Give him a hand," I said, and the willing girl hurried to help the groom with the harnessing. Yet hardly was she beside him when the groom clipped hold of her and pushed his face against hers. She screamed and fled back to me; on her cheek stood out in red the marks of two rows of teeth. "You brute," I yelled in fury, "do you want a whipping?" but in the same moment reflected that the man was a stranger; that I did not know where he came from, and that of his own free will he was helping me out when everyone else had failed me. As if he knew my thoughts he took no offense at my threat but, still busied with the horses, only turned round once towards me. "Get in," he said then, and indeed everything was ready. A magnificent pair of horses, I observed, such as I had never sat behind, and I climbed in happily. "But I'll drive, you don't know the way," I said. "Of course," said he, "I'm not coming with you anyway, I'm staying[149] with Rose." "No," shrieked Rose, fleeing into the house with a justified presentiment that her fate was inescapable; I heard the door chain rattle as she put it up; I heard the key turn in the lock; I could see, moreover, how she put out the lights in the entrance hall and in further flight all through the rooms to keep herself from being discovered. "You're coming with me," I said to the groom, "or I won't go, urgent as my journey is. I'm not thinking of paying for it by handing the girl over to you." "Gee up!" he said; clapped his hands. the gig whirled off like a log in a freshet; I could just hear the door of my house splitting and bursting as the groom charged at it and then I was deafened and blinded by a storming rush that steadily buffeted all my senses. But this only for a moment, since, as if my patient's farmyard had opened out just before my courtyard gate, I was already there; the horses had come quietly to a standstill; the blizzard had stopped; moonlight all around; my patient's parents hurried out of the house, his sister behind them; I was almost lifted out of the gig, from their confused ejaculations I gathered not a word; in the sickroom the air was almost unbreathable; the neglected stove was smoking; I wanted to push open a window; but first I had to look at my patient. Gaunt, without any fever, not cold, not warm, with vacant eyes, without a shirt, the youngster heaved himself up from under the feather bedding, threw his arms round my neck, and whispered in my ear: "Doctor, let me die." I glanced round the room; no one had heard it; the parents were leaning forward in silence waiting for my verdict: the sister had set a chair for my[150] handbag, I opened the bag and hunted among my instruments; the boy kept clutching at me from his bed to remind me of his entreaty; I picked up a pair of tweezers, examined them in the candlelight and laid them down again. "Yes," I thought blasphemously, "in cases like this the gods are helpful, send the missing horse, add to it a second because of the urgency, and to crown everything bestow even a groom—" And only now did I remember Rose again; what was I to do, how could I rescue her, how could I pull her away from under that groom at ten miles' distance, with a team of horses I couldn't control. These horses, now, they had somehow slipped the reins loose, pushed the windows open from outside, I did not know how; each of them had stuck a head in at a window and, quite unmoved by the startled cries of the family, stood eyeing the patient. "Better go back at once," I thought, as if the horses were summoning me to the return journey, yet I permitted the patient's sister, who fancied that I was dazed by the heat, to take my fur coat from me. A glass of rum was poured out for me, the old man clapped me on the shoulder, a familiarity justified by this offer of his treasure. I shook my head; in the narrow confines of the old man's thoughts I felt ill; that was my only reason for refusing the drink. The mother stood by the bedside and cajoled me towards it; I yielded, and, while one of the horses whinnied loudly to the ceiling, laid my head to the boy's breast, which shivered under my wet beard. I confirmed what I already knew, the boy was quite sound, something a little wrong with his circulation, saturated with coffee by his solicitous mother, but sound[151] and best turned out of bed with one shove. I am no world reformer and so I let him lie. I was the district doctor and did my duty to the uttermost, to the point where it became almost too much. I was badly paid and yet generous and helpful to the poor. I had still to see that Rose was all right, and then the boy might have his way and I wanted to die too. What was I doing there in that endless winter! My horse was dead, and not a single person in the village would lend me another. I had to get my team out of the pigsty; if they hadn't chanced to be horses I should have had to travel with swine. That was how it was. And I nodded to the family. They knew nothing about it, and, had they known, would not have believed it. To write prescriptions is easy, but to come to an understanding with people is hard. Well, this should be the end of my visit, I had once more been called out needlessly, I was used to that, the whole district made my life a torment with my night bell, but that I should have to sacrifice Rose this time as well, the pretty girl who had lived in my house for years almost without my noticing her—that sacrifice was too much to ask, and I had somehow to get it reasoned out in my head with the help of what craft I could muster, in order not to let fly at this family, which with the best will in the world could not restore Rose to me. But as I shut my bag and put an arm out for my fur coat, the family meanwhile standing together, the father sniffing at the glass of rum in his hand, the mother, apparently disappointed in me—why, what do people expect?—biting her lips with tears in her eyes, the sister fluttering a blood-soaked towel, I was somehow ready to admit[152] conditionally that the boy might be ill after all. I went towards him, he welcomed

me smiling as if I were bringing him the most nourishing invalid broth
—ah, now both horses were whinnying together; the noise, I suppose,
was ordained by heaven to assist my examination of the patient—and
this time I discovered that the boy was indeed ill. In his right side,
near the hip, was an open wound as big as the palm of my hand. Rose-
red, in many variations of shade, dark in the hollows, lighter at the
edges, softly granulated, with irregular clots of blood, open as a surface
mine to the daylight. That was how it looked from a distance. But on
a closer inspection there was another complication. I could not help
a low whistle of surprise. Worms, as thick and as long as my little
finger, themselves rose-red and blood-spotted as well, were wriggling
from their fastness in the interior of the wound towards the light, with
small white heads and many little legs. Poor boy, you were past helping. I had discovered your great wound; this blossom in your side was
destroying you. The family was pleased; they saw me busying myself;
the sister told the mother, the mother the father, the father told several
guests who were coming in, through the moonlight at the open door,
walking on tiptoe, keeping their balance with outstretched arms. "Will
you save me?" whispered the boy with a sob, quite blinded by the life
within his wound. That is what people are like in my district. Always
expecting the impossible from the doctor. They have lost their ancient
beliefs; the parson sits at home and unravels his vestments, one after
another; but the doctor is supposed to be omnipotent[153] with his
merciful surgeon's hand. Well, as it pleases them; I have not thrust my
services on them; if they misuse me for sacred ends, I let that happen
to me too; what better do I want, old country doctor that I am, bereft
of my servant girl! And so they came, the family and the village elders,
and stripped my clothes off me; a school choir with the teacher at the
head of it stood before the house and sang these words to an utterly
simple tune:

> Strip his clothes off, then he'll heal us,
> If he doesn't, kill him dead!
> Only a doctor, only a doctor.

Then my clothes were off and I looked at the people quietly, my fingers in my beard and my head cocked to one side. I was altogether
composed and equal to the situation and remained so, although it was
no help to me, since they now took me by the head and feet and carried me to the bed. They laid me down in it next to the wall, on the
side of the wound. Then they all left the room; the door was shut;
the singing stopped; clouds covered the moon; the bedding was warm
around me; the horses' heads in the open windows wavered like
shadows. "Do you know," said a voice in my ear, "I have very little
confidence in you. Why, you were only blown in here, you didn't come
on your own feet. Instead of helping me, you're cramping me on my

deathbed. What I'd like best is to scratch your eyes out." "Right," I said, "it is a shame. And yet I am a doctor. What am I to do? Believe me, it is not[154] too easy for me either." "Am I supposed to be content with this apology? Oh, I must be, I can't help it. I always have to put up with things. A fine wound is all I brought into the world; that was my sole endowment." "My young friend," said I, "your mistake is: you have not a wide enough view. I have been in all the sickrooms, far and wide, and I tell you: your wound is not so bad. Done in a tight corner with two strokes of the ax. Many a one proffers his side and can hardly hear the ax in the forest, far less that it is coming nearer to him." "Is that really so, or are you deluding me in my fever?" "It is really so, take the word of honor of an official doctor." And he took it and lay still. But now it was time for me to think of escaping. The horses were still standing faithfully in their places. My clothes, my fur coat, my bag were quickly collected; I didn't want to waste time dressing; if the horses raced home as they had come, I should only be springing, as it were, out of this bed into my own. Obediently a horse backed away from the window; I threw my bundle into the gig; the fur coat missed its mark and was caught on a hook only by the sleeve. Good enough. I swung myself on to the horse. With the reins loosely trailing, one horse barely fastened to the other, the gig swaying behind, my fur coat last of all in the snow. "Gee up!" I said, but there was no galloping; slowly, like old men, we crawled through the snowy wastes; a long time echoed behind us the new but faulty song of the children:

> O be joyful, all you patients,
> The doctor's laid in bed beside you![155]

Never shall I reach home at this rate; my flourishing practice is done for; my successor is robbing me, but in vain, for he cannot take my place; in my house the disgusting groom is raging; Rose is his victim; I do not want to think about it any more. Naked, exposed to the frost of this most unhappy of ages, with an earthly vehicle, unearthly horses, old man that I am, I wander astray. My fur coat is hanging from the back of the gig, but I cannot reach it, and none of my limber pack of patients lifts a finger. Betrayed! Betrayed! A false alarm on the night bell once answered—it cannot be made good, not ever.[156]

BASIL BUSACCA

From "A Country Doctor." In Angel Flores
and Homer Swander, eds. *Franz Kafka Today*.
Madison: University of Wisconsin Press, 1958.
Pp. 45-54. Reprinted by permission of the
copyright owners, the Regents of the University of Wisconsin.

The tales of Aesop, as everyone knows, have two substantive
aspects: 1) the dramatic surface—taken neither as itself or as coating
for the "meaning"; 2) the "meaning," which has little to do, except
nominally, with foxes and grapes, or pelicans and bottles. The *meaning* could be expressed in the $x$'s and $y$'s of symbolic logic more eco-
nomically than in language, albeit less charmingly, because it is concerned with particular *relations* and not with specific *termini* (e.g.,
foxes, grapes). The formula of relations (the meaning) may, like a
proverb such as "A stitch in time saves nine," be applied to any set of
specific *termini* whose relations may be conceived as analogous: thus
we tell the child who says that "spelling is silly," after he fails to
spell correctly, that he should "remember the fox and the grapes."
     The function of both aspects is comic. The stories of Aesop are
droll tales significant of droll patterns of behavior which are available
to rational correction. In reading the tales we are sufficiently detached
from specific *termini* to recognize discrepancy from the rational even
when such discrepancy is analogous to some of our own behavior.
Aesop is an example of the comic poet, whose strategy, as Professor
Julius Weinberg of the University of Wisconsin likes to put it, is to
lift you up beside him, let you look down upon an analogue of your
own irrational behavior, and give you a chance to say, in effect, "Just
look at those ridiculous creatures. *I* would certainly never do anything so silly—and what's more I never will again!"
     The world assumed by Aesop is rational and orderly. The
only[45] variables are the sentient beings. But such a construction of
the world has, in human history, stood only as Working Hypothesis
A. Working Hypothesis B, equally ancient, assumes a world in which
tragedy is natural and inevitable, assumes that order is not a fact of
nature but a limited and fallible human construct. In the "B" world,

which is perhaps as valid as the "A," any rationale of behavior which
assumes a thoroughly orderly universe must be more or less mistaken,
tragic to participate in, comic to view—if viewed, with detachment,
from a "B" world standpoint.

Franz Kafka, who properly regarded his writings as comic, is
clearly of the "B" world. That he is the subtle Aesop of that world
(who lets one smile wryly at one's predicament in a tragic universe) is
apparent from the facility with which his explicators have "proved"
the analogies between given texts and a variety of political, moral, economic, religious, sexual, biographical, historical, and other contexts.
Individual explicators fail only if they are bad workmen and mistake
the essential relations or assign an $x$ or $y$ inappropriately, but almost
all of them share a logical fallacy, which is to assume *not only* that
the story of the fox and the grapes *can* refer to the child who can't
spell, but *also* that it *can refer to no other situation*. The analogues
offered by the explicators are perfectly sound; what is ridiculous is the
insistence of each explicator that the others are wrong. . . .[46]

Here, as in all literary art, what is of first importance is not the
fable but the dramatic surface, the immanent qualitative reality of
the experience of "A Country Doctor" itself. Taken as *oracle*, however, if one picks vocabulary from the "B" world, or as *slide rule*, if
from the "A," the story must be particularized, for those who insist
upon particularizations, in the local contexts of numberless analogues;
for once the primary *relations* are apparent, there is no problem in
providing *termini*. Consider the following examples:

*Sampler A.*—This is simply the paradox of the medical man. The doctor ignores, and in effect, sacrifices, his own household in order to
accept the demands of professional life. Ironically, the sacrifice is[51]
wasted, becomes in fact almost criminal, precisely in those cases in
which he attends patients who are mortally ill. As sooner or later he
comes to realize unless he is a complete fool, his role is more absurd
when he visits a patient beyond medical aid than when he calls on
one "who doesn't really need a doctor," and in the former case, rather
than the latter, it is charlatanism for him to go through the professional motions which reassure the family, because, in his helplessness,
the doctor is, in effect, in the same bed with the patient. Taken against
the whole universe of the situation, moreover, his professional services
are multiply absurd—destructive of his home, of himself, and perhaps (in a more basic sense than the medical) of the patient, if for
example the doctor is called in preference to the priest who might
claim the last moments of the soul. Then the doctor's activity serves
only to confirm the superstitious belief and/or cynicism of the citi-
zenry toward medicine, and works to intensify his own increasing sense

of the hollowness of his own pretensions, of his vulnerability to the horse-laugh of the gods, of the desperation of his loneliness.

*Sampler B.*—The so-called doctor is roused by homosexual desire. In the opening scene he admits to having ignored Rose, and his anger at the rapacious groom is coupled with the motive to have the groom accompany him on a ride. The death of his horse correlates exactly with the rejection of heterosexual desires, and the new horses, which are "magnificent," were concealed in what had been to him a pigsty. He is a doctor in the ironic sense of assuager of (sexual) pain, his own and his "patient's," and in his ambivalent relation to the patient's appeal, itself ambivalent, to "let me die," that is, leave me to my present sexual predilections, and "save me," that is, reconcile me to heterosexuality: resolved for the patient of course when he realizes the "doctor" is willing to accept the "wound." For the "doctor," the realization that he himself has accepted homosexuality, and has passed into another world (with all the reorientations that passage will require), is an awareness that begins slowly, but quickly accelerates as he feels himself alienated, naked, unable to return to "normal" life, betrayed.

*Sampler C.*—Obviously the story is an ironic History of the Jews. At a point when the motive power of the faith has been lost, when the relations between the Learned in the Law (the doctor) and the society[52] (Rose) have degenerated to the mere rituals of institutional housekeeping, there emerges—in what is symbolically the community of the unclean, the pigsty—the ambivalent messianic faith Christianity (Church of the Prince of Peace, and Church Militant). Although Judaism attempts to deal with the problem of the newer faith, it has lost its capacity for healthy growth; it exists in the hothouse atmosphere of the ghetto; the open spaces where the new religion thrives are to it only sterile and icy wastes. Even the faithful (the "patient") view their situation with resignation, or with desperation, or with skepticism. Thus the wound in the side of the false messiah (plotted, but not inflicted, by the Jewish hierarchy: "You brute . . . do you want a whipping?") paradoxically, festers in the society of the ghetto. No matter, then, that the messiah was false. The wound is real, and so are the taunts from the fringes of the community, the echoes of the Gospels, taunting the faith which never achieved its own Messiah. ("Strip his clothes off, then he'll heal us, / If he doesn't, kill him dead!" / Only a doctor, only a doctor.") The ghettos of the victims are the shards of the world of the chosen people, and tragedy eats like acid at the tables of the law: "Never shall I reach home at this rate; my flourishing practice is done for, my successor is robbing me, but in vain, for he cannot take my place; in my house the disgusting groom is raging; Rose is his victim; I do not want to think about it any more."

*Sampler D.*—We have here the situation which would occur if K.'s advocate in *The Trial* were to recognize that his semiofficial status was not only ambiguous but specious, that the logic he brought to K.'s case was irrelevant, that his detachment was merely the illusion of the legalistic mind—if, in short, he were forced to the realization that he is vulnerable to trial just as K. is Like his client he would discover himself in a new dimension, but there would be this difference, for him there would be added the terror of the familiar-become-strange. He could not return to his profession, as K. could not return to the bank; and truly he could say of any successor to his practice that "he cannot take my place"—that is, he cannot understand what I now understand, and he cannot yet know how close he is to the two-edged gift of understanding.

At this point, obviously, all the familiar analogues which have been posited for *The Trial, The Castle,* and no doubt "The Metamorphosis,"[53] might be introduced—even if we left out of account those offered for parallel or related stories—for when the fable is sound, and the oracular genius of Kafka is as sure as the artistic, analogues are not far to seek.[54]

## MARGARET CHURCH

"Kafka's 'A Country Doctor.' " *The Explicator*, XVI (May, 1958), item 45 [no pagination]. Reprinted by permission of the author and the publisher.

"A Country Doctor," like *The Trial* and *The Castle,* is a quest. It centers around the theme of the alienation and frustrations of man in seeking a goal, in this story of those isolated (country) few who seek to help others. Also implied is the false pride of these self-appointed helpers. The doctor's horse is dead; a blizzard rages The only person who stands by him is his servant girl Rose. Fate conjures up in answer to the doctor's need a demonic pair of horses and a demonic groom. He must sacrifice Rose to the groom if he is to reach his patient. Those who would do good must often, ironically enough, utilize evil in order to accomplish their ends.

He arrives at the patient's house. Further frustration comes, however, when the boy begs that he may be left to die. Those whom we want to help do not even wish it. The heads of the demonic horses thrust into the room constantly remind the doctor (symbolically as well as actually) of his sacrifice of Rose, and he is tempted to leave his quest in order to save her. He is about to depart, thinking "he has been called out needlessly," when he discovers on second examination a large wound in the boy's side, and he knows that he is past helping. Now that he knows he cannot save the boy, the boy, of course, begs to be saved.

The wound is the wound of evil in the side of innocence, for instance, the wound (Rose-red) which the groom makes when he bites the servant girl. The wound is also paradoxically "the Rose"—beauty and goodness which "inflict themselves" on sinful man. Thus the boy exclaims that his wound is all he has to contribute, for he selfishly cherishes the sacrificial nature of his role and the beauty of the rose-like wound which stems from his sacrifice.

At the doctor's realization of his inability to cure the boy, the villagers (society or our censors) punish him by stripping him of his clothes, his dignity, and laying him beside the boy, on the same level as the one he would help. Only now is he able to offer the succor he could not give when he had placed himself in a superior position. He tells the boy that one's wounds, the inroads of evil and guilt, are only a matter of perspective: "your mistake is: you have not a wide enough view."

He returns home on the now slowly moving horses (time is an inner affair) bereft of his clothes, his coat, naked, exposed. Still not cured of his pride, he feels betrayed, that the call has been a false alarm. As in Kafka's *The Trial* and *The Castle,* the efforts of the hero avail nothing, for fate (the officials of the novels) is indifferent.

Any interpretation of Kafka requires a point of view toward his works. It is not possible, in this author's opinion, to interpret him in a narrowly religious sense, for instance. On one level, the wound is, perhaps, the wound in the side of Christ. But Kafka's preoccupation with sin and guilt is more general. Likewise the symbolism should not be interpreted in too narrow a Freudian sense. The heads of the horses thrust through the window or the worms in the wound may be phallic in significance, but the action of Kafka's work takes place in a more general area. He writes, in fact, of all human experience and thought, leaving the reader with a wide range of interpretation.

STANLEY COOPERMAN

From "Kafka's 'A Country Doctor'; Microcosm of Symbolism." *University of Kansas
City Review,* XXIV (Autumn, 1957), 75-80.
Reprinted by permission of the author and
the publisher.

"A Country Doctor," like most dream literature, is rooted firmly
in symbolism—so firmly, indeed, that any certain dichotomy between
the literal and the symbolic vanishes. It is necessary to accept a simple
dream narrative as the literal level of "A Country Doctor," since only
a dream can give it any literal meaning whatsoever. On this basis,
symbolic associations move within a psychological landscape and may
be interpreted psychoanalytically. We are introduced to a situation of
anxiety and impotence—the demands of duty cannot be fulfilled by
the doctor. Into this situation comes a potency figure—the groom—
offering what seems to be a solution. Notice the symbolism of birth
permeating the entire "pigsty" sequence (the darkness, the smell, the
groom crawling out on all fours calling "Brother" and "Sister"). This
culminates in the arrival of the horses, "their legs tucked close to
their bodies, each well-shaped head lowered like a camel's, by sheer
strength of buttocking squeezed out through the door hole which they
filled entirely."

The groom, then, is an ambivalent figure; on the one hand, he
aids the doctor by providing "Brother and Sister" and the means for
fulfilling duty; on the other, he is a "brute" who subjects Rose to her
"inescapable fate"—sexual violation. Rose, later called "the pretty girl
who had lived in my home for years almost without my noticing her,"
is a mother figure, domesticity, the love-object, and "servant." In a
sudden and terrible insight, the doctor becomes aware of the violation
of this mother figure ("I could just hear the door of my house splitting and bursting as the groom charged at it").

At that moment time is destroyed, the doctor is plunged back
into the timelessness of the unconscious, and he meets himself as a
youth—the boy with a wound. Here the atmosphere is one of disgust:
"The air was almost unbreathable, I wanted to push open a window."
This is a phrase which appears in many of Kafka's works.

At first this aspect of himself—this youth—seems well, but the
doctor is uncomfortable in his diagnosis. The family—especially the

father—oppresses him. The situation finally becomes one with obvious Oedipus overtones, as well as self-defense of potency: "In the narrow confines of the old man's mind I felt ill; that was my only reason for refusing the drink. The mother stood by the bedside and cajoled me toward it." On his second examination the doctor discovers the boy's wound, the Oedipus fixation ("a fine wound is all I brought into the world, that was my sole endowment"), and he succumbs to an intense feeling of guilt and failure. He is guilty of the rape of Rose because he has left her to the groom's lust. And he is also guilty—a failure—because he is unable to effect a cure.

The doctor feels completely isolated as the family and friends stare at him: "The family and the village elders stripped my clothes off me; a school choir with the teacher at[78] the head of it stood before the house." Religion cannot help him, his sin is too great ("the parson sits at home and unravels his vestments"). He must get back to Rose and combat the groom; he must escape from the family and the nightmare of religious sanctions ("O be joyful, all you patients..."). The result, however, is impotence. He cannot return, or compete with the lustful tyranny of the groom: "Like old men we crawled through the snowy wastes...in my house the disgusting groom is raging; Rose is his victim; I do not want to think about it any more...I cannot reach it." The doctor's narration ends on a note of complete impotency, and the dream stops.

This—a slice of dream life—is one of many possible psychological interpretations. However, it by no means limits the meanings of "A Country Doctor," since the story is rich in associations operating through, but beyond the literal dream level. From another standpoint, the story need not be considered in terms of psychology, but rather as a poetic evocation of the individual buffeted by chaos in an age where all outlines are blurred, and faith has turned to frost. The basic conflict, as in "The Trial," may be considered that of evil breaking suddenly into a rational, well-ordered life (perhaps a life which is over-regulated: "I was the district doctor and did my duty to the uttermost") and finally paralyzing it. The doctor is impotent when faced with the Sacred Wound—which, as Herbert Tauber points out, is the "awakened consciousness of the shattered condition of life."

Viewed in this light, the story becomes a symbolic restatement of the classic existential situation. On the one hand, we have a respectable and adjusted life; on the other, the swift insight, the crisis erupting within the placidly flowing sequence of "duties" and prosaic tasks. "I could see no way out," the doctor cries, and his words are an echo of the philosophers of crisis from Kierkegaard to Sartre.

Suddenly, without warning, the dark, irrational and diabolic forces represented by the beast-groom and the great horses take command. They drive the doctor deeply and instantaneously face to face with the insoluble—the "fear and trembling"—the moment when reasons fail, when "the center will not hold," when nothing is left but the scarlet wound—the beautiful wound—of awareness.

Rose's rape by the dark force of the groom represents the smashing of all that is near, protecting, feminine. But the guilt is strongly the doctor's in this violation; he has failed to realize the true value of Rose ("the pretty girl who had lived in my house for years without my noticing her"); everyday life has become formulistic, conventional, devoid of passion or awareness. As a result of this failure, the doctor is incapable of coping with the crisis when it comes—again, like the other isolated heroes (or victims) of existential literature. His failure delivers him to the disgusting wound and the bitter cold.

Faced with the wound (which represents his own ruined state and so cannot be cured) the doctor is isolated, completely alone before a[79] suddenly meaningless and hostile universe. The traditional answers are gone; they can no longer serve ("the parson sits at home and unravels his vestments"). Although the secular self must be relied upon ("the doctor is supposed to be omnipotent"), it provides neither meaning nor answer ("old country doctor that I am"), and, when the usual prosaic days and nights are shattered ("bereft of my servant girl"), there is nothing but sterility, the empty shell of what once were solutions ("strip his clothes off; then he'll heal us...O be joyful all you patients").

The nightmare ending is the doctor's chaotic spiritual state after meeting the Wound: a wasteland of panicked effort and treadmill motion, a vain attempt to prevent the inevitable crisis. He is caught, now, between "neither—nor" in a ruined secularism ("earthly vehicle"), driven by a desperate necessity for something beyond himself ("unearthly horses"). But it is too late; he is incapable of making the choice made by those who meet the Wound but who arrive finally at acceptance through faith. And so he rides through the snowy wastes, the nightmare storm, an absurd and anguished figure ("I cannot reach it") in a shattered world ("It cannot be made good, not ever").

The two interpretations I have presented concern the same work, and in addition rely to a great extent on the same symbols. But they are not mutually exclusive; in the symbolic art of Kafka two methods of criticism may, and indeed must, occupy the same space at the same time. Kafka is ambiguous and difficult, but his material—the stuff of the human soul—would be violated if he presented a single dimension of meaning. The work has many truths, a weaving and reweaving of many themes, and it cannot be approached bluntly or singlemindedly. We must synthesize, separate and reform with every method at our disposal, without sneering at one method or completely discounting another. This may involve considerable difficulty. It has often been pointed out, however, that in the art of reading fiction, as in the art of living, our satisfactions increase as we are willing to hazard our resources.[80]

## 8. WILLIAM BLAKE—"The Mental Traveller"

From *Poetry and Prose of William Blake,* edited by Geoffrey Keynes. London: Nonesuch Library, 1927.

I travel'd thro' a Land of Men,
A Land of Men & Women too,
And heard & saw such dreadful things
As cold Earth wanderers never knew.

For there the Babe is born in joy
That was begotten in dire woe;
Just as we Reap in joy the fruit
Which we in bitter tears did sow.[110]

And if the Babe is born a Boy
He's given to a Woman Old,
Who nails him down upon a rock,
Catches his shrieks in cups of gold.

She binds iron thorns around his head,
She pierces both his hands & feet,
She cuts his heart out at his side
To make it feel both cold & heat.

Her fingers number every Nerve,
Just as a Miser counts his gold;
She lives upon his shrieks & cries,
And she grows young as he grows old.

Till he becomes a bleeding youth,
And she becomes a Virgin bright;
Then he rends up his Manacles
And binds her down for his delight.

He plants himself in all her Nerves,
Just as a Husbandman his mould;
And she becomes his dwelling place
And Garden fruitful seventy fold.

An aged Shadow, soon he fades,
Wand'ring round an Earthly Cot,
Full filled all with gems & gold
Which he by industry had got.

And these are the gems of the Human Soul,
The rubies & pearls of a lovesick eye,
The countless gold of the akeing heart,
The martyr's groan & the lover's sigh.

They are his meat, they are his drink;
He feeds the Beggar & the Poor
And the wayfaring Traveller:
For ever open is his door.[111]

His grief is their eternal joy;
They make the roofs & walls to ring;
Till from the fire on the hearth
A little Female Babe does spring.

And she is all of solid fire
And gems & gold, that none his hand
Dares stretch to touch her Baby form,
Or wrap her in his swaddling-band.

But She comes to the Man she loves,
If young or old, or rich or poor;
They soon drive out the aged Host,
A Beggar at another's door.

He wanders weeping far away,
Untill some other take him in;
Oft blind & age-bent, sore distrest,
Untill he can a Maiden win.

And to allay his freezing Age
The Poor Man takes her in his arms;
The Cottage fades before his sight,
The Garden & its lovely Charms.

The Guests are scatter'd thro' the land,
For the Eye altering alters all;
The Senses roll themselves in fear,
And the flat Earth becomes a Ball;

The stars, sun, Moon, all shrink away,
A desart vast without a bound,
And nothing left to eat or drink,
And a dark desart all around.

The honey of her Infant lips,
The bread & wine of her sweet smile,
The wild game of her roving Eye,
Does him to Infancy beguile;[112]

For as he eats & drinks he grows
Younger & younger every day;
And on the desart wild they both
Wander in terror & dismay.

Like the wild Stag she flees away,
Her fear plants many a thicket wild;
While he pursues her night & day,
By various arts of Love beguil'd,

By various arts of Love & Hate,
Till the wide desart planted o'er
With Labyrinths of wayward Love,
Where roam the Lion, Wolf & Boar,

Till he becomes a wayward Babe,
And she a weeping Woman Old.
Then many a Lover wanders here;
The Sun & Stars are nearer roll'd.

The trees bring forth sweet Extacy
To all who in the desert roam;
Till many a City there is Built,
And many a pleasant Shepherd's home.

But when they find the frowning Babe,
Terror strikes thro' the region wide:
They cry "The Babe! the Babe is born!"
And flee away on Every side.

For who dares touch the frowning form,
His arm is wither'd to its root;
Lions, Boars, Wolves, all howling flee,
And every Tree does shed its fruit.

And none can touch that frowning form,
Except it be a Woman Old;
She nails him down upon the Rock,
And all is done as I have told.[113]


## W. M. ROSSETTI

In *The Poetical Works of William Blake, Lyrical and Miscellaneous,* edited by William Michael Rossetti, London: George Bell and Sons, 1890.

The "Mental Traveller" indicates an explorer of mental phæ-nomena. The mental phænomenon here symbolized seems to be the career of any great Idea or intellectual movement—as, for instance, Christianity, chivalry, art, &c.—represented as going through the stages of—1, birth; 2, adversity and persecution; 3, triumph and maturity; 4, decadence through over-ripeness; 5, gradual transformation, under new conditions, into another renovated Idea, which again has to pass through all the same stages. In other words, the poem represents the action and re-action of Ideas upon society, and of society upon Ideas.
*Argument of the stanzas.* 2, The Idea, conceived with pain, is born amid enthusiasm. 3, If of masculine, enduring nature, it falls under the control and ban of the already existing state of society (the woman old). 5, As the Idea[184] developes, the old society becomes moulded into a new society (the old woman grows young). 6, The Idea, now free and dominant, is united to society, as it were in wed-lock. 8, It gradually grows old and effete, living now only upon the spiritual treasures laid up in the days of its early energy. 10, These still subserve many purposes of practical good, and outwardly the Idea is in its most flourishing estate, even when sapped at its roots. 11, The halo of authority and tradition, or prestige, gathering round the Idea, is symbolized in the resplendent babe born on his heart. 13, This prestige deserts the Idea itself, and attaches to some individual, who usurps the honour due only to the Idea (as we may see in the case of papacy, royalty, &c.); and the Idea is eclipsed by its own very prestige, and assumed living representative. 14, The Idea wanders homeless till it can find a new community to mould ("until he can a maiden win"). 15 to 17, Finding whom, the Idea finds itself also living

under strangely different conditions. 18, The Idea is now "beguiled to
infancy"—becomes a *new* Idea, in working upon a fresh community,
and under altered conditions. 20, Nor are they yet thoroughly at one;
she flees away while he pursues. 22, Here we return to the first state
of the case. The Idea starts upon a new course—is a babe; the society
it works upon has become an old society—no longer a fair virgin, but an
aged woman. 24, The Idea seems so new and unwonted that, the
nearer it is seen, the more consternation it excites. 26, None can deal
with the Idea so as to develope it to the full, except the old society
with which it comes into contact; and this can deal with it only by
misusing it at first, whereby (as in the previous stage, at the opening
of the poem) it is to be again disciplined into ultimate triumph.[185]

## S. FOSTER DAMON

From *William Blake, His Philosophy and
Symbols*. Boston: Houghton Mifflin, 1924.

*The Mental Traveller* represents very definitely the life of the
Mystic, in . . . five stages. . . . These 'states,' as Blake called them,
are always in existence. . . . In *The Mental Traveller* they are represented as recurring in a vast cycle.

Blake begins, as was his custom, with the Fall, or 'Experience,'
since the State of Innocence is not self-conscious. A child is born, Orc,
the spirit of Revolt; the child which is begot in pain, but brought
forth with joy. As usual, before he can gather strength, he is repressed
and tortured by the 'Woman Old,' who is the Shadowy Female, Vala,
the goddess of Material Nature. His head (intellect) is circumscribed
with the crown of thorns; his heart (emotion) is extirpated, and the
whole crucifixion is re-enacted. Society feeds upon his agony, unconsciously growing younger as he grows more mature.

Then the next stage, the New Life, appears. Orc or Revolt
breaks loose, organizes the world after his own youthful will, and establishes his own family, or system of things. From his previous suffering and his spiritual labours, he has amassed the gems and gold of
'treasures in heaven,' which are freely given to all comers. 'His grief is
their eternal joy.'

But this cannot last. He is growing old; and other errors are
upon him. From his own hospitality (hearth—the liberality of his
opinions), an established code of conduct springs up  a Church, outward religion. This is the 'Female Babe,' so sacred that none dare

touch her. In Blake's later symbolism, she is named Rahab. She chooses her own paramour (ideal), and they drive the 'aged Host' away; they cast out the original impulse which was the beginning of their Church. And thus the Dark Night of the Soul is reached.

The Dark Night is spent in uniting the outcast with his Emanation.[131] Orc is no longer Orc: he is rather Los seeking Enitharmon. In brief, the Man must be made whole. The search is bitter. He explores the world by means of science (stanzas 16 and 17), and all joy flees. But his Emanation (who might also be named Jerusalem) is nearby. She flees from him; he pursues her. Gradually they become accustomed to each other; in their 'various arts of love,' he is regenerated again, while she grows more mature.

Thus the ultimate stage of the Mystic Way is reached; which Blake also identifies with the first stage, Innocence. Again the instinctive, pastoral existence appears in their Unitive life.

But it is not final, for nothing is final. Jerusalem becomes Vala; spiritual freedom becomes aged into the outward form of Nature; and again the Man takes on the form of Orc, the 'Frowning Babe,' ready again to revolt against any stagnation of the universe.[132]

## MONA WILSON

> From *The Life of William Blake*. New York: Jonathan Cape and Robert Ballou, 1932. Reprinted by permission of The Nonesuch Press, Ltd., London.

"The Mental Traveller" presents a fascinating problem, of which no satisfactory solution has yet been offered. Damon identifies the mental traveller with the mystic and endeavours to trace the five stages of the mystic way, but, even if this part of his argument carried conviction, the one thing clear about the poem is that it is dealing with a cycle. The mystic way is not a cycle: it is a figure for progress towards a definite goal through five states or regions traversed by every mystic. . . .[156]

Another explanation may be tentatively suggested. The dichotomy of male and female throughout the poem is analogous to that of spectre and emanation. The old woman ill-treats the frowning babe who, as youth, "binds her down for his delight." The female babe is pursued by her lover. There is a continuing cycle with no true and harmonious union. The frowning babe suggests Orc, the spirit of Revolt, and the "little female babe," too precious to be touched,

moral and religious ideals. Does Blake . . . here deny the possibility
of progress in the world of space and time, since it seems to him to
consist only in the vain and fruitless alternation of revolutionary and
of moral and religious ideals, which in their turn beguile mankind
with false hopes?[157]

JOYCE CARY

> From *The Horse's Mouth* [1944]. Harper's
> Modern Classics. New York: Harper &
> Brothers, 1959. Copyright 1944 by Joyce Cary.
> Reprinted by permission of the publisher.

If, while I am dictating this memoir, to my honorary secretary,
who has got the afternoon off from the cheese counter, I may make
a personal explanation, which won't be published anyhow; I never
meant to be an artist. You say, who does. But I even meant not to be
an artist because I'd lived with one and I couldn't forget seeing
my father, a little gray-bearded old man, crying one day in the garden.
I don't know why he was crying. He had a letter in his hand; perhaps
it was to tell him that the Academy had thrown out three more Jimson
girls in three more Jimson gardens. I hated art when I was young,
and I was very glad to get the chance of going into an office. My
Mother's cousin, down at Annbridge, near Exmoor, had pity on us,
and took me into his country office. He had an engineering business.
When I came to London in '99, I was a regular clerk. I had a bowler,
a home, a nice little wife, a nice little baby, and a bank account. I
sent money to my mother every week, and helped my sister. A nice
happy respectable young man. I enjoyed life in those days.

But one day when I was sitting in our London office on Bank-
side, I dropped a blot on an envelope; and having nothing to do
just then, I pushed it about with my pen to try and make it look more
like a face. And the next thing was I was drawing figures in red and
black, on the same envelope. And from that moment I was done for.
Everyone was very sympathetic. The boss sent for me at the end of
the month and said, "I'm sorry, Jimson, but I've had another com-
plaint about your work. I warned you last week that this was your
last chance [55] But I don't want to sack you. You might never get
another job, and what is going to happen then to your poor young
wife and her baby. Look here, Jimson, I like you, everyone likes you.
You can trust me, I hope. Tell me what's gone wrong. Never mind

what it is. I'm not going to be stupid about it. Is it debts? You haven't been gambling, I suppose. Is your petty cash all right? Take a couple of days off and think it over."

But of course I couldn't think of anything except how to get my figures right. I started as a Classic. About 1800 was my period. And I was having a hell of a time with my anatomy and the laws of perspective.

> Her fingers numbered every nerve
> Just as a miser counts his gold.

I spent my holiday at a life class, and when I went back to the firm, I didn't last two days. Of course, I was a bad case. I had a bad infection, galloping art. I was at it about twelve hours a day and I had a picture in the old Water Color Society that year. Very classical. Early Turner. Almost Sandby.

My wife was nearly starving, and we had pawned most of the furniture, but what did I care. Well, of course I worried a bit. But I felt like an old master. So I was, very old. I was at about the period when my poor old father was knocked out. I'd gone through a lot to get my experience, my technique, and I was going to paint like that all my life. It was the only way to paint. I knew all the rules. I could turn you off a picture, all correct, in an afternoon. Not that it was what you call a work of imagination. It was just a piece of stuff. Like a nice sausage. Lovely forms. But I wasn't looking any more than a sausage machine. I was the old school, the old Classic, the old church.

> An aged shadow soon he fades
> Wandering round an earthly cot
> Full filled all with gems and gold
> Which he by industry has got.

I even sold some pictures, nice water colors of London churches. But one day I happened to see a Manet. Because some chaps were[56] laughing at it. And it gave me the shock of my life. Like a flash of lightning. It skinned my eyes for me, and when I came out I was a different man. And I saw the world again, the world of color. By Gee and Jay, I said, I was dead, and I didn't know it.

> Till from the fire on the hearth
> A little female babe did spring.

I felt her jump. But of course the old classic put up a fight. It was the Church against Darwin, the old Lords against the Radicals. And I was the battleground. I had a bad time of it that year. I couldn't paint at all. I botched my nice architectural water colors with impressionist smudges. And I made such a mess of my impressionist landscapes that I couldn't bear to look at them myself. Of course, I

lost all my kind patrons. The first time, but not the last. But that
didn't upset me. What gave me the horrors was that I couldn't paint.
I was so wretched that I hardly noticed when we were sold up and my
wife went off, or even when my mother died. It was a good thing she
did die, or she would have had to go to the workhouse. And really,
I suppose she died of a broken heart at seeing her youngest go down
the drain.

Of course I was a bit upset about it. I thought my heart was
broken. But even at the funeral I couldn't tell whether I was in
agony about my poor mother's death, or about my awful pictures.
For I didn't know what to do with myself. My old stuff made me sick.
In the living world that I'd suddenly discovered, it looked like a rotten
corpse that somebody had forgotten to bury. But the new world
wouldn't come to my hand. I couldn't catch it, that lovely vibrating
light, that floating tissue of color. Not local color but aerial color, a
sensation of the mind; that maiden vision.

> And she was all of solid fire
> And gems and gold, that none his hand
> Dares stretch to touch her baby form
> Or wrap her in her swaddling band
> But she comes to the man she loves
> If young or old, or rich or poor,
> They soon drive out the aged host
> A beggar at another's door.[57]

I got her after about four years. At last I got rid of every bit
of the grand style, the old church. I came to the pure sensation
without a thought in my head. Just a harp in the wind. And a lot of
my stuff was good. Purest go-as-you-please.

And I sold it too. I made more money then than I ever did again.
People like impressionism. Still do, because it hasn't any idea in it.
Because it doesn't ask anything from them—because it's just a nice
sensation, a little song. Good for the drawing-room. Tea cakes.

But I got tired of sugar. I grew up.

And when they showed me a room full of my own confections, I
felt quite sick. Like grandpa brought to a nursery tea. As for icing any
more eclairs, I couldn't bring myself to it. I gradually stopped painting and took to arguing instead. Arguing and reading and drinking;
politics, philosophy and pub-crawling; all the things chaps do who
can't do anything else. Who've run up against the buffers. And I got
in such a low state that I was frightened of the dark. Yes, as every
night approached, I fairly trembled. I knew what it would be like. A
vacuum sucking one's skull into a black glass bottle; all in silence. I
used to go out and get drunk, to keep some kind of illumination going
in my dome.

> He wanders weeping far away
> Until some other take him in
> Oft blind and age bent, sore distrest
> Until he can a maiden win.

And then I began to make a few little pencil sketches, studies, and I took Blake's Job drawings out of somebody's bookshelf and peeped into them and shut them up again. Like a chap who's fallen down the cellar steps and knocked his skull in and opens a window too quick, on something too big. I did a little modeling and tried my hand at composition. I found myself wandering round the marbles at the Brit. Mus. and brooding over the torso of some battered old Venus without any head, arms or legs, and a kind of smallpox all over the rest of her. Trying to find out why her lumps seemed so much more important than any bar-lady with a gold fringe; or water lily pool.

> And to allay his freezing age
> The poor man takes her in his arms;
> The cottage fades before his sight,
> The garden and its lovely charms.[58]

Good-by impressionism, anarchism, nihilism, Darwinism, and the giddy goat, now staggering with rheumatism. Hail, the new Classic. But you might say it was in the air about them, at the turn of the century when the young Liberals were beginning to bend away from *laissez-faire* and to look for their Marx, and science took a mathematical twist, and the old biologists found themselves high and dry among the has-beens, blowing their own trumpets because no one else would do it for them. And I studied Blake and Persian carpets and Raphael's cartoons and took to painting walls.

But I rubbed most of them out again. They looked like bad imitations of the old masters; or made-up, pompous stuff. They didn't belong to the world I lived in. A new world with a new formal character.

I had a worse time than the last time. I drank more than ever. To keep up my self-respect. But it didn't have the same effect. I was gloomy even in drink. I didn't seem to be getting anywhere very much. If there was anywhere to get to.

> The stars, sun, moon all shrink away,
> A desert vast without a bound,
> And nothing left to eat or drink
> And a dark desert all around.

And of course no one would buy anything. They didn't know what I was driving at. I probably didn't know myself. I was like a chap under witchcraft. I didn't know if I was after a real girl or a succubus in the shape of a fairy.

> The honey of her infant lips
> The bread and wine of her sweet smile
> The wild game of her roving eye
> Does him to infancy beguile.
> Like the wild stag she flees away
> Her fear plants many a thicket wild
> While he pursues her night and day
> By various wiles of love beguiled.

The job is always to get hold of the form you need. And nothing is so coy. Cezanne and the cubists, when they chucked up old doddering impressionism, caught their maidens. But the cubists did it too easily. They knocked them down with hammers and tied up the fragments[59] with wire. Most of 'em died and the rest look more like bird cages than forms of intuition and delight. Cezanne was the real classic. The full band. Well, I suppose poor old Cezanne did more wandering in the desert even than me—he wandered all his life. The maiden fled away so fast that he hardly caught her once a year. And then she soon dodged off again.

> By various arts of love and hate
> Till the wide desert planted o'er
> With labyrinths of wayward love
> Where roams the lion, the wolf, the boar.

I painted some cubists myself once and thought I'd got my maiden under padlock at last. No more chase, no more trouble. The formula of a new classical art. And of course a lot of other people thought so too. A lot of 'em are painting cubistry even now; and making a steady income and sleeping quiet in their beds and keeping their wives in fancy frocks and their children at school.

> The trees bring forth sweet ecstasy
> To all who in the desert roam
> Till many a city there is built
> And many a pleasant shepherd's home.

Cubiston. On the gravel. All services. Modern democracy. Organized comforts. The Socialist state. Bureaucratic liberalism. Scientific management. A new security. But I didn't live there long myself. I got indigestion. I got a nice girl in my eye, or perhaps she got after me. After 1930, even Hickson stopped buying me. And tonight it seems that I can't paint at all. I've lost sight of the maiden altogether. I wander weeping far away, until some other take me in. The police. It's quite time. I'm getting too old for this rackety life.[60]

# SUGGESTIONS FOR STUDY

NOTE: *The following suggestions for study include questions on the selections, topics for papers, and recommended additional readings. Suggestions marked with an asterisk (\*) call for reading and research of material not included in this manual.*

## Part One: The Nature of Symbolism

### Preliminaries

1. One of the main purposes of Part One is to give you the tools by means of which you can form your own definitions of *symbol*. As you read the selections, underline or list separately as many one-sentence definitions of *symbol* as you can find. Note also any distinctions between different types of symbols. These lists will prove useful later.

2. You will notice that a good many of the writers represented here define *symbol* and *symbolism* by distinguishing these words from related terms. With the help of your instructor, a good dictionary, or, preferably, a modern glossary of literary terms such as M. H. Abrams's *A Glossary of Literary Terms* (New York: Rinehart, 1957) or Joseph T. Shipley, ed., *Dictionary of World Literature* (New York: Philosophical Library, 1943), write definitions of the following:

| | |
|---|---|
| Allegory | Myth |
| Archetype | Objective correlative |
| Emblem | Sign |
| Image | Simile |
| Metaphor | Symbol |

You will probably want to revise some of your definitions after you have read the selections, but a preliminary knowledge of these terms will help you better understand the readings.

## 1. The Boundaries of Symbolism

1. Dickens is the author of the first selection; Thomas Gradgrind is the unidentified speaker. Does Dickens agree with Gradgrind? Analyze the style carefully. Find examples of similes, metaphors, and symbols. What is the function of the cave-cellarage-warehouse imagery? Why is the word *square* repeated several times? Is the name Gradgrind a symbol? On the basis of such an analysis, what conclusions would you draw concerning the ways in which Dickens implies an attitude towards Gradgrind without explicitly stating it?

2. Briefly state the thesis of Saul Bellow's essay. Is the main target of his attack symbolism itself, the overemphasis on symbolism in modern criticism, or the excesses of certain ingenious symbol-hunters? What strengths and weaknesses do you find in his argument? Is Bellow a Gradgrind?

3. Emerson, Symons, Feibleman, and Wilson offer four different justifications for symbolism. What are they? Which do you find the strongest argument? Which is the weakest? Would each of the four writers accept the justifications given by the other three? Can you accept all four, or must you choose among them?

4. It is apparent from the readings in this section that a writer's attitude towards symbolism depends on his concept of reality. Gradgrind, Bellow, Emerson, and Wilson seem to take attitudes towards reality that emphasize, respectively, the material, the emotional, the spiritual, and the relative. Which seems to provide the best basis for literary criticism?

5. George Santayana concludes his novel *The Last Puritan* (New York: Scribner's, 1936) with this sentence: "After life is over and the world has gone up in smoke, what realities might the spirit in us still call its own without illusion save the form of those very illusions which have made up our story?" Explain. Write an essay in which you show that Santayana's statement may or may not be applied to literature in general.

\* 6. Mark Twain's short novel *The Mysterious Stranger* deals with the relation of dream to reality. Read the story, then write a paper which not only explains the symbols of the story, but also shows how the story provides a good introduction to the problem of the relation of symbolism to an author's view of reality.

\* 7. The following short stories deal with an artist's attempt to turn either the real or the ideal into a work of art:

Nathaniel Hawthorne—"The Artist of the Beautiful"
Honore de Balzac—"The Hidden Masterpiece"
Henry James—"The Madonna of the Future"
Henry James—"The Real Thing"
Albert Camus—"The Artist at Work," in *Exile and the Kingdom* (1958).

Read one or several of these stories, then write a paper showing how the fiction does or does not illuminate the problem of art versus reality.

## 2. Intention—Standard or Fallacy?

1. In this section J. E. Spingarn has been chosen to represent what H. L. Mencken named the "Goethe-Carlyle-Croce-Spingarn theory" which asks these three questions about a work of literature:

(1) What has the author tried to do?
(2) How well has he succeeded in doing it?
(3) Was it worth doing?

Do the selections that follow Spingarn's destroy the validity of these questions as effective standards for the evaluation of art? If you think so, what three questions would you ask instead?

2. Do all the writers in this section, including Spingarn, seem to agree with Von Abele that "the only 'intention' with which we, as readers, have any business is what might be called 'intention realized' "? Explain and evaluate.

3. Defend or dispute Wimsatt and Beardsley's statement that "practical messages . . . are more abstract than poetry." Compare an advertisement with a poem on the basis of the abstract versus the concrete, then consider what light your comparison throws on the question of intention as a standard for evaluation.

4. Can you reconcile Frost's statement that a poem must be ". . . judged for whether any original intention it had has been strongly spent or weakly lost" with "Calculation is usually no part in the first step in any walk"? In studying an author's intentions, where would you begin?

5. William Faulkner once rated American writers of his generation in this order: Thomas Wolfe, Faulkner, John Dos Passos, Erskine Caldwell, and Ernest Hemingway. Asked to explain why he rated Wolfe first and Hemingway last, Faulkner replied: "I made my estimate on the gallantry of the failure, not on the success or validity of the

work. . . . I meant only that Hemingway had sense enough to find a method which he could control and didn't need or didn't have to, wasn't driven by his private demon to waste himself in trying to do more than that. So, he has done consistently probably the most solid work of all of us. But it wasn't the splendid magnificent bust that Wolfe made in trying to put the whole history of the human heart on the head of a pin, you might say."—Frederick L. Gwynn and Joseph L. Blotner, eds., *Faulkner in the University* (Charlottesville: University of Virginia Press, 1959), pp. 143-144. Do you feel that this is a valid standard for judging novelists? Is it a valid standard for judging novels?

* 6. Compare a story or novel by Henry James with (1) the author's statement of his intentions before the story was composed—see *The Notebooks of Henry James,* ed. F. O. Matthiessen and Kenneth Murdock (New York: Oxford University Press, 1947)—and (2) his post-composition view of his intentions as given in the Prefaces of the New York Edition of his works—see *The Art of the Novel: Critical Prefaces by Henry James,* ed. R. P. Blackmur (New York: Scribner's, 1934).

* 7. Analyze D. H. Lawrence's novel, *Sons and Lovers,* in terms of the author's statement of intentions as given in his *Letters,* ed. Aldous Huxley (New York: Viking Press, 1932), pp. 78-79. Your instructor can suggest other works of literature for which the author's statements of intention are available.

*Additional readings:* See "The Problem of Intentions," in R. W. Stallman, ed , *The Critic's Notebook* (Minneapolis: University of Minnesota Press, 1950), pp. 205-254; and Bibliography, pp. 289-293.

## 3. Definitions and Touchstones

1. M. H. Abrams cites several examples of the rose as symbol which you may wish to compare with the Rose of Kafka's short story, "The Country Doctor" (Part Two, Problem 7). Is Kafka's Rose a "public symbol" or a "private symbol"? See also Walcutt's discussion of the rose symbol in Housman's "To an Athlete Dying Young," Part One, Section 4.

* 2. Additional examples of the rose as symbol are given in Harold Bayley, *The Lost Language of Symbolism* (New York: Barnes and Noble, 1951), Vol. II, pp. 224-265; and Barbara Seward, *The Symbolic Rose* (New York: Columbia University Press, 1960). Read either or both of these discussions and some of the examples cited, then write a paper on the rose as symbol, showing how different writers use the same symbol in very different ways.

3. What basic attitudes towards reality and symbolism (see above, section 1, question 4) would you attribute to Coleridge, Carlyle, Baudelaire, Yeats, and Lawrence? Which of the four justifications of symbolism (see above, section 1, question 3) would each be most likely to accept?

4. Carlyle's Professor Teufelsdröckh says, "Thus certain *Iliads*, and the like, have in three thousand years, attained quite new significance." Relate this to the problem of intention, and consider the effect of time upon the interpretation of literature.

5. Baudelaire's sonnet "Correspondences" is a symbolic poem about symbolism. Analyze the poem in detail and show what new concept of symbolism it seems to introduce. Consider especially

> And man goes through this forest, with familiar
> eyes of symbols watching him.

6. What further light does the incident of the dropped pen in Yeats's "The Symbolism of Poetry" throw on the problem of intention? What is "inspiration"? What part does it play in the creative process?

* 7. Discuss one of Lawrence's literary works, such as the poem "Snake" or the short story, "The Rocking-Horse Winner," on the basis of his distinctions between allegory, symbol, and myth.

8. Do you feel that Joyce's three qualities of art suggest a valid critical aproach to literature? In what ways is his "epiphany" similar to or different from "symbol"?

9. W. H. Auden says: "A symbol is felt to be such before any possible meaning is consciously recognized; i.e. an object or event which is felt to be more important than the reason can immediately explain is symbolic"—*The Enchaféd Flood, or The Romantic Iconography of the Sea* (New York: Random House, 1950), p. 65. Do you feel that this is an adequate definition of *symbol?*

## 4. The Interpretation of Symbols

1. State in expository terms Melville's attitude towards symbolic interpretation as you find it implied in "The Doubloon." (You may wish to compare your statement with Melville's own more expository discussion in "The Whiteness of the Whale," Chapter 42 of *Moby-Dick.*)

2. Is the essay by Walcutt in any way a reply to the kind of interpretation of symbols presented in Melville's "The Doubloon"? On the basis of your understanding of the previous readings, defend or attack Walcutt's position on the limits of symbolic interpretation

3. Compare Mary McCarthy's attack on excesses of symbol-hunting with that of Saul Bellow. Which is the more convincing?

4. Do you agree with Mary McCarthy's view that intentionally planted symbols are an indication of poor art? Can you reconcile this view with Bellow's statement, "A true symbol is substantial, not accidental"?

5. Mary McCarthy admits that a writer does not always know beforehand just what he intends to accomplish in a story, which is always for him, as well as for the reader, "a little act of discovery." If this is true, then do you feel that the author is a better or more final authority on the meaning of a work of literature than is the reader?

\* 6. Read Mary McCarthy's story, "Artists in Uniform" (Harper's Magazine, CCVI [March, 1953]), then decide whether you as reader would feel justified in going beyond her explanation as author in interpreting the story.

7. Now that you have completed the readings in Part One, decide whether or not it is ever possible for criticism to be completely objective or scientific. If not, do you feel that anything goes—that one man's interpretation is as good as any other's? What checks would you suggest to keep criticism from becoming entirely relativistic or impressionistic?

8. Look back over your list of definitions of *symbol* (see above, p. 155, question 1). Can you find any underlying principle which all of these definitions—or most of them—seem to have in common? Using this principle as a basis, write your own one-sentence definition.

9. Test your definition by stating briefly how it differs from your understanding of the related terms listed above, p. 155, question 2. How would you revise these preliminary definitions? How many of them refer to types of symbols? Is *symbol* a term capable of including all the others, or would you subordinate *symbol* to some other?

10. List as many distinctions between types of symbols as you have found in the selections. Which seem to you particularly useful?

11. Write a paper in which you explain in detail your definition of *symbol*, showing in what ways it is similar to or different from the definitions offered by some of the writers in Part One. Give examples of true and false symbols, and work out a system of symbol classification which you feel would be useful in the interpretation of literature.

*Additional readings:* Probably the best introduction for the general reader to modern philosophical theories of symbolism is Susanne K. Langer, *Philosophy in a New Key: A Study in the Symbolism of Reason, Rite, and Art* (Cambridge: Harvard University Press, 1942)—also available in a paper-bound Mentor edition. Miss Langer's translation of Ernst Cassirer's *Language and Myth* (New York: Harper, 1946) presents in brief resumé the main conclusions in his monumental *The Philosophy of Symbolic Forms*, trans. Ralph Manheim (New Haven: Yale University Press, 1953-1957), 3 vols. Alfred North Whitehead's *Symbolism: Its Meaning and Effect* (New York: Macmillan, 1927) deals primarily with the impact of symbolism upon society. More difficult philosophical discussions of symbolism are the following: R. M. Eaton, *Symbolism and Truth: An Introduction to the Theory of Symbolism* (Cambridge: Harvard University Press, 1925); Wilbur Marshall Urban, *The Philosophy of Language and the Principles of Symbolism* (London: Allen and Unwin, 1939); and Charles W. Morris, *Signs, Language, and Behavior* (New York: Prentice-Hall, 1946).

Probably the best single book on literary symbolism in general—at least for the reader beginning a study of the subject—is William York Tindall's *The Literary Symbol* (New York: Columbia University Press, 1955). Other good introductions are the chapter "Symbols in Poetry" in Isabel C. Hungerland's *Poetic Discourse* (Berkeley: University of California Press, 1958), pp. 135-160; and the discussion of "Image, Metaphor, Symbol, and Myth" in René Wellek and Austin Warren, *The Theory of Literature* (New York: Harcourt, Brace and Company, 1949), pp. 190-218. More advanced students may wish to consult Northrop Frye, *Anatomy of Criticism* (Princeton, New Jersey: Princeton University Press, 1957), pp. 71-128; Charles Feidelson, *Symbolism and American Literature* (Chicago: University of Chicago Press, 1953); Philip Wheelwright, *The Burning Fountain: A Study in the Language of Symbolism* (Bloomington: Indiana University Press, 1954); Robin Skelton, "The Creation of Symbol," in his *The Poetic Pattern* (Berkeley: University of California Press, 1956), pp. 118-133; and Elder Olson, "A Dialogue on Symbolism," in R. S. Crane, ed., *Critics and Criticism: Ancient and Modern* (Chicago: University of Chicago Press, 1952), pp. 567-594. *The Journal of Aesthetics and Art Criticism* devoted its September, 1953, issue to a symposium on symbolism.

On the symbolic interpretation of fiction, three recent essays have been particularly influential: Harry Levin, *Symbolism and Fiction* (Charlottesville: University of Virginia Press, 1956)—reprinted in his *Contexts of Criticism* (Cambridge: Harvard University Press, 1957), pp. 190-207; Philip Rahv, "Fiction and the Criticism of Fiction," *Kenyon Review*, XVIII (Spring, 1956), 276-299; and Norman Friedman, "Criticism and the Novel," *Antioch Review*, XVIII (Fall, 1958), 343-370.

## Part Two: Problems in Symbolism

## 1. Humpty Dumpty

1. Knieger describes a class discussion of "Humpty Dumpty." Criticize this discussion on the basis of what you have learned about symbolism from the readings in Part One.

2. What reply could the anti-eggian make to the argument in the third paragraph that "Humpty Dumpty's eggness cannot be disputed"? Assuming, for the sake of argument, that Humpty Dumpty is not an egg, interpret the poem on the basis of internal evidence alone.

3. Interpret the symbolism in the following nursery rhymes:

I

This little piggy had roast beef.
This little piggy had none.
This little piggy went to market.
This little piggy stayed home.
And this little piggy went wee-wee all the way home.

II

Ride a cock-horse to Banbury Cross,
To see a fine lady upon a white horse;
Rings on her fingers and bells on her toes,
And she shall have music wherever she goes.

III

I had a little husband,
    No bigger than my thumb;
I put him in a pint-pot
    And there I bade him drum.
I bought a little horse
    That galloped up and down;
I bridled him, and saddled him
    And sent him out of town.
I gave him some garters
    To garter up his hose,
And a little silk handkerchief
    To wipe his pretty nose.

* 4. Using the above and other examples, write a paper on symbolism in nursery rhymes.

* 5. Robert Penn Warren's novel, *All the King's Men,* takes its title from "Humpty Dumpty." Analyze the novel in terms of the nursery rhyme.

* 6. Interpret the symbolism in a work of children's literature, such as Cinderella, Sleeping Beauty, or Beauty and the Beast; one of Grimm's fairy tales (see Joseph Campbell's "Folkloristic Commentary" in *Grimm's Fairy Tales* [New York: Pantheon Books, 1944], 831-864); or Lewis Carroll's *Alice in Wonderland* (compare your interpretation with William Empson's Freudian analysis, "Alice in Wonderland: The Child as Swain," in his *Some Versions of Pastoral* (1935).

## 2. Henry David Thoreau—A Hound, A Bay Horse, and a Turtledove

1. Consider the three quite different explanations offered by Thoreau himself. What do these tell you about the authority of the author in the interpretation of a work of literature? If the third explanation were proved to be valid, would it destroy the validity of other interpretations?

2. Using Walcutt's standards for symbolic interpretation, briefly evaluate the interpretations offered by Emerson, Burroughs, Jones, Van Doren, Girdler, Peairs, and Davidson as summarized by Harding. Which of these can be dismissed as subjective readings with too little evidence from the text? Which seem to be based on the most promising approaches?

3. To what extent would you qualify Harding's statement that "the individual critic is left free to interpret as he wishes"?

4. Here is Emerson's poem "Forerunners":

Long I followed happy guides,
I could never reach their sides;
Their step is forth, and, ere the day
Breaks up their leaguer, and away.
Keen my sense, my heart was young,
Right good-will my sinews strung,
But no speed of mine avails
To hunt upon their shining trails.
On and away, their hasting feet
Make the morning proud and sweet;
Flowers they strew,—I catch the scent;
Or tone of silver instrument
Leaves on the wind melodious trace;
Yet I could never see their face.
On eastern hills I see their smokes,
Mixed with mist by distant lochs.
I met many travellers
Who the road had surely kept;
They saw not my fine revellers,—
These had crossed them while they slept.
Some had heard their fair report,
In the country or the court.
Fleetest couriers alive
Never yet could once arrive,[85]
As they went or they returned,
At the house where these sojourned
Sometimes their strong speed they slacken,
Though they are not overtaken;

In sleep their jubilant troop is near,—
I tuneful voices overhear;
It may be in wood or waste,—
At unawares 't is come and past.
Their near camp my spirit knows
By signs gracious as rainbows.
I thenceforward and long after
Listen for their harp-like laughter,
And carry in my heart, for days,
Peace that hallows rudest ways.[86]

    —FROM *Poems*. Concord Edition.
    Boston: Houghton Mifflin, 1904.

Do you agree with Harding that this poem "hints of the combination of hound, horse, and dove"? What other parallels can you find between the poem and the passage by Thoreau? Ignoring the question of direct source, make a comparative analysis of the two works. Does the one throw light on the other if considered as parallels rather than cause and effect? (After you have done this, you may want to investigate the possibility of direct influence. If you can prove that one work definitely influenced the other, would you feel that this finally solves the riddle of the Thoreau passage?—See the debate between R. W. Stallman and F. W. Bateson on the question of sources in *College English*, XVII [1955-1956], 20-27, 131-135, 180.)

    * 5. Look up some of the other possible sources cited in the last section of Harding's notes, then write a paper showing what light these sources throw on the interpretation of Thoreau's passage.

## 3. Robert Frost—"Stopping by Woods on a Snowy Evening"

    1. What is the basic difference between the student interpretations quoted by Daniels and those offered by Walcutt (see above, pp. 39-42), Unger and O'Connor, and Ciardi? Can you find any indications of subjective reading in the Unger and O'Connor or Ciardi interpretations? Which seems to be more closely based on the text alone? Which is the more specific in the identification of symbols? Which is the more convincing?

    2. Some interpreters of the poem feel that the first two lines are an allusion to God, whose house in the village is the church. Would you accept this as a valid hypothesis? If so, interpret the remainder of the poem in this light.

    3. Reread the extract from Frost's essay, "The Constant Symbol" (Part One, Section 2), and, if possible, the entire essay, which contains some remarks on "Stopping by Woods on a Snowy Evening." Using Frost's essay as roughly equivalent to a statement of intention, analyze

the poem in terms of the three intentionalist questions (see above, p. 157).

4. Using the methods suggested by Walcutt, Unger and O'Connor, or Ciardi, read and interpret several other poems by Frost, such as "Birches," "Fire and Ice," "Mending Wall," and "After Apple-Picking." Does your analysis support Lionel Trilling's controversial assertion (See *Partisan Review,* Summer, 1959) that Frost's poetry is "terrifying"?

*Additional readings:* Charles W. Cooper and John Holmes, *Preface to Poetry* (New York: Harcourt, Brace and Company, 1946), pp. 605-607; Reginald L. Cook, *The Dimensions of Robert Frost* (New York: Rinehart, 1958), pp. 78-81; Charles A. McLaughlin, "Two Views of Poetic Unity," *University of Kansas City Review,* XXII (Summer, 1956), 309-316; Laurence Perrine, *Sound and Sense: An Introduction to Poetry* (New York: Harcourt, Brace and Company, 1956), pp. 124-125; Lawrance Thompson, *Fire and Ice: The Art of Robert Frost* (New York: Henry Holt, 1942), pp. 25-27.

## 4. Jonah and the Whale

1. Using the psalm in Chapter Two as your main text, determine Jonah's own symbolic interpretation of his experience.

2. Assuming that the author of the Book of Jonah was familiar with folklore of the kind recounted in the second selection, defend or criticize his omission of certain vivid and dramatic details. Do the omissions give the story more universality as poetic statement? Do they make it a better story?

3. Father Mapple's sermon may be studied as both an interpretation of the story of Jonah and a work of literature in its own right. To what extent is his interpretation based on the text of the Book of Jonah? Is he justified in trying to improve upon the Bible? Are his additions in keeping with the spirit of the original? Can Melville's "Jonah Historically Regarded" be read as a kind of comment on Father Mapple's sermon? Ignoring the source of the sermon, evaluate it as a work of literature. Would you agree with the assertion that this chapter of *Moby-Dick* can be read separately as a short story in which the subject is actually not Jonah or the moral lesson that may be derived from Jonah, but the creative process of art—that, in other words, this is a work of art about the creation of art? (Interpreted in this light, Henry James's short story, "The Birthplace," would provide an interesting comparison.)

4. Write a comparative evaluation of the Book of Jonah, the traditional Jewish lore, and Father Mapple's sermon as symbolic short stories.

* 5. George L. Robinson, in *The Twelve Minor Prophets* (New York: Harper, 1926), pp. 83-87, summarizes traditional interpretations of the Book of Jonah and says that they fall within three groups: the mythical, the historical, and the allegorical. Look up some of these earlier interpretations (see the bibliographical note in Robinson, p. 93) and discuss the merits and limitations of each of these approaches. In what category would you place the readings by Harold Watts and Erich Fromm?

* 6. When Jesus was asked for a "sign" by the Scribes and Pharisees, he replied: "An evil and adulterous generation seeketh after a sign; and there shall be no sign given to it, but the sign of the prophet Jonah. For as Jonah was three days and three nights in the whale's belly; so shall the Son of Man be three days and three nights in the heart of the earth. The men of Nineveh shall rise in judgment with this generation, and shall condemn it, because they repented at the teaching of Jonah; and, behold, a greater than Jonah is here." (Matthew, 12: 39-41; compare Luke, 11: 29-32). Write a paper comparing Jonah and Jesus.

* 7. The story of Jonah and the whale is an example of what folklorists call the "swallow story," other examples of which may be found in Longfellow's *Hiawatha* (Book VIII) and the fairy tale Little Red Riding Hood. See Joseph Campbell, *The Hero with a Thousand Faces* (New York: Pantheon Books, 1949), pp. 90-94, and write a paper comparing Jonah with some of the parallels. Or write a paper on the mythical or psychological significance of the "swallow story" in general.


## 5. Nathaniel Hawthorne—"Young Goodman Brown"

1. On the basis of the story alone, what would you say is Hawthorne's own concept of reality? Does it matter whether Goodman Brown merely dreamed the events or actually experienced them?

2. Von Abele (see above, p. 15) says that it is not difficult to exhaust the meanings of "Young Goodman Brown." On the basis of the interpretations presented here, do you agree?

3. Explain the importance of Warren's note on the source of the story. If Cotton Mather's *Wonders of the Invisible World* is "without doubt" Hawthorne's source, do you feel that it restricts possible interpretations of the story and thus disqualifies some of those offered here?

4. F. O. Matthiessen, in *American Renaissance: Art and Expression in the Age of Emerson and Whitman* (New York: Oxford University Press, 1941), p. 284, says, "that damaging pink ribbon obtrudes the labels of a confining allegory, and short-circuits the range of associ-

ation." Compare the interpretations of the pink ribbon offered by the critics in this section, then defend or criticize Matthiessen's statement.

5. Compare this story with Stephen Vincent Benet's "The Devil and Daniel Webster" or some other fictional treatment of a temptation by the devil, such as one of the literary treatments of the Faust legend.

* 6. Write your own interpretation of the symbols in another story by Hawthorne, such as "The Minister's Black Veil," "Rappaccini's Daughter," or "My Kinsman, Major Molyneux."

*Additional readings:* Caroline Gordon and Allen Tate, *The House of Fiction* (New York: Scribner's, 1950), pp. 36-39; Q. D. Leavis, "Hawthorne as Poet," *Sewanee Review,* LIX (Spring, 1951), 197-198; William Bysshe Stein, *Hawthorne's Faust: A Study of the Devil Archetype* (Gainesville: University of Florida Press, 1953), pp. 61-63; Thomas F. Walsh, Jr., "The Bedevilling of Young Goodman Brown," *Modern Language Quarterly,* XIX (December, 1958), 331-336; Norris Yates, "Mask and Dance Motifs in Hawthorne's Fiction," *Philological Quarterly,* XXXIV (January, 1955), 56-70.

## 6. James Joyce—"Clay"

1. "Clay" is a symbolic story *about* symbols. Explain the distinction between implicit and explicit symbols in the story, and analyze the story in terms of different levels of symbolism.

2. The three critics represented here hold quite different opinions of Maria—for Hudson, she is "death-in-life"; for Magalaner, she is a witch who lives in an asylum for delinquent women; and for Noon, she is something of a saint. Which of these views seems to be most justified by the story itself?

3. In "The Background to 'Dubliners,'" *The Listener,* LI (March 25, 1954), 526-527, Joyce's brother Stanislaus took issue with an American critic, presumably Magalaner, for finding in "Clay" three levels of significance: "Though such critics are quite at sea, they can still have the immense satisfaction of knowing that they have dived into deeper depths than the author they are criticizing ever sounded. I am in a position to state definitely that my brother had no such subtleties in mind when he wrote the story." If you were the critic in question, how would you reply to this comment?

4. Magalaner finds in the story evidence to support his view that Maria is both the Virgin Mary and a witch. Do these identifications contradict each other? Can you reconcile them in any way? Would it help to know Joyce's attitude towards religion, or would such information be irrelevant?

5. Interpret the story in terms of the three qualities of art stated by Joyce (see above, pp. 32-33). What is the epiphany of the story?

*Additional readings:* Cleanth Brooks, John T. Purser, and Robert Penn Warren, *An Approach to Literature,* Third Edition (New York: Appleton-Century-Crofts, 1952), pp. 137-140; Brewster Ghiselin, "The Unity of James Joyce's Dubliners," *Accent,* XVI (Spring, 1956), 75-88, and (Summer, 1956), 196-213; Richard Levin and Charles Shattuck, "First Flight to Ithaca: A New Reading of Joyce's 'Dubliners,'" in Seon Givens, ed., *James Joyce: Two Decades of Criticism* (New York: Vanguard Press, 1948), pp. 77-78.

## 7. Franz Kafka—"A Country Doctor"

1. What do the three critical readings offered here have in common? Granting the basic similarity, how do they differ? On the basis of what is now your understanding of the limits of symbolic interpretation, evaluate Busacca's four "samplers," Margaret Church's interpretation, and Cooperman's two readings.

2. Suppose that the country doctor is God and that his patient is Mankind. Can you find evidence with which to develop this hypothesis into an interpretation of the story?

3. State three additional hypotheses. Develop the one which seems to be most promising.

4. Is Kafka's story too obviously symbolical to be an effective short story? Compare it in this regard with Hawthorne's "Young Goodman Brown" and Joyce's "Clay." What conclusion would you draw concerning the proper balance between realistic and symbolic elements in works of fiction?

* 5. Using the conclusion you have reached in the question above, compare "A Country Doctor" with Kafka's "Metamorphosis" or "The Penal Colony."

* 6. Write a symbolic interpretation of a Kafka novel—*Amerika, The Castle,* or *The Trial.*

*Additional readings:* Richard H. Lawson, "Kafka's 'Der Landarzt,'" *Monatshefte,* XLIX (October, 1957), 265-271; and Herbert Tauber, *Franz Kafka: An Interpretation of His Writings* (New Haven: Yale University Press, 1948), pp. 74-76. For general criticism of Kafka, see the selections and the bibliographies in Angel Flores, ed., *The Kafka Problem* (Norfolk: New Directions, 1946) and Angel Flores and Homer D. Swander, eds., *Franz Kafka Today* (Madison: University of Wisconsin Press, 1958).

## 8. William Blake—"The Mental Traveller"

1. Although "The Mental Traveller" may be interpreted by the Blake expert in terms of the poet's private mythology, its imagery is

more generalized and universal than is the imagery of many of his other poems. Evaluate the interpretations given here on the basis of internal evidence from the poem itself. What, for instance, is Rossetti's justification for saying that the poem deals with "an explorer of mental phænomena"? Does Damon have any evidence for his statement that the poem represents "very definitely the life of the Mystic"? Do you feel that the interpretations may stand up even though the premises are shaky?

2. Compare the selection by Joyce Cary with Father Mapple's sermon as examples of symbolic interpretation which become works of art in their own right. What do they have which other critical readings in this book lack? Does this weaken them as criticism?

3. Interpret the story of Gully Jimson. What general principles concerning the artist's intention, the nature of the creative process, and the artist's relation to reality are implied in this chapter from *The Horse's Mouth?* Are these principles in agreement with those held by other writers represented in this book, or is Gully Jimson the exception?

* 4. The extract from *The Horse's Mouth* reprinted here is part of an extended section of the novel containing many references to "The Mental Traveller" and other poems by Blake. In fact, the whole novel is pervaded with Blake allusions. See Andrew Wright, *Joyce Cary: A Preface to His Novels* (New York: Harper, 1959), which contains an appendix identifying all the Blake quotations in the novel. Make a study of these allusions, and write an analysis of the novel emphasizing the Blake influence. Or, if you prefer, interpret the symbols of Cary's novel without regard to Blake.

*Additional readings:* Edwin John Ellis and William Butler Yeats, *The Works of William Blake* (London: Quaritch, 1893), Vol. II, pp. 34-36—compare with Yeats, *A Vision* (London: T. Werner Laurie, 1925), pp. 133-134; Northrop Frye, *Fearful Symmetry* (Princeton, New Jersey: Princeton University Press, 1947), pp. 227-229; Emily S. Hamblen, *On the Minor Prophecies of William Blake* (London: Dent, 1930), pp. 362-365; John H. Sutherland, "Blake's 'Mental Traveller,'" *ELH*, XXII (June, 1955), 136-147; and Hal Saunders White, *A Primer of Blake* (Ames, Iowa: Littlefield, Adams and Co., 1951), pp. 91-94.

## The Symbolic Novel: Suggestions for Independent Study

*Short Novels:*

| | |
|---|---|
| Albert Camus | THE STRANGER |
| Joseph Conrad | HEART OF DARKNESS |
| Stephen Crane | THE RED BADGE OF COURAGE |
| William Faulkner | THE BEAR |
| F. Scott Fitzgerald | THE GREAT GATSBY |
| Ernest Hemingway | THE OLD MAN AND THE SEA |
| Henry James | THE TURN OF THE SCREW |
| James Joyce | THE DEAD |
| Franz Kafka | METAMORPHOSIS |
| Thomas Mann | DEATH IN VENICE |
| Herman Melville | BILLY BUDD |
| Katherine Anne Porter | PALE HORSE, PALE RIDER |
| Mark Twain | THE MYSTERIOUS STRANGER |
| Glenway Wescott | THE PILGRIM HAWK |

*Longer Novels:*

| | |
|---|---|
| Walter Van Tilburg Clark | THE TRACK OF THE CAT |
| Joseph Conrad | VICTORY or NOSTROMO |
| William Faulkner | LIGHT IN AUGUST |
| E. M. Forster | A PASSAGE TO INDIA |
| William Golding | THE LORD OF THE FLIES |
| Henry Green | LOVING |
| Graham Greene | BRIGHTON ROCK |
| L. P. Hartley | EUSTACE AND HILDA |
| Thomas Hardy | THE RETURN OF THE NATIVE |
| Nathaniel Hawthorne | THE SCARLET LETTER |
| Henry James | THE GOLDEN BOWL |
| James Joyce | ULYSSES |
| Franz Kafka | THE CASTLE or THE TRIAL |
| D. H. Lawrence | THE RAINBOW |
| Malcolm Lowry | UNDER THE VOLCANO |
| Thomas Mann | THE MAGIC MOUNTAIN |
| Herman Melville | MOBY-DICK |
| Frank Norris | THE OCTOPUS |
| Edgar Allan Poe | NARRATIVE OF ARTHUR GORDON PYM |
| Marcel Proust | SWANN'S WAY |
| John Steinbeck | THE GRAPES OF WRATH |
| Robert Penn Warren | THE CAVE |
| Virginia Woolf | TO THE LIGHTHOUSE |
| Emile Zola | GERMINAL |

# APPENDIX: WRITING THE CRITICAL PAPER

## The Nature of Criticism[1]

When you are asked to write a critical paper, you may well start by asking yourself what literary criticism is. A possible definition is the stated response of a reader to a created work of verbal art. In terms of this definition, three things would appear to be necessary before we can have criticism: the maker of the art, the art itself, and the perceiver of the art. We may think of criticism as a triangle, the three sides of which represent author, work, and reader. It is possible to write good criticism which deals with only one or two sides of the triangle—in fact, much of the best "new criticism" of the past several decades has ignored the author altogether and, striving for objectivity, has placed its emphasis on the work alone. However, the inexperienced critic will find it safer to assume at the beginning that the triangle is equilateral; otherwise, he is likely to err in one of three basic ways.

## 1. The Author

Too much emphasis on the author leads to what has been called *the genetic fallacy,* the assumption that a work of literature, a *result,* may be equated with its *causes.* The genesis of a work is to be found in the character, attitude, and experience of the author; in his reading and knowledge of literary tradition; and in the social and cultural background of the time in which he lives. Information gained through the study of biography, literary sources, and social background may explain much in a work of literature. We must realize, however, that the causes of any one work are so many and complex that they cannot be exhausted and that the effect of a successful work is always greater than any of its partial causes or combination of causes can account for. The biographer deals with that side of an author which is a matter of public record, but there is a difference between the living person and the creative self of the author. As Henry James said, all we can ever see of the artist *as artist* is "the back he turns to us as he

---

1 Good introductions to literary criticism include (in order of difficulty) David Daiches, *Critical Approaches to Literature* (New York: Prentice-Hall, Inc , 1956); René Wellek and Austin Warren, *Theory of Literature* (New York· Harcourt, Brace and Co , 1949); and Northrop Frye, *Anatomy of Criticism* (Princeton, New Jersey. Princeton University Press, 1957).

bends over his work,"[2] which is to say that we find the creative self only in the work it produces. Biography, sources, and background may be used to the extent that they provide support for critical discussion, but no paper is truly critical if it is primarily concerned with these things or if it confuses them with the finished result.

## 2. The Reader

Too much emphasis on the reader results in subjective impressionism. Before the new critical revolution of the past several decades, criticism tended to be impressionistic—"the adventures of a soul among masterpieces." Such criticism usually tells us more about the critic than about the work he is discussing. It is characterized by unsupported generalizations, an excessive concern with evaluation, and reliance on emotive adjectives such as "moving," "gripping," and "exciting." In the hands of a brilliant reader, impressionistic criticism may be effective; and a man of genius, such as D. H. Lawrence in *Studies in Classic American Literature,* may intuitively arrive at valid conclusions which a less gifted critic could reach only through extended and careful analysis. Unfortunately, few of us are Lawrences.

Impressionism may take many different forms. When students first attempt to write literary criticism, they often reduce the complex and universal meaning of a work of literature to a personal "message," as in the student interpretations of Robert Frost's "Stopping by Woods on a Snowy Evening" quoted by Earl Daniels (see above, pages 64-65). More generally, they confuse a work of art with a fragment of life. To ask such questions as "Is the work true to life?" or "Is a certain character a good person?" is impressionistic because it is asking whether or not the work conforms to the particular view of reality or the notion of goodness which the reader happens to hold. Sometimes impressionism takes the form of what may be called the *argumentative fallacy,* the tendency to quarrel with the ideas or values of an author divorced from the work in which they appear. Editorials on the lack of affirmation in the younger generation of American novelists and the many discussions of the works of Ernest Hemingway which turn out to be criticisms of the Hemingway "code" are examples of this fallacy. We should remember that serious artists appear to have little voluntary control over their way of viewing life and that an artist may produce an esthetically satisfying work even though his philosophy is an inadequate one. Few people today would accept the philosophies held by Homer, Dante, or Ezra Pound, but they remain good artists for all that. If an author's values affect the artistic success of a work, the critic is justified in dealing with the values, but all that really counts

---

[2] *The Art of the Novel,* ed. R. P. Blackmur (New York: Charles Scribner's Sons, 1934), p. 96.

in literary criticism is whether or not the values are effectively drama-
tized within the art.

## 3. The Work

Too much emphasis on the work itself often leads the beginning critic in the direction of mere description, paraphrase, or synopsis.
Often students confuse the "critical paper" with the "book review." The
main purpose of a reviewer is to introduce a new or neglected book.
He must describe the book in order to let the reader know what it is
about, and he must offer some evaluation in order to let the reader know
whether or not it is worth reading. When your instructor asks you to
write a "critical paper," he seldom means a "book review." He has presumably read the work himself and does not need a paraphrase or
synopsis. As for evaluation, chances are he would not have suggested
that you read the work at all unless it had established some claim to
being worthwhile. Therefore, the critical paper, unlike the book review, is usually less concerned with description and appraisal than with
analysis and interpretation.

Historically, criticism tends to move along the sides of the triangle
in such a way that at various periods the emphasis falls on author,
reader, or work. In recent years the work has been the dominant concern of critics, but there are increasing signs that critics are beginning
to return to an awareness that reader and author also participate in
the critical process and cannot be ignored entirely. Failure to consider
the genesis of a work has led to some spectacular blunders in interpretation, and critics are becoming more and more aware that a truly objective analysis of a literary work is impossible. The critic must select
for study those aspects which seem significant to him, but to select is
to distort. All too often "nose to nose, the critic confronts the writer
and, astonished, discovers himself."[3] The skillful reader can find not
only whatever he is looking for in a fairly complex poem or story, but
also, if he looks again and is honest enough, its direct opposite. William
York Tindall, in explaining what he calls *the exhaustive fallacy*, re-
minds us that it is impossible to analyze thoroughly even a short poem
or a story, let alone a complete novel, for we can hardly consider all its
many aspects or see it from every possible angle of vision simultaneously.[4] Even when all interpretations are put together, they cannot
exhaust the entire work; to commit the exhaustive fallacy is to accept
the part as equivalent to the whole. Closely related to this fallacy is
what we may call *the selective fallacy*, demonstrated whenever a critic
selects evidence to support a preconceived conclusion or draws un-
warranted general conclusions from selected, partial evidence. A com-

---

[3] Marvin Mudrick, "Conrad and the Terms of Modern Criticism," *Hudson
Review*, VI (Autumn, 1954), 421.
[4] "The Criticism of Fiction," *Texas Quarterly*, I (February, 1958), 109.

plete view being impossible, there seems to be no way to avoid the selective fallacy entirely. Nonetheless, critics have an obligation to acknowledge the tentative, relative nature of conclusions drawn from partial evidence.

Thinking of criticism in terms of the author-work-reader triangle can help us avoid the distortions which come about when one side of the triangle is overemphasized at the expense of the other two. For practical reasons, it is difficult for the critic, beginning or experienced, to devote equal attention to all three sides; but awareness of the constant interaction of author, reader, and work serves as a check against such extremes of faulty criticism as may be represented in the genetic, argumentative, and selective fallacies.

## Basic Types of Criticism

There is no general, universal agreement on the meaning of most literary terms. In common usage, words like *criticize, analyze, interpret,* and *explicate* are treated as synonyms which may be used interchangeably. Like all synonyms, however, these have subtle differences in meaning. Let us use *criticism* as the general term, then try to distinguish among the different kinds of criticism. Although there is considerable overlapping in the six critical approaches defined below, each has at least one quality that makes it unique. A critical paper may use several or all of these approaches.

## 1. Exegesis

Exegesis is concerned with the literal meaning which is presumed to be intended by the author.[5] Among other things, it provides definitions of terms, explains allusions, identifies sources, clears up obscurities, examines revisions of the text, compares parallel passages, and determines the immediate meaning as it would be understood by the author's ideal contemporary audience. Because the value of exegesis is in ratio to the difficulty of the work being studied, it appears most frequently in studies of earlier literature, as in the notes

---

[5] For this definition I am indebted to Richard M. Kain, "The Limits of Literary Interpretation," *Journal of Aesthetics and Art Criticism,* XVII (December, 1958), 216. In this valuable article Mr. Kain divides literary interpretation into four levels and areas—"the levels of literal, derivative, consequent, and accommodated meanings; the areas, respectively, of exegesis, criticism, interpretation, and subjective 'reading' " (p. 218) I have not used this system in entirety because of what I take to be the awkwardness of subordinating "criticism" to "interpretation" and using the latter term both generally and specifically.

to an edition of a Shakespeare play, or complex modern works like *The Waste Land* or *Finnegans Wake*. A certain amount of exegesis is preliminary to any critical reading, but it is seldom used as the main approach in a critical paper. In part, this is because it is difficult to write a well-unified exegesis, for exegesis is by nature concerned with specific details rather than the work as an artistic totality.

## 2. Explication

Explication is generally understood to mean any close critical reading. If the notes provided by exegesis are presented in the form of an essay, we have one kind of explication. However, explication usually goes beyond intended, literal meaning in the direction of derived, interpreted meaning. It differs from exegesis also in that it is concerned with the whole work rather than isolated details. The explicator usually proceeds chronologically in his discussion of the literary work and provides a line-by-line, episode-by-episode commentary. Thus explication is most conveniently used in the study of shorter works, such as poems, stories, or single chapters, rather than entire plays or novels. In unskilled hands explication can easily slip into mere paraphrase or synopsis.

## 3. Analysis

Analysis means the determining of the elements of something; to analyze is to break a whole thing into its parts. As critical method, analysis differs from exegesis and explication, both of which are usually chronological in organization, in that it divides a work or subject into its component aspects and treats these aspects in turn. Thus the analysis of a short story, for example, may cover (1) plot, (2) characters, (3) theme, (4) imagery, (5) symbolism, and (6) point of view. Or—and this would be preferable in the case of a short paper—any one of these aspects could be analyzed in terms of its sub-divisions, as when we speak of a character analysis, thematic analysis, and so on. Analysis is probably the type of critical approach most frequently used today.

## 4. Interpretation

Interpretation differs from exegesis, explication, and analysis, all of which are assumed to be more or less objective in approach, in that it applies to literature something from outside the work. Sometimes the interpreter proceeds deductively by applying to literature concepts derived from another person, discipline, or philosophy—we may, for instance, identify an interpretation as psychological, socio-logical, or mythic; or Freudian, Jungian, or Marxist. Sometimes the interpreter may try to be inductive in his approach by attempting to derive the meaning of the work from internal evidence alone. But whether interpretation is deductive or inductive, it demands an in-terpreter, who brings to the work his own convictions, values, and way of seeing. That no two witnesses see things in exactly the same way is a commonplace. Most criticism is interpretative in a sense, but the main weaknesses of interpretation as a basic critical approach are that it tends to accommodate literary meaning to some other kind of mean-ing and that it is particularly subject to the selective fallacy.

## 5. Comparison

Comparison is the study of similarities and differences among two or more works or aspects of literature, or between a particular work and the general class to which it belongs (as when we compare *Hamlet* to a hypothetical, "model" Elizabethan tragedy). Whatever we are comparing must be similar enough to justify the comparison, yet dif-ferent enough to yield clear distinctions of one thing from another, for comparison is useful particularly when we want to define the unique-ness of something. Often a certain theme or technique can be clarified by comparing it with its more extended use in other works by the same author. There is danger, of course, in trying to explain the work of A by comparing it with the work of B, for even if we assume that B is a source of A, any significant work alters and transcends its sources. Com-parisons are best organized in terms of the *basis* of comparison rather than the *subjects* of comparison. For example, a paper dealing with the symbol of the rose in Blake, Yeats, and Kafka is less likely to fall into three separate fragments if the critic organizes his discussion in terms of the various levels of symbolic meaning or the different functions of symbolism (basis of comparison), then illustrates his general principles by reference to rose symbols in the works of the three authors (subjects of comparison).

## 6. Evaluation

Evaluation is concerned with appraising the merit of a literary work. Once the main concern of criticism, evaluation has been neg-lected by modern critics, who tend to feel that they ought to devote their attention to works that have already established themselves. How-ever, in a sense any critical study is evaluative: the critic who analyses or interprets a work of literature implies that the work deserves serious attention, and most analyses imply that the work successfully conveys what the critic has succeeded in finding within it. Nonetheless, evaluation is seldom the primary concern of the modern critic unless the book he is discussing is new or neglected or unless he happens to disagree with the general opinion. Evaluation may be a secondary concern of the critic who analyses a work and tries to determine why certain aspects succeed and others fail; no work of literature is perfect in all its parts, and the critic often weighs virtues and defects in reaching a balanced estimate of the work's significance.

Evaluation depends on *criteria*, standards of judgment. The impressionistic standard ("I don't know much about art, but I know what I like!"), the market standard (how many have liked it?), the appeal to authority (who has liked it? whom has it influenced?), and the mimetic standard (is it true to life?) are frequently used criteria, but hardly to be recommended in serious criticism. More valid standards include the following:

*Fulfillment of Intention.* The critic asks three basic questions: (1) what did the author try to do? (2) how well did he do it? and (3) was it worth doing? Many modern critics feel that these questions illustrate *the intentional fallacy;* such critics feel that the only intention which can be studied is the realized intention within the work and that any intention not found in the work is irrelevant. The merits of intention as a standard are discussed pro and con in the second chapter of this book.

*Internal Standards.* The critic asks such questions as these: Are the parts of the literary work in proper proportion? Are the conflicts and tensions resolved, or, if not, are they kept balanced? Is the work well unified? Joyce's three requirements of art—wholeness, harmony, and radiance—may be used as internal standards (see above, pages 32-33).

*Comparison with other works of the same class.* A competent writer may succeed in producing a work that meets the above tests, yet falls short of greatness when it is compared with other works. For example, L. A. G. Strong's novel about a sensitive young boy growing up in Ireland, *The Garden* (1931), seems to do everything the author intended, it was worth doing, and it meets internal standards of balance and harmony. Nonetheless, *The Garden* seems a minor novel when we compare it with another novel about a sensitive young Irishman, Joyce's *A Portrait of the Artist as a Young Man* (1914).

## Suggested Procedure

### 1. Choosing a Subject

After you have considered the nature of criticism and the various types of critical approach and after you have read the work or works you are to discuss, your next task is to select a subject for your paper. The subject should be narrow enough to be treated adequately in the space you have, yet broad enough to seem significant. Just as it is not enough that a literary work fulfill the author's intention if the intention is an inadequate one, so you will be expected to say something of consequence about the literature you discuss. One test of a good subject is that it should tie together several key points or aspects of the work. Thus you may find it useful to think of subjects which involve opposing qualities or elements—the individual versus society, the real versus the symbolic, flat versus round characters, organic versus mechanical unity, black versus white imagery, and so on. If the critic has a one-sided subject, he can usually only count its appearances in the work; a multi-sided subject enables him to move from description to analysis and to show the relation between parts.

### 2. Collecting Data

The more you know about the work, the better qualified you are to criticize it. Ideally, the critic should have a good background of literary knowledge, he ought to know thoroughly the work in question, he should have read everything else written by the author, and he should be acquainted with all available information on the author, his period, and his work—and he ought to have all this information in his mind at once. But, of course, this is the ideal, and even the writer of a Ph. D. dissertation or a professional critic would find it difficult, if not impossible, to attain.

Fortunately, you will find that in most cases much of this ideal preparation has been done for you by earlier writers on your subject. One of the main purposes of criticism is to guide later readers and critics. Thus to the extent that time, interest, and library facilities permit, you ought to acquaint yourself with the secondary material (that is, writings *about* your primary object of study) most relevant to your subject, for if all that you have to say has been already said, there is little point in your saying it at all. Once you have chosen a subject, your instructor may be able to suggest the most helpful secondary material. Or you may wish to consult one of the standard and most recent bibliographies, literary histories, or guides to literary study.[6]

Whether or not you use secondary material, you will be expected to know thoroughly the work you are criticizing. A first reading gives you an over-all conception of the work and suggests the main problems in appreciation or understanding. After you have chosen a subject, you will have to review the work in search of all passages which bear upon your subject. To avoid the selective fallacy, your data collecting ought to be as inductive as possible: if, for instance, you are writing on the pessimistic philosophy of an author, you will be accused of slanting your evidence in favor of a preconceived conclusion if you ignore or overlook the optimistic passages.

## 3. Planning the Paper

After you have chosen your subject and collected the material related to it, your next step is to determine the thesis of your paper. The *thesis*—not to be confused with the *subject*—is the main point of your essay, the central idea, a statement *about* the subject. You should be able to state your thesis in a single grammatical sentence (a simple or complex sentence, not a compound one); if you cannot do so, chances are that your subject is too broad and that you have several main theses.

In planning the paper, you should first determine the logical divisions of your thesis, then work up a plan by means of which each section (in a short paper, perhaps each paragraph) will be related to the thesis. You should prepare a sentence outline before you begin writing. The sentences in the outline will probably provide you with the *topic sentences* (that is, the sub-theses) of the separate sections or paragraphs within your paper. If your outline is a good one, you will find at this point that your paper is virtually written, for once you have the frame, all that remains is to fill it in with the best and most convincing of the evidence you have collected.

The basic organization of a critical essay is usually a simple one: a thesis is stated, then demonstrated or proved. Your thesis ought to be stated early in the paper and in such a way that the reader will recognize it immediately as the thesis. Remember that you are not writing a mystery story and that you should tell the reader at the beginning just what you hope to show him. Some modern critics notwithstanding, the essence of effective criticism is clarity, and the clearest papers are those in which the critic tells the reader immediately what he hopes to estab-

---

6 The best general guide is Arthur G. Kennedy and Donald B. Sands, *A Concise Bibliography for Students of English,* Fourth Edition (Stanford, California: Stanford University Press, 1959) For the most complete and up-to-date checklists of criticism and scholarship dealing with individual topics or writers, see the annual bibliographies published in *PMLA* each April.

lish, then proceeds to give his evidence in a straightforward, direct manner without wordiness, ambiguity, or "double talk."

The three essential parts of a critical paper are the introduction, the demonstration, and the conclusion:

A. *Introduction* or *Proposal*. The opening section of your paper should contain the statement of thesis, a clear indication of your purpose in writing. If your paper is a long one, you may want to describe briefly the plan of what is to follow, outlining for the reader the major steps in your demonstration. In addition to the statement of thesis or purpose, the one essential, your introduction may also include any or all of the following, though not necessarily in this order:

*Survey of Research.* You describe briefly the present position of research on the subject you are discussing and summarize the views held by other critics. Some writers prefer to put such information in a footnote, and some omit it altogether. However, the survey of research often helps to make your subject seem more significant, for you suggest in this way the need for amending the conventional view of the subject. You should avoid setting up a straw-man as opponent; one of the worst sins of critics is a deliberate distortion of current views in order to demolish something which either does not exist or is too weak to need refuting.

*Boost.* You indicate the importance of your discovery or argument. Often the boost may be implied in the survey of research, but if very little or nothing has been said by others on your subject, your boost may consist simply of an expression of wonder at the strange neglect of something which, for reasons you hope your paper will make clear, is actually important for the full understanding of the subject in question. Sometimes the boost consists of the suggestion that your particular thesis opens larger questions concerning the subject in general. For example, in an essay on Hemingway's "The Short Happy Life of Francis Macomber," Warren Beck says in his opening paragraph:

... Wilson's assumption that Mrs. Macomber murdered her husband has been rather generally accepted by readers. "Our clue to the full meaning of the act," says one critical discussion in this vein, "is given by the guide." However, one may question not just Wilson's credibility as a witness but his comprehension of Mrs. Macomber and of the Macombers' human situation. And this, in turn, involves larger questions concerning Hemingway's work, as to both its art and its substance.[7]

*Concession.* Most arguments are stronger if they concede something to the other side. You may wish to acknowledge the existence of

---

[7] "The Shorter Happy Life of Mrs. Macomber," *Modern Fiction Studies,* I (November, 1955), 28.

other valid critical interpretations or approaches, or you may want to point out that yours is but one of many ways of viewing a complex subject that will seem all the richer for the variety of views applied to it.

*Capsule Summary.* Some teachers ask their students to include in their introductory section a brief synopsis or description of the work or works being discussed. If you have reason to believe that your audience may not be well acquainted with the work or if you want to refresh your reader's memory, then a capsule summary may be useful.

B. *Demonstration.* This is the orderly presentation of evidence which supports your thesis. Although it would seem obvious that the demonstration is the most crucial of the three parts and ought to be the longest section of the paper, it is surprising how many critical essays seem to consist entirely of an introduction and a conclusion. In determining the most effective method of demonstration, you may wish to review the six types of critical approach described above. You may use only one, several, or all of the approaches, but it would perhaps be wise to choose one as the basic approach, using any of the others to supplement it. If exegesis or explication is your main concern, then you will probably want to present your evidence chronologically. If you use analysis, you must organize in terms of selected aspects of your subject, building up, if possible, to your strongest and most important point. Comparison is best organized by the basis of comparison rather than the subjects being compared, and evaluation by whatever criteria you select. Interpretation has no set method of organization; it usually combines with explication or analysis.

C. *Conclusion.* Your conclusion may consist of one or all of the following:

*Clincher.* Sometimes, particularly in a shorter paper, your strongest and most convincing evidence provides the only conclusion necessary. But in such cases the clincher ought to be something that ties together the several strands of your subject.

*Summary.* You summarize briefly what you have attempted to show, perhaps restating your thesis more exactly and emphatically. A summary is seldom necessary in very short papers.

*Application of Conclusion.* You may wish to suggest the implications of your discovery or argument as it relates to other works by the author or authors you are discussing, a whole period of literature, or a literary concept.

CPSIA information can be obtained at www.ICGtesting.com
Printed in the USA
LVOW13*1412261113

362908LV00003B/8/P